CARTER

P9-BYU-835

Teaching Fractions and Ratios for Understanding

Essential Content Knowledge and Instructional Strategies for Teachers

Teaching Fractions and Ratios for Understanding

Essential Content Knowledge and Instructional Strategies for Teachers

Susan J. Lamon
Marquette University

1999

LAWRENCE ERLBAUM ASSOCIATES, PUBLISHERS
Mahwah, New Jersey   London

The final camera copy for this work was prepared by the author, and therefore the publisher takes no responsibility for consistency or correctness of typographical style. However, this arrangement helps to make publication of this kind of scholarship possible.

Copyright © 1999 by Lawrence Erlbaum Associates, Inc.
All rights reserved. No part of this book may be reproduced in any form, by photostat, microfilm, retrieval system, or any other means, without prior written permission of the publisher.

Lawrence Erlbaum Associates, Inc., Publishers
10 Industrial Avenue
Mahwah, NJ 07430

Cover design by Kathryn Houghtaling Lacey

Library of Congress Cataloging-in-Publication Data

Lamon, Susan J., 1949–
Teaching fractions and ratios for understanding : essential content knowledge and instructional strategies for teachers / Susan J. Lamon.
        p. cm.
Includes bibliographical references and index.
ISBN 0-8058-2940-7 (pbk : alk. paper)
1. Fractions—Study and teaching (Elementary) 2. Ratio and proportion—Study and teaching (Elementary) I. Title.
QA137.L36 1999
        372.7'2—dc21   98-51379
                                                            CIP

Books published by Lawrence Erlbaum Associates are printed on acid-free paper, and their bindings are chosen for strength and durability.

Printed in the United States of America
10   9   8   7   6   5   4

To Bill
For your love, patience, and support

Contents

Introduction

All too often, children's disenchantment with mathematics begins late in elementary school or in middle school when, even after years of practice, they cannot remember how to "do" fractions after summer vacation, or when they can perform steps, but are totally bored because they do not know what the steps mean or why they are doing them. Understanding fractions marks only the beginning of the journey toward rational number understanding and, by the end of the middle school years, as a result of maturation, experience, and instruction in mathematics, it is presumed that students are capable of a formal thought process called *proportional reasoning*. This form of reasoning opens the door to high school mathematics and science, and eventually, to careers in the mathematical sciences. The losses that occur because of the gaps in conceptual understanding about fractions, ratios, and rational numbers are incalculable. The consequences of "doing," rather than understanding, directly or indirectly affect a person's attitudes toward mathematics, enjoyment and motivation in learning, course selection in mathematics and science, achievement, career flexibility, and even the ability to fully appreciate some of the simplest phenomena in everyday life.

For this reason, the National Council of Teachers of Mathematics asserted in their *Curriculum and Evaluations Standards* (1989), that proportional reasoning "is of such great importance that it merits whatever time and effort must be expended to assure its careful development" (p. 82). Unfortunately, until recently, we have had little understanding of how proportional reasoning develops. By the time one reaches middle school, mathematics and human cognition are of sufficient complexity that studying the development of understanding in fractions, ratios, and rational numbers is a challenging research site. Without a research base to inform decision making about the important conceptual components of proportional reasoning, textbook approaches have unintentionally encouraged simplistic, mechanical treatment of ratios and proportions, highlighting the algebraic representation of a proportion and the manipulation of the symbols. The rules for solving problems using proportions were indelibly printed into our memories: put like term over like term, cross multiply, then divide. For most people, the rule is a proxy for reasoning about quantities and their relationships.

This book represents an attempt to shorten the inevitable time lag between the completion of research and the translation of that research into usable ideas for the classroom. In recent years, those who do research in the teaching and learning of fractions, ratios, and rational numbers have developed a deeper understanding of the complexity of the mathematics, the ways in which these domains are related, and some of the critical components of understanding. While there is still much to be learned about children's thinking and learning in relation to rational numbers, there are some fundamental ideas that should be made accessible to teachers and others who care about mathematics curricula and instruction.

This book addresses the urgent need for curriculum materials that cross traditional boundaries to include many of the elements that are integrated in the teaching—learning enterprise: mathematics content, teacher understanding, student thinking, teaching methods, instructional activities, and assessment. The job of preparing preservice teachers has always been unnecessarily difficult because the content they need is in one book, the teaching methods in another, and the material they use with students in yet another. In reality, the work of teachers and students is complex and cannot be chopped into little pieces and packaged separately.

Undoubtedly, this material pushes you beyond the limits of your understanding of rational numbers. It challenges you to refine and to explain your thinking and to make sense—without falling back on the rules and procedures you have relied on throughout your life. All of the activities in this book are to be solved using reasoning alone. You may find it difficult to abandon fraction rules and procedures, but forcing yourself to work without them will unleash powerful ways of thinking.

This book is not a textbook as much as it is a resource book. One of its underlying assumptions is that facilitating teacher understanding using the same questions and activities that may be used with children, is one way to help teachers to build the comfort and confidence they need to talk to children about complex ideas. Unlike a textbook that is used to study formal theory and then is discarded when it comes to putting ideas into practice, the many problems and activities included here are valuable resources for use in elementary and middle school classrooms. There are no prescriptions for incorporating these ideas into instruction, however. My experience with teachers suggests that they are thoughtful practitioners. When they feel confident in their own understanding, they know how to use new knowledge to enhance what they do in the classroom.

This book is intended for researchers and curriculum developers in mathematics education, for preservice and inservice teachers of mathematics, for those involved in the mathematical and pedagogical preparation of mathematics teachers, and for graduate students in mathematics education. Its methods and activities have been tested with students from third grade through eighth grade, with preservice and inservice teachers, and with other adults. Some of ways in which it has been used are discussed here.

Mathematics or Math Methods for Preservice Elementary Teachers. In some states, certification requirements include three or more math or math methods courses for preservice elementary teachers. In two states where this is the case, an entire three-credit course was devoted to the study of rational numbers. This book provided enough material for a 15-week course. Because not all of the preservice teachers had adequate access to classrooms or individual students while taking the course, middle school students visited and were interviewed in the university classroom.

Integrated Mathematics and Math Methods for Preservice Middle School Mathematics Teachers. This book has also been used as one of several required books in a course for prospective middle school teachers with a major in mathematics. They studied a chapter a week, worked and discussed all of the problems, and then videotaped and analyzed interviews with middle school students solving the same problems.

Inservice Courses. This material provided the basis for several inservice projects for elementary and middle school teachers. In one school district, several chapters were introduced during a two-week summer institute, and one chapter was discussed on each of six in-service days during the academic year. The remaining chapters were finished during the following summer. The teachers incorporated some of the ideas and activities into their mathematics curriculum, discussed their classroom activities with their colleagues, and shared student work.

Family Mathematics. Activities in this book provided the basis for biweekly family night activities at several elementary schools. Teachers selected topics for parent—student discussion during family night activities, and assigned homework problems to be worked on together by parents and students each week throughout the school year. Parents reported that they enjoyed and benefited from the activities their children brought home from school. They were lured into territory in which they were uncomfortable, but they soon discovered how easily they could engage in mathematical conversations with their children.

In all of these contexts, abundant discussion of the activities and sharing of explanations, strategies, and solutions, was the key to helping people change their perspectives and engage in high-level reasoning. Whether the reader is working alone, in a class, or in an inservice group, it is suggested that you include time for personal problem solving and reflection and time to meet with others. To maximize the benefits of using this book, first work the problems yourself so that you will know exactly what is entailed in each solution. Second, discuss your solution with others and compare it with alternate solutions they may have produced. In adults' work as well as in students' work, you meet diverse reasoning that affords a broad and deep experience and understanding of mathematics. After you have worked out misconceptions, misunderstandings, disagreements, and alternative solutions with your colleagues or fellow students, you will be better prepared to orchestrate discussions in your classroom. The vocabulary and the important content is clearer. You are better prepared for the range of responses students give when they work the same problems.

To help you understand the intended uses of this book, the various components of each chapter are described here.

Self Assessment. When you see the invitation to "stop and work these examples before going on," it is advantageous to do so. If you look ahead, you may find that the problems are discussed later in the chapter, or later in the book. However, there are many ideas that are deceptively easy when someone else is talking about them, but far more difficult when you try to use them yourself. To get a full appreciation of the complexity of a problem, and to fully understand what is entailed in achieving a solution, it is much better to try it on your own before moving ahead.

Activities. Problems and investigations in each chapter will help you to try out the new ideas presented in the chapter and to use them in examples that are not exactly like those shown in the text. The exercises help you to explore connections among the topics within and between chapters of the book. The activities are designed to build a broad base of understanding before the introduction of the standard algorithms for operating with fractions, ratios, and proportions. Some are presymbolic. Problems are to be solved with reasoning alone, using no rules or algorithms.

Children's Strategies. Excerpts of children's work are included in every chapter for your analysis. Because many of the ideas and the problems you encounter have not been part of the traditional elementary and middle school mathematics curricula, you may not be able to anticipate how children will handle them. Samples of student work are provided to give an indication of some of the responses you can expect.

More. A book containing in-depth discussions of all of the problems is available as a supplement to this book. This book is not merely an answer key. It develops and extends discussions of the issues, teaching problems, and other considerations raised in the chapters. It should be consulted only after the reader has had time to work the exercises and to discuss them with others. It contains additional problems with solutions that instructors may find helpful for assessment purposes, and a set of problems that require both good reasoning and computational skills.

The issues and discussion raised by many of the activities invite both young and old to adopt new perspectives. The activities exploit some of the simplest, everyday situations and contexts wherein lie the roots of more complex ideas and ways of thinking. The book is written in a colloquial style. Hopefully, this will make the mathematics more approachable by those who are afraid to tackle unfamiliar topics.

Chapter 1
Proportional Reasoning: An Overview

STOP *Children's Strategies*

Some middle school children were given the tree tower problem, in which their task was to consider the remarks of the two characters in the picture and decide the height of the tower. The responses from students A, B, C, D, and E are given here. Before reading on, decide the height of the tower for yourself, then explain your reasoning to someone else and rank the student responses according to the sophistication of their mathematical reasoning.

Why don't you climb the ladder? It's only 10 feet high.

It can't be! I am 6 feet tall, so it must be 30 feet.

A. 15 feet

If the tower was in front of me and I look up it would look near 15 feet tall.

B. 9ft Tall

Mrs peshKi said the gold part of our pencil is a inch so I Kept adding the inches and I got nine.

C. It about 18 feet. I figured out thes it takes about 3 people the size of that man to be as tall as the town. I found that out by counting the ☐☐ I knew that every 8 of those would be 6 feet. So I just count every eight.

D. I thank its about 30 feet because one man said it ten feet. It cant be because the other man is feet and the tower is more than 10 feet so I think its 30 feet.

E. It is 24 feet. I took my thumb and pointer finger measured the man 3 times.

* *

This chapter provides a backdrop for all that follows. The goal of this book is to share some teaching methods and materials that may be used throughout the elementary and middle school years to promote the ideas and ways of thinking that contribute to proportional reasoning. Before we get started, it might help to have some idea of where we are headed and to develop a sense of what proportional reasoning is and why it is important. We begin with a brief summary of what researchers have found when they talk to children about fractions, rational number ideas, ratios and rates, and proportional thinking, so that we can better appreciate the need for enhancing instruction. The conclusions from research also provide a rationale for the inclusion of the content, material, and teaching methods used in this book.

Components of Understanding

One of the most compelling tasks for researchers has been to discover the kinds of understanding, thinking processes, and contexts that are essential to powerful reasoning. By deeply analyzing mathematical content, children's thinking, and adult thinking, we have begun to understand some of the knowledge that contributes to proportional reasoning and how it develops. We know that it is impossible to teach the reasoning process directly because, in short, the whole is greater than the sum of the parts. It is not a priori data in the mind, nor does it result merely from empirical observation. The development of proportional reasoning is not an all-or-nothing affair. That is, it is not the case that suddenly, a light goes on, the student has an "ah-ha" experience, and "gets it." Rather, competence grows over a long period of time and in many different dimensions. The operating theory for instruction is that by providing children experiences with some of the critical components of proportional reasoning before proceeding to more abstract, formal presentations, we increase their chances of developing proportional reasoning. This book suggests ways to provide experiences in each of six areas that are known to contribute to powerful ways of thinking. These are shown in the following diagram.

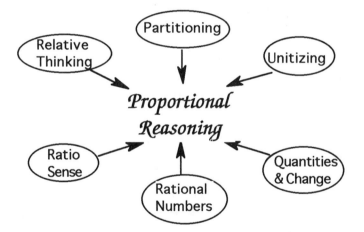

Relative thinking and unitizing are cognitive functions. Partitioning involves concrete activity, active "doing" to promote insight. Ratio sense is an intuition, acquired through experience in appropriate contexts, about what to do and when to do it. Knowing rational numbers entails being able to move around flexibly in the world of rational numbers, connecting various meanings and operations. Finally, quantitative reasoning, the ability to interpret and operate with changing quantities, plays a role in proportional reasoning. We expand each of these ideas in later chapters, but for now, it is important to note that to achieve the goal of proportional reasoning, one needs extensive time and experience to build up many kinds of knowledge: concepts, ways of thinking, and ways of acting (operations)—all linked to appropriate contexts.

When referring to this content-context thinking and operating interaction, researchers use the term *multiplicative conceptual field*. Although we restrict ourselves to the topics in the diagram just presented, the multiplicative conceptual field contains more advanced mathematical ideas as well. The term refers to the fact that all of these ideas are part of a tightly connected web of ideas built on multiplicative rather than on additive ideas. These ideas do not develop in isolation of each other. The more connections a person can build between these topics, the better his or her reasoning power is.

Changing Instruction

No one knows better than teachers who have had experience teaching fractions that current instruction is not serving many students. However, in addition to having a *need* to change, there must be a viable direction for change. Research has now gone beyond documenting problems and moved toward uncovering promising new activities and teaching methods. A few of the most compelling reasons to change fraction and rational number instruction are given here. For those who wish to study the research literature in greater detail, a bibliography is included at the end of this book.

· Fraction, ratio, and rational number ideas are psychologically and mathematically complex and interconnected.
A long-term learning process is required for understanding the web of ideas related to proportional reasoning. Current instruction that gives a brief introduction through part—whole fractions and then proceeds to introduce computation procedures does not give children the time they need to construct important ideas and ways of thinking.

· Students whose instruction has concentrated on part-whole fractions have an impoverished understanding of rational number.
Many different interpretations of a rational number are represented by a single fraction symbol (for example, $\frac{3}{4}$). Instruction needs to provide children the opportunity to build a broad base of meaning for fraction symbols, to become flexible in moving back and forth among meanings, to establish connections among them, and to understand how the meanings influence the operations one is allowed to perform. It is simply not sufficient to use only part—whole fractions as a basis for building an understanding of rational numbers.

· Instruction needs to take an active role in facilitating thinking that will lead to proportional reasoning.

It is estimated that more than half the adult population cannot reason proportionally. This means that for most people, maturation and experience, even when they are supplemented by current instruction, are not sufficient to develop sophisticated mathematical reasoning.

• Long-term studies show that instruction can be improved.
Studies in which children were given the time to develop their reasoning for at least 3 years without being taught the standard algorithms for operating with fractions and ratios, have produced a dramatic increase in students' reasoning abilities, including their proportional reasoning. Some of the student work in the following chapters illustrates the powerful thinking that they produced.

What is Proportional Reasoning?

Proportional reasoning results after one has built up competence in a number of practical and mathematical areas. This is typical of many ideas in mathematics. For example, what is a function? What is space? What is a limit? Someone may give you definitions of those terms, but truly understanding them is a more difficult task. They are not absolute ideas with a single source of meaning. Instead, meaning is built over time and is facilitated by interactions with many closely related situations, each of which embodies some, but maybe not all, of the critical aspects of an idea. This is true of proportional reasoning. It draws on a huge web of knowledge.

So, the answer is that we cannot say in a very concise way what proportional reasoning is, nor can we say exactly how a person learns to reason proportionally. Nevertheless, you can gain some sense of what is entailed in proportional reasoning by trying the next two problem sets. The first is a set of 10 questions that may be answered quickly and mentally if you reason proportionally. The second set is composed of more substantial problems whose solutions require proportional reasoning or some form of thinking critical to proportional reasoning. Because you know that many of these problems may be solved using proportions, you may be tempted to use an equation of the form $\frac{a}{b} = \frac{c}{d}$, but using those symbols is not reasoning. Think about each problem and explain the solution without using rules and symbols.

 Stop and answer the following set of questions. Solve the problems mentally. Use your pen or pencil only to record your answers. Do not perform any computation!

1. Six men can build a house in 3 days. Assuming that all of the workmen work at the same rate, how many men would it take to build the house in 1 day?

2. Eighty candies will be divided between two boys in the ratio 2:3. How many will each boy receive?

3. If 5 chocolates cost $.75, how much do 13 cost?

4. Between them, John and Mark have 32 marbles. John has 3 times as many as Mark. How many marbles does each boy have?

5. Jane loves to read. She can read a chapter in about 30 minutes. Assuming chapters are all about the same length, how long will it take her to read a book with 14 chapters?

6. Six students were given 20 minutes to clean up the classroom after an eraser fight. They were angry and named 3 other accomplices. The principal added their friends to the clean-up crew and changed the time limit. How much time did she give them to complete the job?

7. If 1 football player weighs 280 pounds, what is the total weight of the 11 starters?

8. Sandra wants to buy a boom box costing $210. Her mother agreed to pay $5 for every $2 Sandra saved. How much did each pay?

9. A company usually sends 9 men to install a security system in an office building, and they do it in about 96 minutes. Today, they have only three men to do the same size job. How much time should be scheduled to complete the job?

10. A motor bike can run for 10 minutes on $.30 worth of fuel. How long could it run on $1.05 worth of fuel?

$$* * * * * * * * * * * * * * * * * * * *$$

When you are finished, discuss your reasoning with someone else. As you listen to other explanations, you may discover that there is more than one way to think about each problem. The next set of problems is more challenging.

 The following problems are not quickies. You may need to spend a considerable amount of time on them. Do not give up if you do not have a solution in 5 minutes. Remember that the goal is to support each solution with reasoning. Do not solve any of the problems by applying rules or by using a proportion equation (e.g., $\frac{a}{b} = \frac{c}{d}$).

11. On a sunny day, you and your friend were taking a long walk. You got tired and stopped near a telephone pole for a little rest, but your nervous friend couldn't stand still. He paced out your shadow and discovered that it was eight feet long even though you are really only 5 feet tall. He paced the long shadow of the telephone pole and found that it was 48 feet long. He wondered how high the telephone pole really is. Can you figure it out?

12. Which is more square, a rectangle that measures 35" x 39" or a rectangle that measures 22" x 25"?

13. Two gears, A and B, are arranged so that the teeth of one gear mesh with the teeth of another. Gear A turns clockwise and has 54 teeth. Gear B turns counterclockwise and has 36 teeth. If gear A makes 5.5 rotations, how many turns will gear B make?

14. Mr. Brown is a bike rider. He considered living in Allentown, Binghamton, and Chester. In the end, he chose Binghamton because, as he put it, "All else being equal, I chose the town where bikes stand the greatest chance on the road against cars." Is Binghamton town A, B, or C?
    A. Area is 15 sq. mi.; 12,560 cars in town.
    B. Area is 3 sq. mi.; 2502 cars in town.
    C. Area is 17 sq. mi.; 14,212 cars in town.

15. Mrs. Cobb makes and sells her own apple-cranberry juice. In pitcher A, she mixed 4 cranberry flavored cubes and 3 apple flavored cubes with some water. In pitcher, B, she used 3 cranberry and 2 apple flavored cubes in the same amount of water. If you ask for a drink that has a stronger cranberry taste, from which pitcher should she pour your drink?

16. Jim's mother asked him to go to her desk and get his dad's picture and its enlargement, but when Jim went into her office, he found five pictures of his dad in various sizes:
    A. 9 cm. x 10 cm.   B. 10 cm. x 12 cm.   C. 8 cm. x 9.6 cm.
         D. 6 cm. x 8 cm.   E 5 cm. x 6.5 cm.
    Which two did she want?

17. From Lewis Carroll: If 6 cats can kill 6 rats in 6 minutes, how many cats will be needed to kill 100 rats in 50 minutes?

18. Two identical balance beams are placed on a table and a number of weights are added while the beams are held in place. Would you expect each beam to tip toward the right or toward the left when it is released?

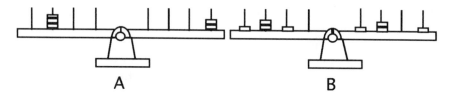

A   B

19. What is the ratio of men to women in a town where $\frac{2}{3}$ of the men are married to $\frac{3}{4}$ of the women?

20. In a gourmet coffee shop, two types of beans are combined and sold as the House Blend. One bean sells for $8.00 per pound and the other for $14.00 per pound. They mix up batches of 50 pounds at a time and sell the House Blend for $10.00 a pound. How many pounds of each kind of coffee go into the blend?

* * * * * * * * * * * * * * * * * * * *

Do not worry if you were not able to solve all of problems 11—20 on your first try. They are some of the types of problems that you should be able to explain by the time you are finished with this book. It would be a good idea to return to them periodically to apply new insights. Now that you have some impression of what proportional reasoning entails, let's try to be more explicit about what it means to reason proportionally.

Some Definitions

One way to define proportional reasoning is to say that it is the ability to recognize, to explain, to think about, to make conjectures about, to graph, to transform, to compare, to make judgments about, to represent, or to symbolize relationships of two simple types. The first type of relationship, a *direct proportion*, occurs when two quantities change in the same direction, that is, as one quantity gets larger (or smaller), the other also gets larger (or smaller), but the size of one quantity relative to the size of the other always stays the same.

Example of a simple direct proportion

For every 2 cups of water in a punch recipe, you add $\frac{1}{3}$ cup sugar. If you start with 8 cups of water, the amount of sugar needed is $1\frac{1}{3}$ cups. The amount of water (w) as compared to the amount of sugar (s) is always the same no matter how large a batch you make. There is always 6 times as much water as there is sugar. So the amount of water as compared to the amount of sugar is given by an index of 6, or $\frac{w}{s}=6$.

The second kind of relationship, an *inverse proportion*, occurs when one quantity increases and the other decreases in such a way that their product always remains the same. A good example of this type of change occurs in work situations where an increase in the number of people on a job decreases the time required to do the job.

Example of a simple inverse proportion

Suppose it takes 6 men 4 days to complete a job. Then,
\# men • \#days = \#man-days to complete the job.

Keeping the number of man days constant, observe what happens to the number of days when the number of men decreases or increases.

# men		#days	# man-days
6	•	4	=24
4	•	6	=24
2	•	12	=24
8	•	3	=24

Decreasing the number of men (m) increases the number of days (d); increasing the number of men decreases the number of work days. This means that when one factor increases, the other decreases (or vice versa), but their product remains constant. Symbolically, md = 24.

Proportions may be more complex than those just described (for example, they may involve more than two variables and one of the variables may change simultaneously in the same direction as one of the others and in the opposite direction from another) but we restrict our attention to the simpler types just mentioned.

There are many mathematical ideas closely related to proportions. These ideas begin with elementary multiplication and division, and include a host of mathematical topics encountered in middle school, high school, and beyond, including fractions, decimals, ratios, percents, probability, similarity, linear functions, equivalence, measurement, and others. Thus, proportional reasoning is critical in mathematics and many sciences, including such courses as algebra, geometry, chemistry, physics, biology, geography. It is equally useful in many everyday contexts, such as those involving recipe conversions, gas consumption, map reading, scale drawings, steepness, fluid concentrations, speed, reducing and enlarging, comparison shopping, and monetary conversions.

Analyzing Children's Thinking

Because critical ideas develop and mature over a period of time, children should begin to think about the activities in this book early in elementary school and continue to discuss and write about these ideas all the way through middle school. As you try problems in this book with children in real classrooms, you will find that many elicit a broad range of responses. The tree tower problem is one such problem.

Student C used the most sophisticated reasoning to solve the problem. The tree house is 18 feet above the ground. Student A is the only student who indicated no reasoning at all. A said that he or she would just look up at the tower and guess. Student D failed to pick up on any of the clues in the picture and focused only on what the child and the man had to say. Unfortunately, this student used faulty reasoning and assumed that one of the characters had to be correct, arguing that if the child in the tree house is wrong, the man on the ground must be right. Students B and E both used measurement as the basis for their arguments. Student E, who measured using the man, could have gotten a correct answer if he or she had known that $3 \cdot 6 = 18$, but student B, who measured with the end of a pencil, probably had some misconceptions about measurement and scale. He or she assumed that 1 inch in the picture converted to 1 foot in real distance. On the other hand, student C used three quantities to help discover the missing height: the height of the man, the total number of rungs on the ladder, and the number of rungs corresponding to the man's height. This thinking was closest to proportional reasoning. Based on this analysis, the levels of thinking, ranked from lowest to highest, are A-D-B-E-C.

The tree tower problem makes a good assessment item. If you asked children to respond to it in September and again in June, you would see a dramatic change in their thinking. The more you analyze children's work at various stages of development, the better you become at discerning levels of sophistication in their thinking. This information, in turn, can help you to make instructional decisions. But even more important than recognizing good reasoning when it occurs, is knowing how to facilitate it. The following chapters serve all of these goals.

 Spend some time thinking about the following questions. Write down your thoughts.

Reflection

1. As you solved the problems in this chapter, did you get a sense of your own ability to reason proportionally? Did your own experience and schooling adequately prepare you for explaining the problems without setting up a proportion?

2. Your school is planning to incorporate major changes in the teaching of fractions and rational number topics. It is your job to justify the changes to some concerned parents. What would you say?

Chapter 2
Relative and Absolute Thinking

STOP **Children's Strategies**
Before going on, read and discuss the three student responses
to the following question. Which responses are correct? How
are they different? Order the responses according to
sophistication of reasoning.

Before, tree A was 8 feet tall and tree B was 10 feet tall. Now, tree
A is 14 feet tall and tree B is 16 feet tall. Which tree grew more?

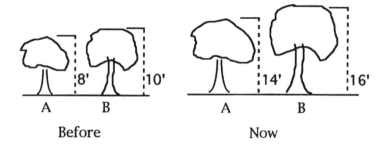

Before   Now

Robert

Both trees grew the same amount 6 ft.
B is always gone to be 2 ft. taller
then A.

P.J.

B climbed higher but not *higher*. I
mean its higher but it didn't climb
more feet because it was already
higher. It didn't grow more. Its
just higher. It seem like A grew
more even though it didn't grow
higher than B.

Dan

A grew 75% of it height, but B
grew a little less — 60% of its
height.

* * * * * * * * * * * * * * * * * * * *

Two Perspectives on Change

The following situation highlights one of the most important types of thinking required for proportional reasoning: the ability to analyze change in both absolute and relative terms.

> Jo has two snakes, String Bean and Slim. Right now, String Bean is 4 feet long and Slim is 5 feet long. Jo knows that two years from now, both snakes will be fully grown. At her full length, String Bean will be 7 feet long, while Slim's length when he is fully grown will be 8 feet. Over the next two years, will both snakes grow the same amount?

Now...

String Bean (4 feet)   Slim (5 feet)

5 years from now...

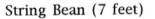

String Bean (7 feet)   Slim (8 feet)

Certainly, one answer is that snakes will grow the same amount because both will add 3 feet of length. So, if we consider only absolute growth—that is, actual growth independent of and unrelated to anything else—the snakes will grow the same amount.

Another perspective, however, relates the expected growth of each snake to its present length. For example, String Bean will grow 3 feet or $\frac{3}{4}$ of her present length. Slim will grow 3 feet, or $\frac{3}{5}$ of his present length. Which snake will grow more in the next two years? If we consider growth relative to present length, String Bean will grow more than Slim because $\frac{3}{4} > \frac{3}{5}$. Therefore, from a comparative or relative perspective, the snakes will not grow the same amount!

Suppose that, in this comparative sense, Slim will grow the same amount as String Bean. What should be his full-grown length? He should grow $\frac{3}{4}$ of his present length, or $3\frac{3}{4}$ feet. Therefore, Slim's length when fully grown would be $8\frac{3}{4}$ feet. Notice that you had to multiply—not add—to find Slim's new length. For this reason, relative thinking is also called multiplicative thinking. Absolute thinking is additive thinking.

Our problem about String Bean and Slim highlights the first and most basic perspective that students need to adopt before they reason proportionally. It is essential that they are able to understand change in two different perspectives: actual growth and growth compared to present length, or absolute change and relative change. As we have seen, these are two very different ideas. Relative thinking attaches significance or meaning to a particular quantity by comparing it to another quantity. Consider another context.

The quantity "5 people" tells the numerosity of a single set, and is nonambiguous in meaning. But if we compare "5 people" to other quantities, it conveys different information.

5 people in a 2-seat car

5 people in a football stadium

5 people on an 8-person elevator

These comparisons convey substantially different messages about crowdedness!

A *ratio* is a comparative index; it always makes a statement about one measurement in relation to another. A person cannot possibly grasp the notion of a ratio if he or she can recognize only the actual change or how much was added to some initial quantities. Ratios ask us to think multiplicatively: how many times its present length did each snake grow? Relative thinking is critical even in initial fraction instruction. Part—whole comparisons may, in fact, be considered a special kind of ratio in which the compared measures refer to the same quality in a set and some subset of that set.

In fraction instruction, relative thinking is entailed in the understanding several important notions. These include:

• the relationship between the size of pieces and the number of pieces.

• the need to compare fractions relative to the same unit.

• the meaning of a fractional number. Three parts of five equal subdivisions of something conveys the notion of "how much" in the same way that the above example conveyed the notion of "crowdedness."

• the relationship between equivalent fractions. The fraction numeral $\frac{3}{5}$, for example, names the same relative amount as when the unit is quartered ($\frac{12}{20}$) or halved ($\frac{6}{10}$).

• the relationship between equivalent fraction representations. For example, to understand the number $\frac{2}{3}$, it is necessary that the student focus on the relative amount represented by the various shaded regions described by $\frac{2}{3}$, as shown here, without regard for the size, shape, color, orientation, location, number of equivalent parts in each partition, and so forth.

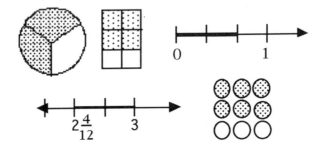

Encouraging Multiplicative Thinking

The children's responses to the opening question about the trees demonstrates how difficult it is for children to move away from the additive thinking with which they are so familiar and to begin to think relatively. P.J.'s response also suggests the great difficulty children have in describing a relative perspective even when they recognize it as an alternative to thinking in absolute terms. Robert's response doesn't indicate that he is thinking relatively about this situation—which doesn't mean that he never does. Dan used percent of growth to show that he is comparing the amount of growth to the starting heights of the trees.

   Discussing problems such as the snake problem or the tree problem in a group setting is often helpful in encouraging a relative perspective, but it is difficult to predict the context in which children first begin to think relatively. Even when they do, it may be in only in a limited number of situations. It may take time until a child begins to think relatively across a variety of situations, so children need to be presented the absolute-relative choice in many different contexts. You can find many contexts in which to encourage relative thinking. Become conscious of the way in which you ask questions and use every opportunity to ask questions both types of questions: one that asks children to think additively and one that asks them to think about one of the quantities in relation to the other. Here are some examples.

Marcus   Crystal

Example of questions that require additive or absolute thinking.

Who has more cookies, Marcus or Crystal?

How many more cookies does Crystal have than Marcus?

How many fewer cookies does Marcus have?

Example of questions that require relative or multiplicative thinking.

How many times would you have to stack up Marcus' cookies to get a pile as high as Crystal's?

What part of a dozen cookies does Crystal have?

Each child has three chocolate chip cookies. What percent of each child's cookies are chocolate chip?

If Crystal ate one cookie each day, how many weeks would her cookies last?

Cookies come 6 to a package. What part of a package does each child have?

Marcus and Crystal put all of their cookies into a box and took them to school to share with their 3 friends.   What part of the box will each friend eat?

Early fraction activities often include questions about pizza. Students tend to answer "how many slices" were eaten rather than "how much" of the pizza was eaten. To determine the number of slices is merely a counting problem and it signals a reluctance to move beyond thinking with whole numbers.   The question "How much pizza?" implies "What part of the original amount of pizza?" and requires relative thinking.

Example. A pizza is cut into 8 equal slices. 3 people have two slices each.

How many slices did they eat? 6 slices

How much (of the) pizza did they eat? $\frac{3}{4}$ of the pizza

Example. Mr. Thomas had 3 vacation days last week.

How many days did he work? 4 days

How much (of a week) did he work? $\frac{4}{7}$ of a week

When you are trying to assess whether your students think absolutely or relatively, you can ask questions in an ambiguous way to see what sort of answer students will give without any prompting, or you can ask your question in a way that directs students to answer relatively. You will obtain more information by first asking your question in an ambiguous form. For example, in the question about the number of girls in each family (#1 in the activities section), notice that the question is asked in its more ambiguous form. That is, "Which family has more girls?" Clearly, the additive response is correct and most children say that both families have the same number of girls. However, if a student suggests that there is another way to look at the situation and can explain his or her perspective, you can be sure that the student is thinking relatively. If you are having a class discussion of the problem, usually someone suggests that there is another way to think about the problem. However, if none of the students answers using relative thinking, you can always suggest the relative perspective with the question "Which family has a larger portion of girls?"

STOP Work the following problems and share your thinking with someone else. Consult the discussions in *More* only after you have thoroughly discussed them.

Activities

1. Which family has more girls?
The Jones Family

The King Family

2. Each of the cartons below contains some white eggs and some brown eggs. Which has more brown eggs?

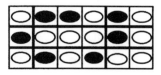   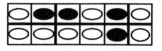

3.

        A   B

How much more pizza is in pan B?
How many times could you serve the amount of pizza in pan A out of the pizza in pan B?

4. Describe how you would decide which ski ramp is steeper, ramp A or ramp B.

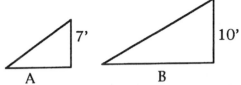

A   B

5. Dan and Tasha both started from home at the same time, 10 am. Dan walked 2 miles to the post office, 3 miles from the post office to the zoo and then 1 mile from the zoo to home. Tasha walked 2.5 miles to her friend's house, then 1.5 miles from her friend's house to the drug store, then 3 miles from the drug store to home. Both Dan and Tasha arrived home at exactly the same time, 12:30 pm. Describe exactly how you can tell who walked farther, Dan or Tasha?

6. Describe exactly how you can tell who walked faster, Dan or Tasha.

7. One of your favorite stores is having a sale. It is more helpful to you to know that an item is $2.00 off or 20% off?

8. What kind of information is necessary to describe the "crowdedness" of an elevator?

9. Here are the dimensions of three rectangles. Which one of them is most square?

     75'x114'   455'x494'   284'x245'

10. Analyze Fred's comment.

Oh, one more thing! Cut that pizza into 4 slices. I can't eat 8.

11. Ty, a third grader, said that because 9 is bigger than 5, $\frac{1}{9}$ is bigger than $\frac{1}{5}$. What does he not understand, and what will you say to him?

12. Sam and Jason, two third graders, commented on the following pictures:

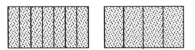

Sam said that $\frac{7}{7}$ is larger because there are more pieces. Jason said that $\frac{4}{4}$ is larger because the pieces are larger. What do you think?

* * * * * * * * * * * * * * * * * * * *

STOP Before going on to the next chapter, take some time to think and to write about the following questions.

Reflection

1. When children are first introduced to multiplication, the operation is defined as repeated addition. Is this a good idea? Is multiplication always repeated addition?

2. When children are taught about measurement, it is important they understand the compensatory principle, which involves relative thinking. It states that the smaller the unit of measure, the more of those units you need to measure something, and conversely, the larger the units of measure you are using, the smaller the number of those units it will take to measure the same amount. What does the compensatory principle have to do with fractions?

3. Think of some mathematical contexts that children would not be able to understand if they were not relative thinkers.

Chapter 3
Fractions and Rational Numbers

STOP

Children's Strategies

The students who answered the following question were just beginning to study fractions. Think about the division of whole numbers and discuss the ways it might have influenced their solutions.

There are fifteen students in your class, including you. On your birthday, your mom made 5 pounds of cookies for the students to share. How much will each person get?

Eva. $15/5 = 3$ pounds per person

Mary Elizabeth

5 pounds isn't big enough so I changed it to oz. 16 oz. = 1 lb.

16 oz. × 5 = 80 oz in 5 pounds

$$15\overline{)80} \quad \begin{array}{r} 5 \\ \end{array}$$
$$\underline{75}$$
$$5$$

Give everybody 5 oz. and give the other 5 cookies to the teacher.

* * * * * * * * * * * * * * * * * * *

Many people have a fear of mathematics. In high school, they were reluctant to take more than the minimum required courses. They had feelings of "being lost" or "in the dark" when it came to mathematics. For most of these people, their relationship with mathematics started downhill early in elementary school, right after they were introduced to fractions. They may have been able to pass courses—perhaps even get good grades—beyond the third and fourth grades by memorizing much of what they were expected to know, but they can remember the anxiety of not understanding what was going on in their mathematics classes. This chapter looks at some of the reasons why fractions present such a big mathematical and psychological stumbling block.

New Units and A New Notational System

As one encounters fractions, the mathematics takes a qualitative leap in sophistication. Suddenly, meanings and models and symbols that worked when adding, subtracting, multiplying, and dividing whole numbers are not as useful.

Several very large conceptual jumps contribute to the children's difficulty in learning fractions. In the preschool years, a child learns to count by matching one number name to each object in the set being counted. The unit "one" always referred to a single object. When the child begins to study fractions, however, the unit may consist of more than one object or it might be a composite unit, that is, it may consist of several objects packaged as one. Furthermore, that new unit is partitioned (divided up into equal parts) and a new kind of number is used to refer to parts of that unit.

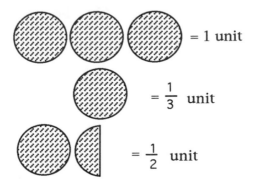

Furthermore, that unit changes. In each new situation, the unit may be something different.

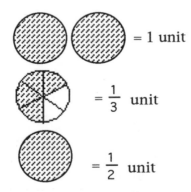

Even perceptual clues are no longer reliable. What *looks* like the same amount can actually be represented by different numbers. For example:

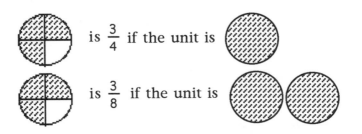

Finally, there is not a unique symbol to refer to part of a unit. The same part can be referenced by different names.

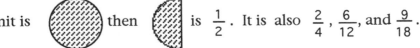

Types of Units

There are many different types of units with which one can study fractions. A language has developed for talking about the kind of unit involved in a fraction problem. If the unit is a single pizza and you buy more than one pizza, say three of them, then you have 3 one-units (or 3 units). If you purchase a package containing three frozen pizzas, then you have purchased one unit that is a composite unit. It is called a three-unit. Here are more examples:

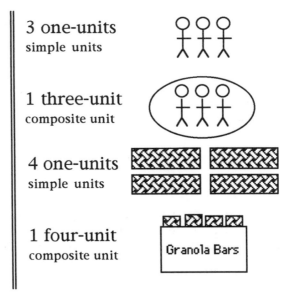

One four-unit and 4 one-units are very different. If it is difficult for children to think about composite units or units that contain more than one item, then it is even more difficult for them to interpret operations on these units. Taking $\frac{1}{4}$ of 4 single granola bars (4 one-

units) is different from taking $\frac{1}{4}$ of a box of granola bars (1 four-unit).
In the first case, you get one granola bar, but in the second case, you get
$\frac{1}{4}$ box. If you want your share of the food to be intact, you might be
concerned about which unit is going to be shared.

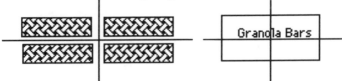

New Operations and Quantities

When children worked with whole numbers, they operated on them
principally by adding and subtracting. They began to develop some
meaning for the operations of multiplication and division, but only in
carefully chosen contexts using carefully chosen numbers and labels.
Before the introduction of fractions, children develop only a very
limited understanding of multiplication and division. This is because
true understanding of the operations of multiplication and division can
only come about when a student is able to construct composite units or
units composed of multiple entities, and fraction notation is needed to
help represent the complex quantities that result from multiplication
and division.

When working with whole numbers, quantities had simple labels
that came about by counting or measuring: 5 candies or 7 feet. The
operations of multiplication and division often produce quantities that
are relationships between two other quantities. Furthermore, the label
attached to the new quantity (the relationship) is not the label of either
of the original quantities that entered into the relationship.

Example
6 candies in every bag is $\frac{6 \text{ candies}}{1 \text{ bag}}$ or 6 candies per bag—not 6 candies
and not 6 bags.

Whole number quantities could be physically represented.
Students could draw a picture of candies or they could use beans or
blocks or chips to represent things being counted. However, a quantity
expressing a relationship such as $\frac{2.5 \text{ children}}{\text{family}}$ or 12 miles per hour
(mph) cannot be easily represented or conceptualized.

To further complicate the labeling issue, sometimes a quantity
that is really a relationship between two quantities is given a single
name. For example, consider the relationship between a certain
distance traveled and the time it took to travel that distance. That
relationship is so familiar that we chunk the two quantities into a single

entity and refer to it as "speed." When we refer to speed or to other chunked quantities in the classroom, it is important to remember that we have disguised the fact that we are really talking about the comparison of two quantities. Many students, well into their middle school years, do not realize that speed involves the comparison of two quantities, time and rate!

Interference of Whole Number Ideas

In whole number operations, many students came to rely on the model of repeated addition to help them think about multiplication, and the model of sharing some set of objects among some number of children to help them think about the process of division. In rational numbers, both of these models are defective. Consider these examples:

Example

A car traveled an average speed of $\frac{52 \text{ mi.}}{\text{hr.}}$ on a trip that took 3.4 hours. How far did it travel?

$$\frac{52 \text{ mi.}}{\text{hr.}} \times 3.4 \text{ hours} = 176.8 \text{ mi.}$$

Example

A car traveled an average speed of $\frac{51 \text{ mi.}}{\text{hr.}}$ and consumed $\frac{1.5 \text{ gal.}}{\text{hr.}}$ on a certain trip. What was the car's fuel efficiency on that trip?

$$\frac{51 \text{ mi.}}{\text{hr.}} \div \frac{1.5 \text{ gal.}}{\text{hr.}} = \frac{34 \text{ mi.}}{\text{gal.}}$$

You can see that in these examples, the repeated addition and sharing models will not help a student to answer the questions asked. It is necessary to build up new ways to think about these situations because the ways of thinking that were useful when working with whole numbers simply do not work any more. A student must learn to think about the quantities and how they are related to each other in order to determine appropriate operations.

Children experience cognitive obstacles as they encounter fractions because they try to make connections with the whole numbers and operations with which they are familiar. Some of the ideas children develop while working with whole numbers actually interfere with their later ability to understand fractions and their operations. For example, most children think that multiplication makes larger and division makes smaller. They experience considerable confusion when they encounter fraction multiplications such as the following:

$\frac{2}{3} \cdot \frac{1}{4}$ (Start with $\frac{2}{3}$, multiply, and end up with a product that is smaller.)

$\frac{5}{8} \div \frac{1}{4}$ (Start with $\frac{5}{8}$, divide, and end up with a quotient that is larger.)

The children whose work is shown at the beginning of this chapter probably remembered that in whole number division, the dividend (the number being divided) was always larger than the divisor. Each used a different method to deal with numbers that were "too small" to fit their concept of division, but then they both ran into the problem of deciding how to label the quantity their division produced. Mary Elizabeth's work shows what a bright little girl she is, but that all students—even the brightest—must take a huge conceptual leap when they begin to work with fractions.

The problems are many. Even those we have mentioned here do not exhaust the list. For example, in whole number operations, multiplication is commutative, that is, 3 x 4 will give the same result as 4 x 3. However, as quantities become more complex, many people begin to question ideas as basic as commutativity.

Example

3 (5-units) or taking 3 bags each of which contains 5 candies is not the same as taking 5 (3-units) of 5 bags each containing 3 candies.

Example

Driving for 3 hours at 45 miles per hour is a very different trip from driving for 45 hours at 3 miles per hour.

Some of the structural properties that were more transparent when working with whole numbers are still true on a more abstract level, but when placed in real contexts, psychological differences may stand in the way of recognizing them.

Problems with Terminology

Sometimes we get careless with the way we use words and this can cause additional difficulties in communicating about an already-complicated topic. Often the word "fraction" is used when rational number is intended, and vice versa. An analogous abuse occurs with the words "number" and "numeral." The word fraction is used in a variety of ways inside the classroom as well as outside the classroom. The many uses of the word are bound to cause confusion.

In particular, the word fraction has several meanings, not all of which are mathematical. For example, a fraction might be a piece of undeveloped land, while in church, it would refer to the breaking of the Eucharistic bread. In the statement "All but a fraction of the townspeople voted in the presidential election," the word fraction means "a small part." When you hear that "The stock rose fractionally," it means "less than one dollar." In math class, it is disconcerting to students that they need to learn a technical definition of the part—whole fraction when they already know from their everyday experience of the word that it means "any little bit." When a fraction such as $\frac{4}{3}$ refers to more than one whole unit, the interpretation "a small part" does not apply very well. To further complicate things, not only the colloquial usage of the word, but also the mathematical usage is problematic. In mathematics, the word fraction may refer specifically to the part—whole meaning of fractions, or it may refer to anything written in the symbolic form $\frac{a}{b}$. Most people are even further confused by the relationship of both meanings to rational numbers.

Fractions As Symbols

Sometimes the word fraction refers to a certain form for writing numbers. In this sense of the word, a fraction is a pair of numbers written in the form $\frac{a}{b}$, usually with the stipulation that the bottom number should not be zero. The top number is called the numerator and the bottom number is called the denominator. The order of the numbers is important. So the fraction $\frac{3}{4}$ is not the same as the fraction $\frac{4}{3}$.

Example

All of these are fractions: $\frac{3}{4}, \frac{\pi}{2}, \frac{\sqrt{4}}{2}, \frac{12.2}{14.4}, \frac{\frac{1}{2}}{\frac{1}{4}}$.

This use of the word fraction refers to a form for writing a number, a notational system, a symbol, two numbers written with a bar between them.

Part-Whole Fractions

Sometimes the word fraction is used to refer to one of several interpretations of rational numbers, traditionally called the *part—whole interpretation*. That is, a fraction represents one or more parts of a unit that has been divided into some number of equal-sized pieces. In this case, the word fraction refers not to the notation, but to a particular interpretation or meaning or conceptual understanding underlying the fraction symbol. Fraction symbolism may be used to represent many different interpretations or personalities of a rational number, but the first that children meet, at least in the present curriculum, is the part—whole comparison. Part—whole fractions have been the traditional inroad to the rational numbers in instruction because, in large part, operations on fractions—equivalence, addition, subtraction, multiplication, and division—form a basis for the formal symbolic computation in the field of rational numbers. It is a very important interpretation of rational numbers because it provides the language and the symbolism for the other rational number personalities.

Rational Numbers

The counting numbers (1, 2, 3, 4, 5, ...) are used to answer the question "How many?" in situations where it is implicit that we mean "How many whole things?" The whole numbers (0, 1, 2, 3, 4, ...) are also used to count how many whole objects are in a set of objects, with the added feature that they can answer that question even when the set is empty. The rational numbers are used for answering the question "How much?" They enable us to talk about wholes as well as pieces of a whole.

When you take some unit of measure, divide that unit into b equal-sized pieces and then take some number, say a, of those b pieces of the unit, then you have a way to talk about a piece that is only part of a whole unit.

The fraction $\frac{a}{b}$ is one of the ways that we can denote the rational number composed of some number of equal-sized subunits of a unit. In this case, fraction means both a part—whole comparison and a notation system. Although some people use the words fractions and rational numbers interchangeably, they are not identical concepts.

Example

All fractions are not rational numbers.

$\frac{3}{4}$, $\frac{\sqrt{4}}{3}$ (written as $\frac{2}{3}$), $\frac{2.1}{4.1}$ (written as $\frac{21}{41}$) and $\frac{\frac{1}{2}}{\frac{1}{4}}$ (written as $\frac{2}{1}$) are all fractions and rational numbers.

$\frac{\pi}{2}$ is not a rational number although it is written in fraction form.

Example

All fractions do not correspond to different rational numbers.

There is not a different rational number for each of the three fractions $\frac{2}{3}$, $\frac{6}{9}$, and $\frac{10}{15}$. A single rational number underlies all of the equivalent forms of a fraction.

Example

All rational numbers may be written as fractions, but they may be written in other forms as well.

Terminating decimals are rational and may be written in fraction form.

Non-terminating, repeating decimals are rational and may be written in fraction form.

Percents are rational numbers and may be written in fraction form.

Nonterminating, nonrepeating decimals are not rational numbers and may not be written as fractions.

Fractions as Numbers

When we speak of a fraction as a number, we are really referring to the underlying rational number, the number the fraction represents. Understanding a fraction as a number entails realizing, for example, that $\frac{1}{4}$ refers to the same relative amount in each of the following pictures.   There is but one rational number underlying all of these relative amounts.   Whether we call it $\frac{1}{4}, \frac{4}{16}, \frac{3}{12},$ or $\frac{2}{8}$ is not as important as the fact that a single relationship is conveyed.   When we consider fractions as numbers, rather than focusing on the two parts used to write the fraction symbol, the focus is on the relative amount conveyed by those symbols.

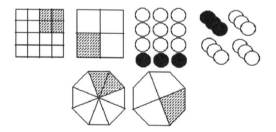

Regardless of the size of the pieces, their color, their shape, their arrangement, or any other physical characteristic, the issue is that $\frac{1}{4}$ refers to the relative number shaded.

Many Sources of Meaning

As one moves from whole number into fractions, the variety and complexity of the situations that give meaning to the symbols increases dramatically. Understanding of rational numbers involves the coordination of many different but interconnected ideas and interpretations. There are many different meanings that end up looking alike when they are written in fraction symbols. Unfortunately, instruction has traditionally focused on only one interpretation, that of part—whole comparisons, after which the algorithms for symbolic operation are introduced. Having a mature understanding of rational number entails much more than being able to manipulate symbols. It means being able to make connections to many different situations modeled by those symbols. Part—whole comparisons are not mathematically or psychologically independent of other meanings, but to ignore those other ideas in instruction leaves a child with a deficient understanding of the part—whole fractions themselves, and an impoverished foundation for the rational number system, the real numbers, the complex numbers, and all of the higher mathematical and scientific ideas that rely on these number systems.

Interpreting the Fraction $\frac{3}{4}$

To get an idea of the complexity and the rich set of ideas involved when a person truly understands the meaning of a fraction symbol, look at some interpretations for just one fraction, say $\frac{3}{4}$. The 12 interpretations we use here do not exhaust all of the possibilities, but they give a fair sample of the nuances in meaning that are hidden under the symbol $\frac{3}{4}$.

 Do the following tasks before reading on.

Twelve different interpretations of the fraction $\frac{3}{4}$ are described. Think carefully about each situation, seeking out the meaning of $\frac{3}{4}$. Then draw a picture to represent the meaning of $\frac{3}{4}$ that is conveyed in the situation.

1. John told his mother that he would be home in 45 minutes.

2. Melissa had three large circular cookies, all the same size--one chocolate chip, one coconut, one molasses. She cut each cookie into four equal parts and she ate one part of each cookie.

3. Mr. Alberts has 3 boys to 4 girls in his history class.

4. Four little girls were arguing about how to share a package of cupcakes. The problem was that cupcakes come three to a package.

Their kindergarten teacher took a knife cut the entire package into four equal parts.

5. Baluka Bubble Gum comes four pieces to a package. Three children each chewed a piece from one package.

6. There were 12 men and $\frac{3}{4}$ as many women at the meeting.

7. Mary asked Jack how much money he had. Jack reached into his pocket and pulled out three quarters.

8. All of the rational numbers can be matched with a point on the number line. $\frac{3}{4}$ must correspond to a point on the line.

9. Jaw buster candies come four to a package and Nathan has 3 packages, each of a different color. He ate one from each package.

10. Martin's Men Store had a big sale—75% off.

11. Mary noticed that every time Jenny put 4 quarters into the exchange machine, three tokens came out. When Mary had her turn, she put in twelve quarters.

12. Tad had 12 blue socks and 4 black socks in his drawer. He wondered what were his chances of reaching in and pulling out a sock to match the blue one he had on his left foot.

* * * * * * * * * * * * * * * * * * * *

Teaching Problems

Traditionally, fraction instruction has failed to put a proper emphasis on the unit. Many people were introduced to fractions by dividing up a single pizza. Teachers and textbook authors did not realize that by always using the same unit—one pizza—children were getting the idea that a unit was always a single pizza. An analogous situation occurs when a triangle is always pictured as an equilateral triangle. Children develop a faulty concept image and may fail to classify the figures shown here as triangles.

Similarly, many adults cannot identify the appropriate operation for solving this problem because instruction focused on a very narrow range of problems types when they were learning whole number multiplication:

> The local lunch stand sells three types of sandwiches, two kinds of soda, and three different desserts. How many different lunches consisting of a sandwich, a drink, and a dessert can be purchased there?

Hopefully, as you worked with the previous questions, you could detect some of the characteristics of situations that were varied to create different nuances. These situations varied along several dimensions:

• A unit whole may consist of a single object (one cookie) or it may consist of more than one object (three cookies).

• The unit may be a single object that has a number of pieces inside (a package of gum) or it may consist of several objects, with multiple pieces inside of each (four packages of jaw busters).

• The fraction $\frac{3}{4}$ was connected to many different ideas and contexts: percents, ratios, decimals, the number line, probability, fair sharing, exchanging, and so forth.

These situations suggest that instruction should employ many strategies and should expose children to a variety of contexts and models to highlight the various interpretations of $\frac{3}{4}$. To teach only the part—whole interpretation of rational number exposes a child a very limited interpretation of the symbols.

Some Pictures of $\frac{3}{4}$

1. John told his mother that he would be home in 45 minutes.

◯ is the unit. 45 minutes out of 60 minutes is $\frac{3}{4}$ of one hour.

2. Melissa had three large circular cookies, all the same size—one chocolate chip, one coconut, one molasses. She cut each cookie into four equal parts and she ate one part of each cookie.

The unit is 3 (1-units) or 3 single cookies.

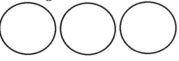

$\frac{3}{4}$ means 3 ($\frac{1}{4}$-cookies).

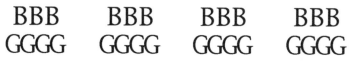

3. Mr. Alberts has 3 boys to 4 girls in his history class.

$\frac{3}{4}$ means 3:4 or 3 boys for every 4 girls.

BBB   BBB   BBB   BBB
GGGG   GGGG   GGGG   GGGG

4. Four little girls were arguing about how to share a package of cupcakes. The problem was that cupcakes come three to a package. Their kindergarten teacher took a knife and cut the entire package into four equal parts.

The unit is a composite unit:

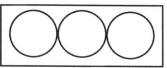

$\frac{3}{4}$ means $\frac{1}{4}$ of the 3-unit taken as a composite unit or $\frac{1}{4}$(3-unit) considered as one whole piece, rather than as three individual pieces.

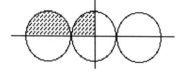

5. Baluka Bubble Gum comes four pieces to a package. Three children each chewed a piece.

 is the unit. $\frac{3}{4}$ means three pieces, each of which is $\frac{1}{4}$ of the unit, or $3(\frac{1}{4}$ -units).

6. There are 12 men and $\frac{3}{4}$ as many women as men at the meeting.

The unit is the group of men. The number of women (W) is $\frac{3}{4}$ the number of men (M) or W = $\frac{3}{4}$ M.

This is a multiplication problem. To get the number of women, either
a) multiply the number of men by 3 and divide the result by 4   o r
b) divide the number of men by 4 and multiply the result by 3.

For example, say the number of men is 12. The number of women is 9.

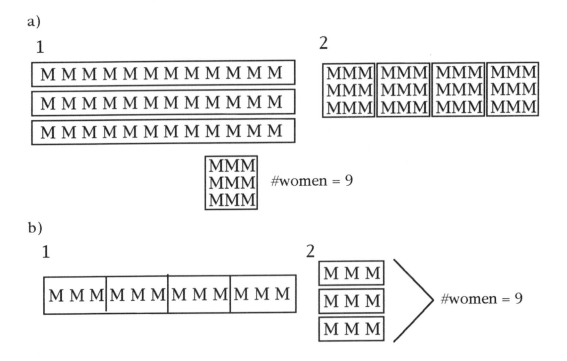

7. Mary asked Jack how much money he had. Jack reached into his pocket and pulled out seven dimes and one nickel.

$.75 is another way of writing $\frac{3}{4}$ of a dollar. $.75 is a decimal number.

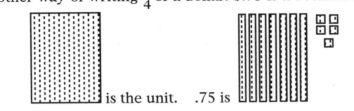

is the unit.   .75 is

or 7 tenths of a dollar and 5 hundredths of a dollar.

8. All of the rational numbers can be matched with a point on the number line. So $\frac{3}{4}$ must have a corresponding position on the following line. Its position is found by taking 3 of 4 equal subunits of the unit interval.

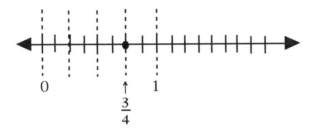

9. Jaw buster candies come four to a package and Nathan has 3 packages, each of a different color. He ate one from each package.

The unit is ⬜⬜⬜⬜, 3 different composite units. $\frac{3}{4}$ means 3 pieces, each of which is $\frac{1}{4}$ of one of the packages.

10. Martin's Men Store had a big sale—75% off.

75% or $\frac{75}{100}$ (75 out of 100) is another way of writing $\frac{3}{4}$.

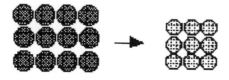

11.   Mary noticed that every time Jenny put 4 quarters into the exchange machine, three tokens came out. When Mary had her turn, she put in 12 quarters.

$\frac{3}{4}$ defines a way of operating on another number in a way that replaces every 4 objects with 3 (a 3-for-4 exchange). So $\frac{3}{4}(12) = 9$.

12. Tad had 12 blue socks and 4 black socks in his drawer. He wondered what were his chances of reaching in and pulling out a sock to match the blue one he had on his left foot.

Twelve out of the 16 socks in the drawer are blue. This means that $\frac{3}{4}$ is the probability that the sock he chooses will be blue.

Do not worry if all 12 meanings were not immediately clear to you. We develop these ideas in more depth throughout this book. In order to build a rich, well-connected web of meanings for rational numbers, we explore five major interpretations: part—whole comparisons, operators, quotients, measures, and ratios.

STOP

Work the following problems and share your solutions with other people. Consult the discussions in *More* only after you have thoroughly discussed them.

Activities

1. Write two problems that are appropriately solved by multiplication but which cannot be easily modeled by repeated addition.

2. Write a division problem whose quotient has a label different from the labels on the divisor and the dividend.

3. Write a problem appropriately solved by division that demonstrates that division does not always make smaller.

4. Write a multiplication problem whose solution demonstrates that multiplication does not always make larger.

5. Suppose something costs $.44 per 88 grams. Is that $.02 per gram or $.005 ($\frac{1}{2}$ of a cent) per gram?

6. Mark went wind surfing and traveled 4 miles in 15 minutes. At what speed was he traveling? What operation is suggested here?

7. Name some "chunked" quantities other than speed.

8. What is the same about all of these?

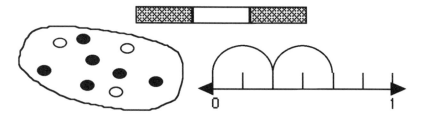

9. Draw a picture to show that taking $\frac{1}{4}$ of a 2-unit is psychologically and mathematically different from 2 one-fourth units. What is the result of each operation?

* * * * * * * * * * * * * * * * * * * *

Before going on to the next chapter, take some time to think about the following questions. Write down your thoughts.

Reflection

1. Why are fractions called equivalent rather than equal?

2. Which abbreviation should we teach children to write, mph or $\frac{mi.}{hr.}$? Is there a good reason for choosing one above the other?

3. Explain what is meant by the statement that these two pictures show the same relative amount.

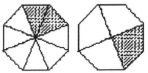

Chapter 4
Units and Unitizing

STOP

Children's Strategies

Analyze these student responses to the following problem, thinking about these questions: 1) What is the unit? 2) How did each child think about the unit?

Jim ordered two pizzas. The shaded part is the amount he ate. How much of the pizza is shaded?

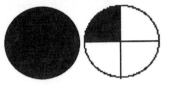

Kristin

$\frac{5}{4}$ because 5 little $\frac{1}{4}$ pieces are shaded.

Jean

$\frac{5}{8}$ because there are 8 pieces and 5 are colors.

TOM

1 And A bite.

Joe

It must be $\frac{5}{8}$ because $\frac{5}{4}$ is impossible. You can't have more than a whole pizza.

* * * * * * * * * * * * * * * * * * * *

Determining the Unit

To answer the question "How much?" we need to use a unit of measure by to determine the amount of stuff in question. Units are closely related to early measurement ideas. If you measure the same amount of stuff with different-sized measuring cups, the number of measures you get for your answer will be smaller or larger, depending on the size of your measuring unit.

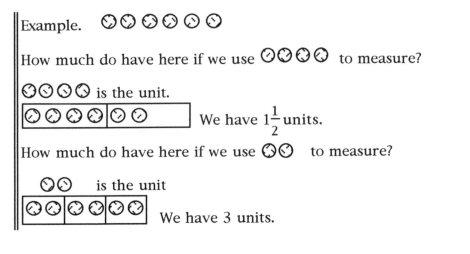

We begin by solving a few problems. These will give some background for talking about units.

STOP   Stop and solve problems A—E before going on.

A. Steve took a case of cola to Marcia's party, but it turned out that most of his friends drank water. He ended up taking three quarters of the cola home again. How much cola did he take home?

B. Mr. McDonald took six of his basketball players out for pizza. They ordered 2 large pizzas, a cheese and a pepperoni, and the seven of them each ate 1 slice of each pizza. If each pizza was machine cut into 12 equal slices, how much of the pizza was eaten?

C. Tony ordered a small cheese pizza and a medium pepperoni. Each came sliced into 8 equal-sized pieces. He ate three slices from each pizza. How much pizza did he eat?

D. Three children in Chris' class solved the cola problem (Problem A) and they gave the following answers.

Tom: 3
Dick: 18
Harry: $1\frac{1}{2}$

Suppose Chris asked you to respond to the children's work that day. What would you say to each of them?

E. Some children also solved the problem about Mr. McDonald's pizza party with his basketball players (Problem B).

John M. wrote: They ate $\frac{14}{24}$ of the pizza.

Sally J. wrote: They ate $\frac{14}{12}$ of the pizza.

Andy S. wrote: They ate 14 pieces.

Their teacher wrote a reminder: Talk to John M. He is adding denominators.
What would you say to each of these people about their solutions or comments?

* * * * * * * * * * * * * * * * * * * *

The chief issue in each of the situations is: What is the unit? In initial fraction instruction, the meaning of fractions derives from the context in which they are used, and each context, either implicitly or explicitly, should define the unit. Deciding on the unit should not be a matter of personal interpretation. The problems we give children to solve should either specify the unit or give enough information that the unit may be determined with a little reasoning. Some of the most widely used kinds of fraction questions in traditional texts confuse students, give them the impression that the unit is not important, or give them the impression that the unit is a matter of personal choice. The following question is not a good fraction question for beginners because the unit is not specified and it is impossible to tell which kind of comparison is indicated, a part—whole comparison or a ratio comparison.

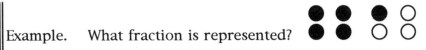

Example.   What fraction is represented?

Several answers could be given:
5 (each dot is a unit); $2\frac{1}{2}$ (each column is a unit); $\frac{5}{3}$ or $\frac{3}{5}$ (a ratio interpretation); $1\frac{1}{4}$ (each set of 4 is a unit)

The significance of the unit and the fundamental changes that must occur in one's thinking at the beginning of fraction instruction cannot be overestimated. Children need to learn early in their fraction instruction that the unit is something different in every new context and that the first question they should always ask themselves is "What is the unit?" Children who do not learn to look for that starting point, that reference point around which the entire meaning of the problem is built, usually make an inappropriate assumption (for example, the unit consists of a single whole entity, just as it did in whole number operations). For many students, progress in fraction thinking is greatly delayed, while for others, rules for computing are practiced without any accompanying reasoning capacity—all because they never grasped the importance of the unit. Many adults who revisit fractions are surprised to learn for the first time that the unit may be something other than one pizza, or one cookie or one cake!

At the beginning of this chapter, the fourth graders' responses illustrate how resistant most children are to fraction ideas. In particular, they are struggling with the question "What is the unit?" Jean seems to understand that the amount eaten must be compared to the total amount available, but the others—a full year after the beginning of their fraction instruction— are reluctant to adopt the perspective that a unit may include more than 1 pizza. Tom's answer avoids fractions. Kristin and Joe realize that Jim ate 5 pieces, but they were not sure whether to compare the 5 to 4 pieces (meaning the unit is 1 pizza) or to 8 pieces (meaning that the unit is 2 pizzas). Joe is trying to make sense of the numbers, but he is still confused. A correct statement would have been that $\frac{5}{4}$ was impossible because "You can't eat more than you ordered."

Unitizing

Another important issue in the problems you just solved **does** refer to a subjective preference or way of thinking. It is a cognitive process that occurs after deciding on the unit and it anticipates or sets the stage for operating on the unit. That cognitive process is called *unitizing*. Unitizing refers to the size of the mental "bite" in terms of which you think about the unit. It is a different process from deciding on the unit. It is process that goes on in a person's head.

Unitizing is the cognitive assignment of a unit of measurement to a given quantity; it refers to the size chunk one constructs in terms of which to think about a given commodity. For example, if you are asked to think about a case of cola, what sort of mental picture comes to your mind? Do you think about a huge cardboard carrying case full of cans or do you picture 24 individual cans of cola? Do you think about two twelve-packs? Four six-packs? Certainly, any of these is a reasonable alternative. You could be thinking of that case as 24 cans or (1-unit), 2 (12-packs), or 4 (6-packs).

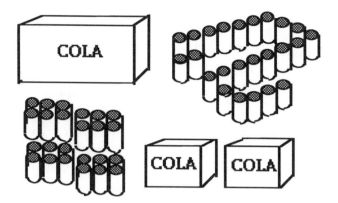

It is easy to understand how gross miscommunication can happen in a classroom. If the teacher asks students to think about a case of cola, the teacher might have one picture in mind, while each student might be picturing a case of cola in terms of the size packages his or her family typically buys. Ultimately, we want students to be able to think flexibly about any unit they are given. There are advantages in being able to conceptualize a unit in terms of many different-sized pieces.

Units Defined Implicitly

A problem's context or wording provides some means of determining the unit. Sometimes the unit is defined explicitly, that is, it is stated in the problem.

Example of a unit defined explicitly

John and his friends ordered two pizzas, each cut into 8 equal slices. They ate 13 slices. How much of the pizza was left?

The unit is the two pizzas, or 16 slices.
$\frac{3}{16}$ of the pizza was left.

More often, the unit is implicit. To say that the unit is defined implicitly means that there is built into the situation a way to determine what the unit is. Discerning the unit when it is defined implicitly is one of the most difficult fraction tasks for beginners. When a unit is defined implicitly, you can ask a series of questions to help you get to the unit.

Example of a unit defined implicitly

●● ●● is $\frac{2}{3}$. Find the unit.

You are given 2 one-thirds.

Ask yourself: "What does $\frac{1}{3}$ look like?"

Then, "What does $\frac{3}{3}$ (one whole or one unit) look like?

Sometimes, after determining the unit, you may need to use the unit to determine another fractional part. A useful way of thinking is to work up or down from where you are to get to the unit. Then work from the unit to the amount you want.

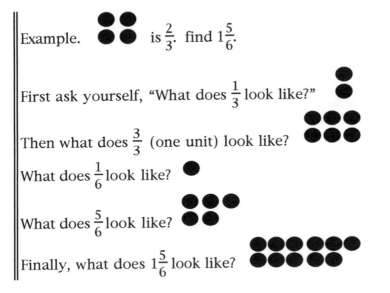

Example. ●● is $\frac{2}{3}$. find $1\frac{5}{6}$.

First ask yourself, "What does $\frac{1}{3}$ look like?"

Then what does $\frac{3}{3}$ (one unit) look like?

What does $\frac{1}{6}$ look like?

What does $\frac{5}{6}$ look like?

Finally, what does $1\frac{5}{6}$ look like?

This reasoning process is an extremely important way of thinking. Children should be encouraged to think aloud and not to do these problems by writing. The following example illustrates the verbal reasoning process that should encouraged.

Example. If 6 stars represent $\frac{3}{4}$, then how many represent $1\frac{1}{8}$?

"If 6 stars are $\frac{3}{4}$, then 2 stars must be $\frac{1}{4}$. If 2 stars are $\frac{1}{4}$, then 8 stars must be $\frac{4}{4}$ or 1 unit. If 8 stars are 1, then 1 star is $\frac{1}{8}$. So $1\frac{1}{8}$ must be 9 stars."

The following type of activity entails the use of more abstract units defined implicitly. Again, encourage students to reason aloud rather than doing these as written exercises.

Example.   2 zips + 1 zip = ▢▢▢▢▢▢. What does 1 zip look like?

Jason: "3 zips have 6 boxes, so 1 zip must be two little boxes next to each other with dots in them."

Example. 4 bleeps = ⬚BⷧB B B B B B B B B B B⬚ . 5 bleeps - 2 bleeps = ?

Megan: "4 bleeps have 12 little squares, so 1 bleep must have 3 squares. So 5 bleeps have 15 little squares and 2 bleeps have 6 little squares. That means the answer is 15 - 6 or 9 little squares."

      Children enjoy these activities and they have fun making up their own problems and challenging their classmates.

Teaching Problems

Now we can talk about some of the opening problems in greater detail.

> Steve took a case of cola to Marcia's party, but it turned out that most of his friends drank water. He ended up taking three quarters of the cola home again. How much cola did he take home?
>
> Tom said 3; Dick said 18; Harry said $1\frac{1}{2}$.

The problem explicitly specifies the unit: one case of cola. Depending on the size of chunk by which you think about the case, you can get different but equivalent answers. Tom, Dick, and Harry all failed to label their responses and should be reminded to so. However, we make the assumption that each of them knew that a case referred to some configuration of 24 cans. Then it is possible that each of them was thinking correctly about the problem. Each boy could have used a different but equivalent form of the unit, 1 case. Tom could have been thinking that a case consisted of 4 six-packs, in which case 3 six-packs would be correct. Harry could have been thinking that a case consisted of 24 individual cans. In that case, 18 cans would be $\frac{3}{4}$ of a case. If Harry was thinking of a case as two 12-packs, then $1\frac{1}{2}$ (12-packs) would also be a correct response. Correctly labeled, their answers should have been 3(6-packs), 18 cans, $1\frac{1}{2}$ (12-packs).

> Mr. McDonald took six of his basketball players out for pizza. They ordered 2 large pizzas, a cheese and a pepperoni, and the seven of them each ate 1 slice of each pizza. If each pizza was machine-cut into 12 equal slices, how much of the pizza was eaten?

John: $\frac{14}{24}$ of the pizza. Sally: $\frac{14}{12}$ of the pizza. Andy: 14 pieces.

Their teacher thought that John was adding denominators.

The problem tells us that McDonald and his boys started with two large pizzas. The unit consists of the two pizzas or 24 slices. This means that if each person ate a slice of each pizza, 14 slices of the 24 total slices were eaten. John is correct.

Sally failed to identify the unit. She thought that 1 pizza or 12 slices was the unit, so she concluded that $\frac{14}{12}$ or $1\frac{1}{6}$ of the pizza was eaten.

This actually says that they ate more pizza than they had! $1\frac{1}{6}$ of the pizza ordered would be $2\frac{1}{3}$ pizzas. They bought only 2 pizzas!

Andy did not answer the question. The question asks how much of the pizza was eaten, meaning how much of the pizza purchased was eaten. His response answers the question "How many slices were eaten?" Andy merely counted slices. This is not a counting question. The words "how much" demand a response that compares what was eaten to what they ordered.

The teacher is not sure what the unit is either. If he or she thinks that John was adding denominators, then we can safely assume that the teacher thinks that the unit is 1 pizza or 12 slices. The teacher thinks that John incorrectly added $\frac{7}{12} + \frac{7}{12}$ and got $\frac{14}{24}$.

Tony ordered a small cheese pizza and a medium pepperoni. Each came sliced into 8 equal-sized pieces. He ate 2 slices of the cheese pizza and 3 of the pepperoni. How much pizza did he eat?

The first question we need to ask as we consider this problem is "What is the unit?" We should notice that a small pizza and a medium pizza were ordered, so that we cannot combine then and say there were 16 slices. Those 16 slices are of different sizes! The unit is 8 small slices + 8 large slices. How much as eaten? The only way to say it is $\frac{2}{8}$ or $\frac{1}{4}$ of the small pizza and $\frac{3}{8}$ of the large pizza.

Using Units of Various Types

It is important that children learn to work with units of many different types. If all they see is round pizzas, they try to use round pizzas even when they need to divide a pizza into thirds. Why not use a rectangular pizza in that case? Children have to know that the representation they choose will not affect the answer. Another reason for varying the type of unit is that it is psychologically different to divide a set of hard candies into three equal-size groups than it is to divide a rectangular pizza into three equal-size pieces. Different types of units can provide challenges for different children. Sometimes, one of the factors that affects a child's thinking about a problem is related to whether they can see all of the pieces under consideration. For example, a package of cupcakes is not the same as a package of gum. Therefore, it is important that children's experiences not be limited. Problem difficulty may be varied by using problems involving units of all the following types:

one continuous item, such as one pizza

more than one continuous item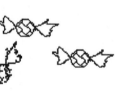

one or more continuous objects that are perforated or
prepartitioned, such as a candy bar

discrete objects (separate things, distinct parts), such as a group
of hard candies

discrete objects that typically come arranged in a special way,
such as chocolates or eggs in an array

composite units, that is, units consisting of single packages that have multiple objects inside, such as a package of cupcakes [1(3-pack] or a pack of gum [1(5-pack)].

One of the long-term goals of fraction instruction is to have children realize is that a fraction refers to a relative amount. This means that no matter what unit or which diagram you start with, no matter how many pieces it has in it, no matter what shape it is, and no matter what color, the number $\frac{a}{b}$ always describes the same relative amount. However, it requires a long, cognitively demanding process to get to that level of abstraction. The best way to help facilitate that understanding is to give children experiences with many different contexts and many different units.

Flexibility in Unitizing

Not only is it important for students to be able to identify the unit in a particular situation, but, in order to develop sophistication in reasoning, it is important to reconceptualize the unit in terms of different-sized chunks, that is, it is useful to be able to unitize and reunitize in the course of solving problems. Some examples illustrate what this means.

Suppose you go to the store and you see a sign that says oranges are 3 for $.67. You want to buy 9 oranges. If you think in terms of single oranges, or 9 (1-units), you will figure out that one orange costs 22.33333... cents. Now you need to multiply by 9 to get the cost of 9 oranges. If you round before multiplying by 9, you magnify the error due to rounding by a factor of 9. In this case, it would definitely be easier to think about a group of 3 oranges. If we unitize 9 oranges as 3 (3-packs), then the cost of 9 is just 3 times $.67 or exactly $2.01.

Think about that "case" of cola we have been discussing. If you need to share a case among 4 people, it is more convenient to think of a case as consisting of 4 six-packs. If you need to share a case between two people, would you deal out one can at a time? There is nothing wrong with using single cans, but it would certainly be faster to measure out each share and more convenient to carry home if your unit was 4 (six-packs) or 2(12-packs). In mathematics, the ability to conceive of a commodity in terms of more than one size chunk frequently adds convenience, simplicity, speed, and sophistication to one's mathematical reasoning.

Textbooks rarely encourage this flexibility; in fact, some of the procedures they ask children to practice work against the development of a flexible use of units. A little experiment will illustrate this point.

STOP Stop here and solve the following problem. Then check with a number of other people to see how they solved it.

Imagine that you are faced with this decision in the supermarket and you do not have your calculator or even a pencil and paper. The only tool you have is your ability to reason. How would you do it?

Which cereal is the better buy?

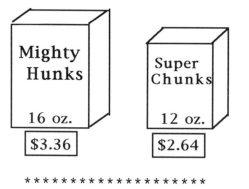

* * * * * * * * * * * * * * * * * * * *

You are likely to find many different solutions among those you ask. Adults rarely solve it the way that textbooks encourage students to solve it. Books recommend that students divide $3.36 by 16 to find the cost for one ounce of Mighty Hunks. Then divide $2.64 by 12 to find the cost of one ounce of Super Chunks. Most people find it difficult to divide mentally by a two-digit divisor, so this method of thinking about single units requires a calculator or pencil and paper.

But if you check with a large sample of adults, the most frequently used solution strategy takes each of the units and unitizes them in terms of 4-ounce chunks probably because it is easier to divide using a single-digit divisor. That is, most adults think of 16 ounces as 4(4-ounces) and 12 ounces as 3(4-ounces). Thus, for the 16 ounce box, the cost of 4 ounces is $3.36 ÷ 4 or $.84 and for the 12 ounce box, the cost of 4 ounces is $2.64 ÷ 3 = $.88.

If we are truly interested in helping children to develop their reasoning ability, rather than their facility in following procedures, it is not useful to have them practice finding unit prices. To help children develop flexibility in their use of units, in situations like the best buy problem, encourage multiple solution strategies and discuss which of them is easier, faster, or more reasonable. Under the conditions that you had no paper and pencil and no calculator, thinking in terms of 4 ounces makes the problem easier to do in your head. In the case of the problem about buying oranges, using a chunk of 3 oranges is nicer because it avoids the problem of a repeating decimal.

Particular conditions in the context of the problem usually suggest which unitization is easiest or most efficient.

Sometimes it is important to reunitize (think in terms of different-sized chunks) several times during the course of solving one problem. For example, consider the following problem:

> Mrs. Alvarez had 4 pizzas, each of a different type. She had 1 pepperoni pizza, 1 double cheese pizza, 1 onion and mushroom pizza, and 1 anchovy pizza. Juan and his two friends, Dave and Luis will share the pizzas. How can they do it so that each gets a fair share of each type? How much pizza does each boy get?

We begin with 4(1-units).

But in order that each boy get a fair share of each pizza, we need to re-unitize each of the 1-units as 3(1/3-units):

Then we distribute 1(1/3-unit) of each pizza to each boy.

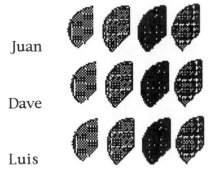

Juan

Dave

Luis

To determine how much of the pizza each boy gets, one share or $4(\frac{1}{3}$-units) must then be compared to the original $12(\frac{1}{3}$-units) in the original amount to get $\frac{1}{3}$ of the pizza. This analysis also helps us to see that it does not make much sense to say that each boy gets $1\frac{1}{3}$ pizzas in the case where each person gets a portion of each of 4 different types of pizza. If you put together each person's shares, do you really get a whole pizza? It makes more sense to say $4(\frac{1}{3}$-units) or $4(\frac{1}{3}$-pizzas).

Notice that the reunitizing process would have been very different if the pizzas had all been the same. Then we might have started with 4(1-units), given each boy 1(1-unit) and re-unitized the fourth (1-unit) as $3(\frac{1}{3}$-units) so that each could receive $1(\frac{1}{3}$-units).

This type of analysis of units and of the reunitizing process helps researchers to gauge the complexity of the thinking required in fraction situations. It is clear that students who can think of a quantity in only one way are disadvantaged, whereas those who have more flexibility in the unitizing process have an advantage in quantitative reasoning when fractional numbers are involved. Unitizing plays an important role in several of the processes needed to understand fractions, especially in sharing (partitioning) and in equivalence.

There are several ways to build on children's everyday experience and to encourage flexibility in unitizing. Young children (third graders) handle this type of thinking very well, but they may need to draw pictures as they work.

Example. 7 sticks of gum and 1(18-pack) of gum = _____ (5-packs) of gum.

5(5-packs)

Another context in which to talk about units and unitizing is called "the unitizer." It is an area model. This means that rather than using a unit that counts things (for example, a 6-unit is 6 of something), the units are blocks that each cover an area of a certain shape. They are nonstandard units of area. This means that the units are not units that are commonly used to measure area, such as square inches or square meters. These are units that we have invented and named just for this activity.

We begin with a unit rectangle. Several different rectangles are provided, but introductory activities should begin with Rec 1. The idea is to cover the rectangle or fractional parts of it with the smaller pieces. Each piece is given a name. A 2-square x 3-square piece is called a mini-rec. A 1-square x 6-square piece is called a stick. A 2-square x 12-square piece is called a railroad track. We can set up equivalencies, designating the pieces by their names:

4 sticks = 4 mini-recs = 2 longs = 8 mini-longs.

Pieces may be copied, cut, and used as manipulatives, but students can just as readily generate equivalent names for an area by inspection. The following dialogue illustrates the use of the unitizer.

"Tell me a way in which I can cover Rec 1 using railroad tracks."
(3 railroad tracks)
"Can you cover it using longs?"
(Yes, 6 longs)
"Can you find other names?"
(72 mini-blocks, 2 blocks, 24 mini-longs, 36 mini-sticks)

Your questions may help students anticipate fraction operations. The following dialogue anticipates the need to use a common denominator in addition and subtraction.

"Can you tell me a way to name 1 mini-long + 1 mini-rec?"
(3 mini-longs)
"Can you tell me a way to name 1 mini-rec + 1 long?"
(3 mini-recs)
"Can you name Rec 1 - $1\frac{1}{2}$ blocks?"
($\frac{1}{2}$ block)

Questions may also anticipate fraction multiplication and division. However, be careful about how division questions are asked and answered. Area divided by area is not area!

"Can you rename 4 copies of 1 railroad track?"
($1\frac{1}{3}$ recs)
"How many times can you fit 1 railroad track into 1 long?"
($\frac{1}{2}$)
"How many times can you fit $1\frac{1}{2}$ longs into Rec 1?
(6 times)

New subunits may also be created and named.

"What do you get when you combine a stick and a mini-rec?"
(2 mini-recs or 2 sticks)
(But it looks like a flag)
"Suppose we call it a flag. How many times can you fit a flag into Rec 1?"
(5 times)

The Unitizer

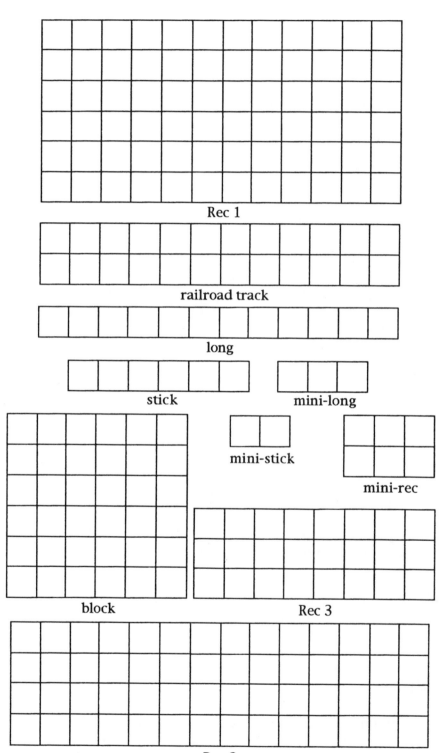

Rec 1

railroad track

long

stick   mini-long

mini-stick

mini-rec

block   Rec 3

Rec 2

Changing the size of the rectangle can change the difficulty of answering the same types of questions. For example, using Rec 2 requires mixed number responses.

"Name Rec 2 in terms of railroad tracks."

($2\frac{1}{3}$ railroad tracks)

Using Rec 3 requires fractional responses.

"Name Rec 3 in terms of longs."

(three copies of $\frac{2}{3}$ of a long)

"How many thirds of a long is that?"

(6 thirds)

"How many longs is that?"

(2 longs)

After working with the unitizer for a while, students increasingly visualize the process of covering pieces. Visually and mentally, they learn to change their perspective and reinterpret situations in terms of different pieces. Once they have the idea, encourage them to generate different ways to name quantities without relying on visual support.

Examples

1 case of cola = 24 cans = 2 (12-packs) = 4 (6-packs) = 3 (8-packs)

23 shoes = $11\frac{1}{2}$ pair

18 eggs = $1\frac{1}{2}$ dozen = 3 (half dozen) = 6 ($\frac{1}{4}$-dozen) = $4\frac{1}{2}$ (4-packs)

1 chocolate bar = 12 squares = 6 pair = 3 (4-chunks) = 2 (6-chunks)

These unitizing activities help to build the notion of equivalence and lay a foundation for fraction operations.

STOP Use the reasoning processes you learned in this chapter in the following problem set.

Activities

1. Specify the unit defined implicitly in each of the following examples. Do not do any writing. Explain your reasoning aloud.

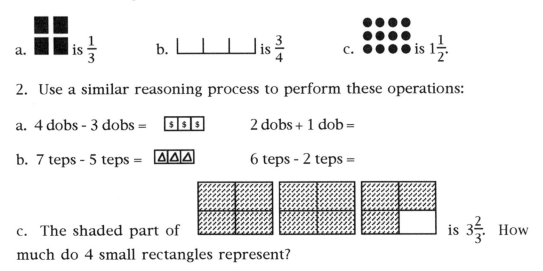

a. ▪▪ is $\frac{1}{3}$ b. └─┴─┴─┘ is $\frac{3}{4}$ c. ●●●● ●●●● ●●●● is $1\frac{1}{2}$.

2. Use a similar reasoning process to perform these operations:

a. 4 dobs - 3 dobs = [s|s|s]   2 dobs + 1 dob =

b. 7 teps - 5 teps = [△|△|△]   6 teps - 2 teps =

c. The shaded part of is $3\frac{2}{3}$. How much do 4 small rectangles represent?

3. Jake went on a diet and decided to measure portions of his food. He was allowed to have 4 ounces of turkey breast, so he went to the deli counter and asked for 4 ounces. After the person behind the counter sliced 3 uniform slices of turkey breast, she said, "This is a third of a pound—about as close as I can get." Jake needs some help to figure out how much of the turkey he can eat. Can you tell him?

4. How does unitizing affect the unit? Explain.

5. Would you purchase the following poster to hang in your classroom?

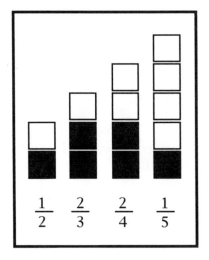

6. Jack and three friends wanted a snack. Mrs. Johnson had only 1(3-pack) of cupcakes. She gave Jack the package and told him to split it fairly. How should Jack share the package of cupcakes with his friends?

Amy and Seth, fourth graders, solved this problem, and they unitized the package of cupcakes differently. How did Amy think about the package of cupcakes? How did Seth think about it?

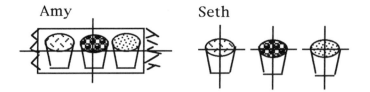

Amy   Seth

7. Two examples of children's work are given. Explain how each child reunitized to solve this problem:

Six children have these four candy bars to share. How can they do it?

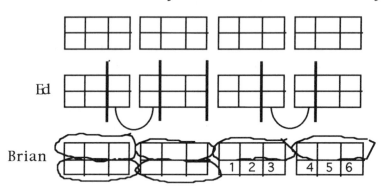

Ed

Brian

8. Unitize the given quantities in terms of the designated chunks. Write your answers using the unitizing notation. (e.g., 3 (6-packs) or $8\frac{1}{2}$(2-packs))

a. You drank 30 colas last month. How many 6-packs is that? How many 12-packs? How many 24-packs?

b. You and your friends chewed 14 sticks of gum. How many 5-packs is that? How many 18-packs is that?

c. 2 (6-packs) of cola + 3 (12-packs) of cola = _____ (24-packs) of cola.

d. 7 pair of shoelaces + 8 shoelaces = _____ pair

9. We commonly use a 2-group when referring to shoelaces (a "pair" of shoelaces) and a 12-group of eggs (a "dozen"). Think of other items that are commonly chunked into groups of more than one object.

10. Generate as many equivalent names as you can for $\frac{1}{3}$ Rec 1.

11. Use Rec 1 to answer the following questions.
a. 1 railroad track ÷ 1 block = _____
b. 1 rec + 1 stick + 1 railroad track = _____
c. 1 rec ÷ 1 mini-block = _____
d. 7 x 1 mini-rec = _____
e.   railroad track ÷ 1 rec = _____
f. 1 mini-long ÷ 1 mini-stick = _____
g. 1 mini-stick + 1 stick + 1 mini-rec = _____

12. When you are working with children, why might it be better not to generate additional names for your answers in #11?

13. Using Rec 2, create three questions whose answers are mixed numbers (numbers that combine wholes and parts). Give the answers.

14. My mom made a rectangular birthday cake and said I could share it with my friends. Abby took $\frac{1}{6}$ of the cake. Ben took $\frac{1}{5}$ of what was left. Then Charlie cut $\frac{1}{4}$ of what remained and gave it to Deena before helping himself to $\frac{1}{3}$ of the remaining cake. After they had all taken their cake, my best friend Marvin and I split the piece that was left in the pan. Did everyone get a fair share?

* * * * * * * * * * * * * * * * * * * *

STOP

Take some time to think about the following questions and to discuss them with others. Then explain your responses in writing.

Reflection

1. Use the process of unitizing to explain equivalent fractions.

2. Analyze each of the following problems, using the number of times that the unit must be reunitized. Use your analysis to form a hypothesis about which of these problems might be more cognitively demanding for sixth grade students:

a. There are $7\frac{1}{3}$ pies left in the pie case. The manager has a fresh supply coming in and she wants to sell the rest of the pie in a hurry, so she offers a deal: Buy one super piece ($\frac{1}{3}$ of a pie) and get a second super piece free. How many customers can get the special deal?

b. Steve shared his 4 Choco-Stix candy bars with four of friends. They had all just eaten 1 stick when another person came along. The five boys decided to give the new guy a fair share of what remained. How much candy did each of the six boys get?

Choco-Stix

3. Explain this statement: The choice of a unit quantity determines the amount represented by a fraction.

Chapter 5
Part-Whole Comparisons

STOP

Children's Strategies

Analyze the work of each fourth grade student shown below and try to determine what he or she probably understands and does not understand about part—whole comparisons. Discuss the children's responses with someone else before going on.

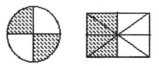

Name the part that is shaded in each picture.
Do these fractions name the same amount? How do you know?

Mike

In the circle $\frac{2}{2}$ is shaded. In the box $\frac{4}{4}$ is shaded. They can't be the same amount because one is a box and one is a circle,

Adam

$\frac{1}{2}$ is shaded in both pitcures. It is the same fraction but not the same amount. You can tell like this

DEREK

$\frac{2}{4}$ IS COLORED IN THE CIRCEL AND

$\frac{4}{8}$ IS COLORED IN THE RECTANGEL.

THEY ARE THE SAME BECAUSE

HALF THE PICTURE IS SHADE.

* * * * * * * * * * * * * * * * * * *

Unitizing and Part-Whole Comparisons

A *part—whole comparison* is used to compare one or more equal portions of a unit to the total number of equal portions into which the unit is divided.

• One portion is not the same as one piece. Sometimes a portion consists of more than one piece.

• One portion is not of some fixed size. The amount in a portion depends on how many equal-sized portions are formed.

• A part—whole comparison uses fraction notation. The two numbers of portions being compared are always present, both in the way you say the name of the fraction and in the way you write the fraction.

• The numbers form an ordered pair; that is, the second number or denominator always refers to the total number of equal portions in the unit, while the first number or numerator always refers to some designated number of those equal portions. The order in which the two quantities are written is meaningful. If the two numbers are written in a different order, they mean something else.

• The number of portions and size of the portions depend on how the unit is unitized. Both numerator and denominator are unitized in the same way in the same fraction; however, a different unitization results in a different fractional name for the same amount.

Consider the following rectangle. $\frac{3}{5}$ of the rectangle is shaded. This is because the area of the entire rectangle has been divided into 5 equal parts and we are comparing the area of 3 of those parts to the area of all 5 parts.

We could think of this rectangle as being composed of $20(\frac{1}{4}\text{-inch})$ squares. The shaded portion would then be $\frac{12}{20}$ of the rectangle.

If we think of the rectangle as being composed of smaller rectangles, each $\frac{1}{2}$ inch by $\frac{1}{4}$ inch, then the shaded part would be $\frac{6}{10}$ of the rectangle.

However, if we prefer to think about the rectangle as being composed of $\frac{1}{2}$-inch squares, the shaded region would be $\frac{3}{5}$ of the rectangle.

Because the shaded region of the rectangle remains the same in each case, the fractions that we generated are just different names for the same part of the rectangle.

$$\frac{12}{20} = \frac{6}{10} = \frac{3}{5}$$

Notice that the number of pieces in the shaded area in the unit rectangle became smaller as we thought about the rectangle being covered by larger-sized pieces. This is consistent with the measurement principles taught long before children were introduced to fractions. The larger the size of the chunks in which we thought about the unit, the smaller the number of pieces we needed to cover the rectangle. Conversely, the smaller the size of chunks in which we thought about the rectangle, the larger the number of the pieces we needed to cover it.

Example.   Suppose the unit is a U.S. dollar bill and you have 3 quarters.

What part of the unit (the dollar) do you have?

If you think of $1.00 as ◯◯◯◯, then you have

$$\frac{\bigcirc\bigcirc\bigcirc}{\bigcirc\bigcirc\bigcirc\bigcirc} = \frac{3}{4} \text{ dollar}$$

In order to compare the numerator and denominator, we need to unitize the numerator and the denominator in the same size chunks. Note that unitizing does not change the unit whole. It merely changes the size of chunks in which you think about it.

Example.   Suppose that the unit is the U. S. quarter and you have a dollar.

Because ⬛ = ◯◯◯◯, you can write

$$\frac{\boxed{\text{ }}}{\bigcirc} = \frac{\bigcirc\bigcirc\bigcirc\bigcirc}{\bigcirc} = \frac{4}{1} = 4 \text{ quarters}$$

Example. If you have 32 cans of soda, how many 6-packs do you have?

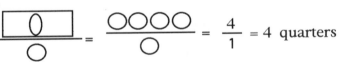

The unit is a 6-pack of soda.

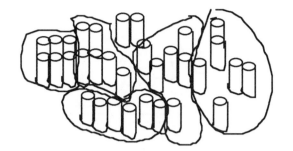

When you separate your 32 cans into 6-packs, you find that you have 5(6-packs) and 2 cans. The 2 cans make up what part of the unit?

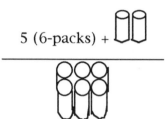

$$5 \text{ (6-packs)} + $$

Unitize the numerator and the denominator using the same size chunks. One way to do this is to think of a 6-pack as 6 individual cans.

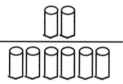

Then you have $\frac{2}{6}$ of a 6-pack. Altogether, you have $5\frac{2}{6}$(6-packs) of soda.

Example. Another way.

You might also think of the 6-pack as 3(2-packs):

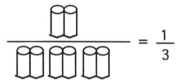 $= \frac{1}{3}$

In this case, you have a total of $5\frac{1}{3}$ (6-packs).

Example. If you have 14 eggs, how many dozen do you have?

The unit is a 12-pack of eggs.

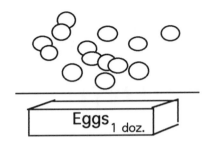

Because there are 12 eggs in a dozen,

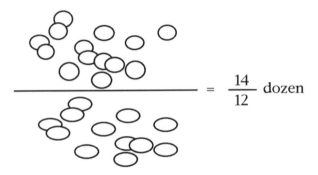

$$= \frac{14}{12} \text{ dozen}$$

Example. Another way.

  I can unitize the numerator by thinking of the 14 eggs as 1(12-pack) and 2 single eggs. I have

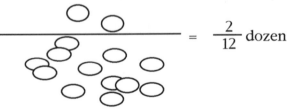

or 1(12-pack) with 2 extra eggs. To find what part of a dozen the 2 eggs are, I could think of a dozen as 12 single eggs. Then I would get:

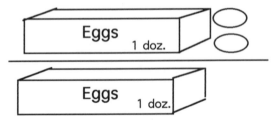

$$= \frac{2}{12} \text{ dozen}$$

14 eggs is $1\frac{2}{12}$ dozen.

Example. Another way.

I could unitize a dozen as 6 pair of eggs and get:

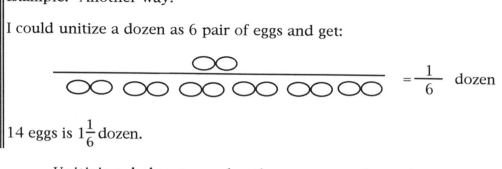

14 eggs is $1\frac{1}{6}$ dozen.

Unitizing helps to make the process of naming equivalent fractions a thoughtful, reasonable process. When children are first introduced to part—whole comparisons and they are also encouraged to draw pictures as we have just done, it also becomes a visual process. Unitizing combined with part—whole comparisons is equally effective when using continuous items such as acres or hours.

Last year you planted 8 different vegetables, each in $\frac{1}{2}$-acre plots. How many acres did you plant?

In this case, you are comparing the amount of land you planted to a standard-sized piece of land called an acre. An acre is 4,840 square yards, so a half acre would be 2,420 square yards. But do we really need to know this? No! The important thing is to be able to look at a model and see a clear picture of the size comparison. When our sets consisted of items such as eggs, we could actually compare by counting eggs, but that is not possible with continuous items such as acres. In this case, it is more convenient to let a rectangle represent the unit, one acre, and to use a rectangle half the size of the acre to represent half an acre.

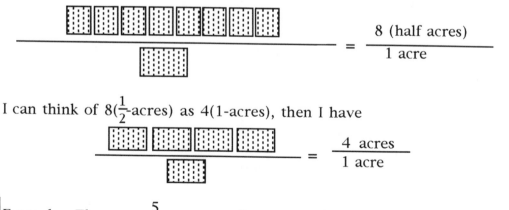

I can think of $8(\frac{1}{2}$-acres) as $4(1$-acres), then I have

Example. There are $\frac{5}{6}$ as many boys as girls in Ashland School. Are there more girls or more boys at Ashland?

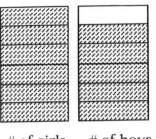

# of girls   # of boys

In this case, I compare the number of boys to the number of girls because the number of girls is the unit. However, I am not told the exact number of girls. As in the last example, I can let a rectangle represent the number of girls because it is not the number per se, but the size comparison between the set of boys and the set of girls that is important.

Children's Difficulties

Although fractions build on a child's preschool experiences with fair sharing, the more formal ideas connected with visual representations, fraction language, and symbolism, are so intellectually demanding that it takes a long time after their first formal introduction to part—whole comparisons before they can coordinate all of the essential details. Mike, Adam, and Derek, the fourth graders whose work you discussed at the beginning of this chapter show a variety of misunderstandings. Mike used a ratio interpretation rather than a part—whole comparison. However, he may have understood that equivalence could not be judged because different units were used. We would probably want more information than can be obtained from a single answer in order to know what he really understands about the unit. Adam seemed to understand that the same fraction numeral described both areas, but appeared to make a visual assessment of the area covered in each picture to determine equivalence, rather than noting that the fraction $\frac{1}{2}$ referred to a different unit different in each picture. Early dependence on visual comparisons can postpone reasoning about relative number and size of pieces. In this problem, Adam was given the pictures and, as it turns out, he was correct. However, using a visual assessment to judge equivalence or to make comparisons is not to be encouraged as a proxy for reasoning. Derek identified the appropriate part—whole fraction in each picture, but answered a different question than was asked. Both fractions are equivalent to $\frac{1}{2}$, but does he realize that they both refer to different areas? We can't tell from his response.

    Part of the reason students have so much difficulty learning the meaning of part—whole fractions and the early ideas of equivalence and comparison is that they inappropriately apply whole number ideas and operations to fraction situations (discussed in chap. 3). Other misunderstandings arise when children draw conclusions about fractions from their own drawings, especially when they have difficulty in controlling size, shape, and number of pieces.

    The following are some of the most common problems for third and fourth graders (and even older students) who do have not well-developed, stable, conceptual knowledge of part—whole comparisons:

- The unit is sometimes not divided into equal-sized shares.

- Decisions about equivalence and order are made when fractions refer to different units or similar units that are not the same size (a small pizza divided into 8 pieces and a large pizza divided into 8 pieces).

- Either because class inclusion is not understood or because a ratio model is more intuitive for some children, a part may be compared to another part of the same whole, rather than comparing a part to the whole.

- Especially when area models are used, fraction equivalence and order may be judged visually, rather than by reasoning, and when the model wears out (that is, when fractions get close in size, such as $\frac{7}{8}$ and $\frac{8}{9}$), children no other means to judge equivalence.

- Not even realizing that their drawings are inaccurate, children use them to reach incorrect conclusions. Thus, having young children use their own drawings may actually deter learning or cause misconceptions.

    Teaching children to reason about fractions gives them the opportunity to think about them before they have the physical coordination to draw fractional parts. It provides an alternate way to attack problems about part—whole fractions when pictures are not useful. It asks children to reason up and down, coordinating size and number of pieces, a mental process useful in the development of proportional reasoning. Finally, unitizing does not require integer results (for example, $\frac{8 \text{ eggs}}{12 \text{ eggs}} = \frac{1\frac{1}{3}(6\text{-packs})}{2(6\text{-packs})}$) and helps to facilitate movement away from "comfortable" or "nice" numbers: whole numbers, halves, and quarters.

Encouraging Flexible Thinking

Too little time is spent on part—whole comparisons before students are introduced to the algorithms for fraction operations. Children should do lots of verbal reasoning, with and without pictures, and should be encouraged, through the kinds of questions we ask them, to use multiple ways of thinking. Ask questions that involve continuous and discrete units. Ask questions whose answers require students to switch from symbols to pictures or pictures to symbols. Ask students to find equivalent fractions and to compare fractions. The following examples show some ways to vary questions so that students may explore various aspects of thinking about part—whole interpretations through unitizing.

Example. Ask children to interpret the fraction symbol using a picture of discrete objects.

How many marbles would I have to give Jim if he won $\frac{2}{3}$ of my marbles?

OOOOOO
OOOOOO

What we really want to know is how to unitize the marbles so that we get a relationship of $\frac{2}{3}$ or

$$\frac{?\ \text{marbles}}{12\ \text{marbles}} = \frac{2}{3}\ \text{of the marbles.}$$

How can I group the unit, 12 marbles, so that I get 3 groups? I can think of 12 marbles as 6(pairs) or 4(triples) or 3(4-packs). In this case, I need three groups, so I will think of the 12 marbles as 3(4-packs).

Two(4-packs) out of the 3(4-packs) gives the required relationship $\frac{2}{3}$.

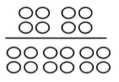

Shading $\frac{2}{3}$ of the marbles means shading 2 of the 3(4-packs) of marbles:

Children should not be encouraged merely to say that $\frac{2}{3}$ of the marbles is 8 marbles. The explanation that $\frac{2}{3}$ arises by thinking about the 12

single marbles as 4-packs is critical both to understanding and to explaining why 8 marbles is the answer to the question.

Example. Ask children to interpret the fraction symbol using a picture of a continuous object.

I have three acres of land. How much land is $\frac{5}{9}$ of my land?

In this case, the unit is 3 acres. I can unitize 3 acres as $9(\frac{1}{3}$ acres). Then $5(\frac{1}{3}$-acres) would give the required relationship.

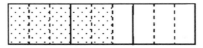

Make sure that children do more than merely draw a picture and shade it. They should be able to identify the shaded portion as $5(\frac{1}{3}$ acres) and as $1\frac{2}{3}$ acres.

Example. Include some fractions whose numerators are larger than 1.

If you want to shade $\frac{7}{6}$ of these dots, how many should you shade?

OOOOOO
OOOOOO

Unitizing the 12 dots as 6(pairs), 7(pairs) would give the required relationship. But you have only 6 pairs, so you need more than one set of marbles to show 7 pairs of marbles or $\frac{7}{6}$ of the marbles.

●●●●●●   ●OOOOO
●●●●●●   ●OOOOO

Example. Ask students to reunitize to produce equivalent fractions (i.e., change symbols to other symbols). Ask questions to which answers are not always whole numbers in the numerator and in the denominator of the fraction.

18 out of my 24 cans of soda remain in the box. Find several ways to name the part of the case that remains.

$$\frac{18 \text{ cans}}{24 \text{ cans}} = \frac{1\frac{1}{2}(12\text{-packs})}{2(12\text{-packs})} = \frac{3(6\text{-packs})}{4(6\text{-packs})} = \frac{\frac{3}{4}(24\text{-pack})}{1(24\text{-pack})}$$

Example. Ask questions that require visual rearrangement of a given picture to produce equivalent fractions.

I baked chocolate and vanilla cookies. What part of the following batch of cookies is chocolate?

$\frac{24}{36}$ chocolate cookies

Suppose I want to package the cookies so that each package contains the same numbers of chocolate and vanilla cookies. What part of each 6-pack should be chocolate? (Look at each row in the picture.) $\frac{4}{6}$ of each 6-pack should be chocolate cookies.

What part of each 3-pack should be chocolate? (Mentally exchange columns 3 and 6 in the picture.) $\frac{2}{3}$ of each 3-pack should be chocolate cookies.

What part of each 12-pack should be chocolate? (Look at 2 rows together.) $\frac{8}{12}$ of each 12-pack should be chocolate cookies.

Example. Ask some comparison questions.

✶✶✶✶✶✶✶✶✶✶✶✶✶✶✶✶✶✶

Which fraction represents the smallest amount of stars? the largest amount?

$\frac{2}{3}$ of the stars, $\frac{5}{6}$ of the stars, or $\frac{5}{9}$ of the stars

$\frac{2}{3}$ would be $\frac{2(6\text{-packs})}{3(6\text{-packs})} = 12$ stars

$\frac{5}{6}$ would be $\frac{5(3\text{-packs})}{6(3\text{-packs})} = 15$ stars

$\frac{5}{9}$ would be $\frac{5(2\text{-packs})}{9(2\text{-packs})} = 10$ stars

$\frac{5}{9}$ of the stars is the smallest amount and $\frac{5}{6}$ of the stars is the largest amount.

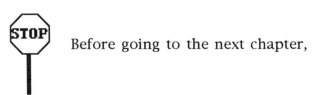

Before going to the next chapter, try the following activities.

Activities

1. a. The triangles are what part of the following group?

b. What is the unit in question 1a?

c. △△ is what part of the set of triangles?

d. How many items are in the unit in question 1c?

e. ◯◯◯ is what part of the set of circles?

f. How many items are in the unit in question e?

2. If the number of cats is $\frac{2}{3}$ the number of dogs in the local pound, are there fewer cats or fewer dogs? Draw a picture to show the answer. What is the unit?

3. One row of seats holds 12 people. What part of a row will four couples occupy? Do this example in two different ways (first by unitizing as couples and then by using people). Which two part—whole comparisons name the same part of a row?

4. Five-eighths of the school band is female. If there were 12 more males, there would be an equal number of boys and girls. How many students play in the band?

5. Answer each of the following questions, clearly indicating the way in which you unitized.
a. 3 days are what part of a work week?
b. 24 shoelaces are what part of a pair?
c. One pair of shoelaces is what part of two dozen?
d. 8 colas are what part of a 12-pack?
e. 8 colas are what part of a 6-pack?
f. 3 quarters are how many half dollars?
g. 17 quarter-acres are what part of an acre?

h. 17 quarter-acres are what part of a half acre?

6. Represent each of the following relationships in a drawing.
a. Five ninths of the committee members are women.

b. I have 4 acres of land and I have $\frac{5}{6}$ of it planted in corn.

c. I have 10 acres of land and $\frac{2}{5}$ of it is a lake.

d. I had 2 cakes, and $\frac{5}{6}$ of them were eaten.

e. I have 2 cupcakes but Jack has $\frac{7}{4}$ as many as I do.

7. What part of the square does the circle cover?

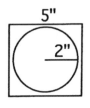

8. Would you have more land if you had $\frac{4}{5}$ of an acre or $\frac{5}{6}$ of an acre? A fourth grade student gave the following response to this question. Prove to her using unitizing that she was fooled by her pictures.

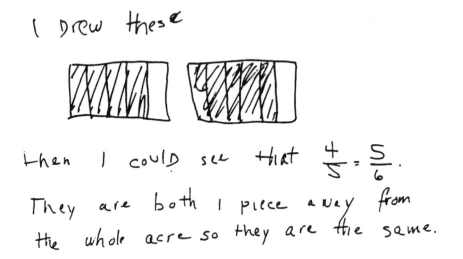

9. Visually reunitize the following picture to answer the following questions:

a. Can you see thirds? How many spots in $\frac{2}{3}$ of the set?

b. Can you see sixths? How many spots in $\frac{5}{6}$ of the set?

c. Can you see ninths? How many spots in $\frac{7}{9}$ of the set?

d. Can you see twelfths? How many spots in $\frac{7}{12}$ of the set?

e. Can you see eighteenths? How many spots in $\frac{11}{18}$ of the set?

10. ♥♥♥♥♥♥♥♥♥♥♥♥♥♥♥♥♥♥

Using this set of hearts, determine the smallest fraction by unitizing:

$$\frac{5}{6}, \frac{2}{3}, \text{ or } \frac{5}{9}.$$

* * * * * * * * * * * * * * * * * * * *

STOP   Think, discuss, then write.

Reflection

1. Can every fraction that is equivalent to $\frac{8}{12}$ be found by multiplying numerator and denominator by some counting number n?

2. Are the following fractions equivalent? $\frac{0}{3}$ and $\frac{0}{7}$

3. Suppose your unit consists of 12 poker chips. Which is the significant quantity in forming fourths: the number in each share or the number of shares?

Chapter 6
Partitioning and Quotients

Children's Strategies
Some fourth grade children answered this question:
Six children share these candy bars. How much candy does each person get?

Analyze the children's responses. Are they correct? Rank the strategies according to their sophistication, giving reasons to support your ranking.

Nicole

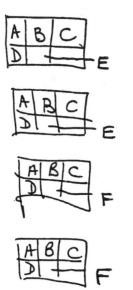

A get ▢ and ▢ and ▢ and ▢

$$\frac{1}{6} + \frac{1}{6} + \frac{1}{6} + \frac{1}{6}$$

B gets the same.

C " " "

D " " "

E "▭ and ▭ $\frac{2}{6} + \frac{2}{6}$

F " " "

Steve

Everybody gets $\frac{2}{3}$ of a candy bar.

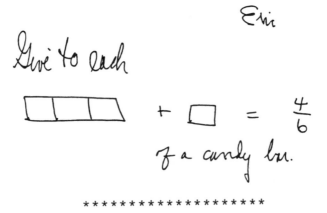

* * * * * * * * * * * * * * * * * * * *

Rational Numbers as Quotients

A rational number may be viewed as a quotient, that is, as the result of a division. For example, $\frac{3}{4}$ may be interpreted as the amount of cake each person gets when 3 cakes are divided equally among 4 people. Later, in high school, one might look at the problem this way: I wish to divide three cakes among 4 people. How much cake will each person receive? Let x = the amount of cake each person will receive. Then the solution will be obtained by solving the equation 4x = 3. To solve the equation, you perform a division to get x = $\frac{3}{4}$. Still later, in more advanced mathematics, one might study the rational numbers as a quotient field. The study of rational numbers as a quotient field is well beyond the elementary and middle school child, but the foundations for building a solid understanding are laid in the early years. In fact, at their most basic level, quotients arise in fair sharing, an activity well known to preschool children.

Partitioning

Partitioning is the process of dividing an object or objects into a number of disjoint and exhaustive parts. This means that the parts are not overlapping and that everything is included in one of the parts. When we use the word in relation to fractions, it is with the additional stipulation that those parts must be of the same size.

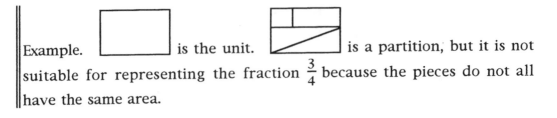

Example. ☐ is the unit. ⊟ is a partition, but it is not suitable for representing the fraction $\frac{3}{4}$ because the pieces do not all have the same area.

It is **not** the case that if the unit contains more than one object, that each object must be divided up in the same manner. Rather, what is critical is that each share you create has the same total area.

Example. Share four cookies among three people.

is ok because the total amount of cookie available is used up; there is no overlap (nothing is assigned to two people at the same time and each share contains the same amount).

The process of partitioning lies at the very heart of rational number understanding. Fractions and decimals are both formed by partitioning. (Note that decimals are based on a division of a unit into 10 equal parts, and each of those parts, into 10 equal parts, etc.). Locating a rational number on the number line depends on the division of the unit into equivalent spaces. The roots of the understanding of equivalence—a mathematical notion that applies far more widely than in the fraction world—are laid when performing different partitions that result in the same relative amounts. We could go on. Partitioning is an action fundamental to the production of numbers, to mathematical concepts, and to reasoning and operations.

In building understanding for rational numbers, there are many good reasons to engage students in lots of partitioning activities. In addition to the fact that partitioning is a fundamental mechanism for building up rational number concepts and operations, it makes use of an activity that has been part of children's everyday experience since they were toddlers: fair sharing. They are very good at sharing cookies and candies, and in that process of sharing, they have experienced the need for fractions when everything did not work out nicely and they had to break food. Thus, these activities build on what children already know and help them to extend their knowledge into new territory.

Unfortunately, instruction has made very little use of partitioning. It is used implicitly in the beginning of fraction instruction when part—whole fractions are defined: the denominator tells the number of equal parts into which the whole is divided. The children usually make some pictures to represent part—whole comparisons, but then picture drawing is abandoned.

Early Partitioning Activities

Some teachers may avoid partitioning activities in the first and second grades because children do not always have excellent hand—eye coordination at that age, and they have trouble drawing the correct number of parts and making them all the same size. However, these problems may be circumvented by giving them prepartitioned pictures so that drawing pictures is not an end it self. The goal should be to keep their concentration on the reasoning process, on the number of shares, and the fairness of shares, rather than on the ability to draw them accurately. For second and third graders, it is a good idea to begin with units in which there are perforations or some form of scored cutting lines. For example, postage stamps come in perforated sheets, and candy bars are scored for breaking.

    A good way to introduce the idea of partitioning is to do it visually. For example, without using your pencil, try to "see" each person's share in the following situation.

Example.   Share 3 pizzas among 6 people.

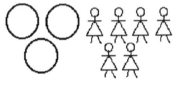

In your mind, you should "see" one share as half a pizza: .

    It is a good idea to ask children to partition visually in order to encourage them to see bigger pieces. When young children in grades K—3 engage in partitioning activities, a common strategy is to divide every piece of the unit into the number of shares needed. This means that if a number of objects are to be shared by three people, they will routinely cut every piece into three parts.

If several objects are to be shared by six people, they will divide every one of the pieces into six parts.

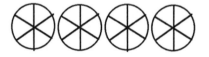

One of the goals of instruction that used partitioning is to create shares as efficiently as possible. More efficient partitioning requires some form of mental comparison of the amount of stuff to be divided to the number of shares. It involves knowing that you have enough stuff that you will not run out if you give each person a little more or make each share larger. Anticipating or estimating or visualizing that relative size before you start cutting reduces the total number of cuts needed to accomplish the job. The object of partitioning is to be able to name how much is in each share. The more fragmented a share is, the more difficult it will be to the total amount in that share. By having students look for one share while the pictures are on an overhead, rather than on a paper in front of them, we can encourage them to "see" shares in larger pieces.

Stages in Partitioning

Children's partitioning strategies show fairly predictable stages. Early on, most children are very good at halving. Soon they get the idea that they can continue to halve when they wish to produce fourths, eighths, and sixteenths. Sometimes they are so concerned with making the right number of pieces that they forget to make them equivalent, but with more practice, they learn to focus on the parts as well as their size.

Producing fractional parts whose denominators are odd is a little harder. When instruction regularly uses objects of different types and shapes, children soon learn that choosing a different shape makes drawing easier. If students are trying to create thirds, for example, and they have been encouraged to move among many different shapes to represent their unit, they will know that it is easier to produce thirds using a rectangle than it is with a circle.

It is important that students realize that the picture makes no difference. $\frac{1}{3}$ refers to a relative amount—1 part out of 3—no matter what the unit looks like.

Partitioning and Equivalence

When children are able to draw more accurately, problems may be presented without accompanying drawings so that the students must decide on an appropriate representation as well as how to partition it. For each problem, there are several possible correct ways to create fair shares. For example, for the problem "6 people share 4 pizzas," here are just a few of the pictures that are possible. In each example, the shaded part represents 1 share.

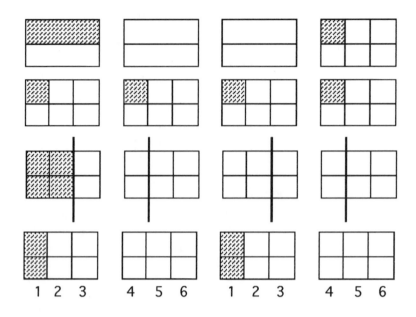

It is important for the teacher to elicit drawings from several children who may have produced different ways to partition a unit. Children should also be encouraged to write the symbols that name all of the pieces of one share.

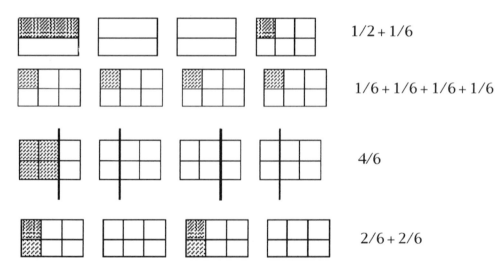

$1/2 + 1/6$

$1/6 + 1/6 + 1/6 + 1/6$

$4/6$

$2/6 + 2/6$

If the children agree that no matter which picture you use, a person always receives the same amount of pizza, then all of the amounts written as fractions must be equivalent.

Next, look for equivalent fractions.

$\frac{1}{2}$ must be the same amount as $\frac{1}{6} + \frac{1}{6} + \frac{1}{6}$.

$\frac{1}{6} + \frac{1}{6}$ must be the same amount as $\frac{2}{6}$.

$\frac{2}{6} + \frac{2}{6}$ must be the same amount as $\frac{4}{6}$.

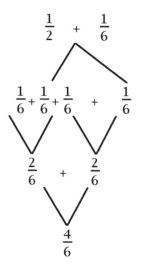

Have children keep a record of the fractions that represent the same amounts. For example, after discussing all of the different partitions just shown, they may conclude that $\frac{1}{2} = \frac{1}{6} + \frac{1}{6} + \frac{1}{6}$.

Example.   4 children share 3 pizzas.

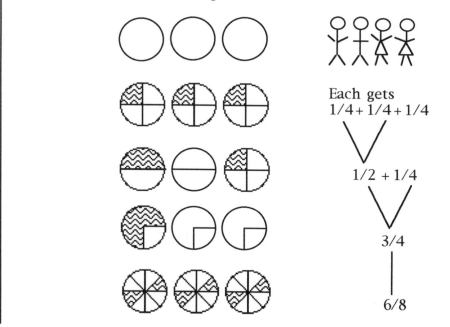

Notice how easily the ideas of equivalence and addition naturally emerge from partitioning activities. However, it is not sufficient to ask children to draw pictures and describe one share by shading. After determining fair shares, it is important that students look for equivalent pieces as we have just done, in order to help answer the important questions that should accompany every partitioning activity.

Quotient and Part-Whole Questions

The important question related to quotients is: How much is one share? Or how much does one person receive? A second and equally important question is: What part of the pizza does each person eat? Or what part of the unit is one share of pizza? Note that this second question concerns a part—whole comparison. For example, take the problem of sharing 3 pizzas among 6 people.

The quotient question is "How much pizza will each person receive?"

The answer is $\frac{3}{6}$ or $\frac{1}{2}$ pizza.

Notice that the answer to the quotient question is a division: the number of objects divided by the number of shares, $\frac{3}{6}$ or $\frac{1}{2}$ pizza per person.

The part—whole comparison question is "What part of the pizza will each person receive?"

This question asks us to compare $\frac{1}{2}$ pizza (one share) to the unit, 3 pizzas.

$$\frac{\frac{1}{2} \text{ pizza}}{3 \text{ pizzas}}$$

Unitizing the 3 pizzas into half pizzas, we get

$$\frac{1 \text{ (half pizza)}}{6 \text{ (half pizzas)}} = \frac{1}{6} \text{ of the unit.}$$

Notice that the answer to the part—whole question is always 1 unit divided by the number shares.

> Example. Suppose 4 children share 3 pizzas.
> One share will be $\frac{3}{4}$ of a pizza.
> What part of the original amount is one share?

Compare $\frac{3}{4}$ pizza to 3 pizzas.

$$\frac{\frac{3}{4} \text{ pizza}}{3 \text{ pizzas}}$$

Unitize the 3 pizzas into ($\frac{3}{4}$ pizzas)

$$\frac{1 \ (\frac{3}{4}\text{-pizza})}{4 \ (\frac{3}{4}\text{-pizza})}$$

One share is $\frac{1}{4}$ of the unit.

It is important that children understand the relationships among several critical quantities: (a) the number of people; (b) one share; and (c) the unit. Children cannot be said to understand quotients until they can readily answer both questions: "How much is one share?" and "What part of the unit is that share?" Another way to ask these questions is: "How much pizza does one person receive?" and "How much of the pizza does one person receive?" ("The" pizza implies the amount of pizza with which we started.) It takes children a long time until they can answer both questions. Next we will explore some of the reasons for this long-term learning process and note the characteristics of children's work that indicate increasing competence.

Partitioning and Unitizing

There is a powerful relationship between unitizing and partitioning that can help teachers decide when children need more partitioning experiences and when they fully understand quotients. Put simply, it is this: the larger the pieces into which a child partitions an object or objects to be shared, the closer that child is to answering the quotient and the part—whole questions.

We have already defined unitizing as thinking about a quantity in terms of different-sized chunks and we have already seen that the partitioning of a unit may be accomplished using different-sized chunks. It is easier to use small pieces in sharing problems, and it takes a long time to discover that two or more of the smaller pieces could have been put together to make larger pieces. Students who are more mature in terms of understanding fraction equivalence are able to use larger chunks when partitioning. If a child splits an object into many little pieces and then distributes them, each person's share is fragmented and it is difficult for the child to determine a single fraction name for one share. Another way to think about this is in terms of reversibility: naming a quantity and then chopping it up into little pieces is much easier than going the opposite way (putting a bunch of little pieces together and naming the quantity they form). Research on partitioning has shown that greater economy in marking and cutting corresponds to a more mature understanding of fractions.

Suppose you ask students to show how 3 people might share 4 pizzas. Students will use many different strategies that can be put into a hierarchy from least sophisticated to most sophisticated by observing (a) the number of pieces in a share; (b) how much excess cutting is used; and (c) how much excess marking is used.

STOP Stop here and rank the following strategies according to their sophistication.

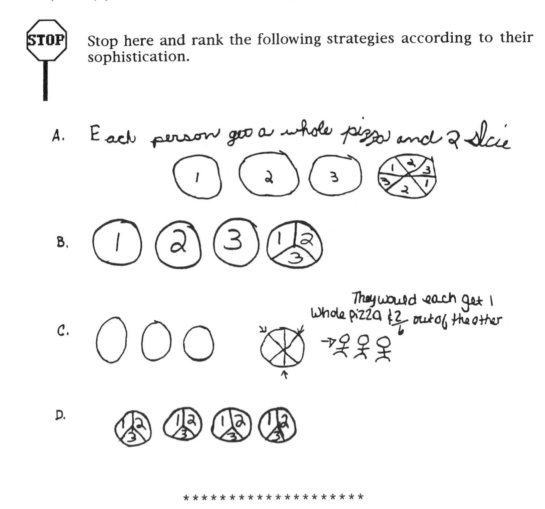

A. Each person gets a whole pizza and 2 slice

B.

C.

They would each get 1 whole pizza & 2 out of the other

D.

* * * * * * * * * * * * * * * * * * *

The most mature strategy (B) marks and cuts as little as possible. The least sophisticated strategy (D) marks and cuts every piece. Students whose strategies lie between these two extremes use a little more marking than is necessary, or a little more cutting than is necessary. The less, the better (C is better than A).

As the ability to think with fractions increases, student strategies become more and more economical in terms of the marking and cutting. This is a consistent pattern that may be observed within and across grade levels. There is a shift from the use of many pieces to the use of fewer pieces; there is a shift from marking every piece to marking only pieces that must be cut; there is also a shift from thinking in terms of single items toward thinking in terms of composite items (such as packs of gum). However, this is not to say that students always use the most economical strategy. Even when a more economical strategy could be used, they respect social practices with regard to whatever type of food you have asked them to partition. For example, they partition pizzas differently when the pizzas are all of the same type (4 cheese pizzas), than when they are all different (one cheese, one pepperoni, one mushroom, and one anchovy) because it is customary for each person to have some of each when different toppings are ordered.

You may have detected some differences in the children's work you analyzed at the beginning of the chapter, based on the characteristics of partitioning just discussed. Compare the children on the first criterion: number of pieces. Nicole used many cuts, Eric used few, but Steve was most economical. The ability to look at how much stuff you have and make an estimate of how large a chunk each person will receive, as opposed to cutting and distributing pieces to see how far you get, is a more mature approach to partitioning.

Compare the students on their ability to give a single fraction name to one person's share. Nicole, whose shares were most fragmented did not answer the question. Eric's shares were less fragmented and he was able to identify $\frac{4}{6}$ of a candy bar as one share. Steve, who had done the least cutting was able to see that each person would receive $\frac{2}{3}$ of a candy bar.

Partitive and Quotitive Division

The type of division we have been considering, that which involves partitioning or determining equal parts or shares, is called partitive division. There is another type of division, called *quotitive division*. In quotitive division, one is quoted a "per share" quantity, and the question is how many such shares can be measured out of some larger quantity.

Example. If each boy needs a piece of rope $\frac{5}{8}$ of a yard long, how many boys can cut a piece from a hank of rope 6 yards long?

Measure out pieces $\frac{5}{8}$ of a yard long from the 6-yard piece.

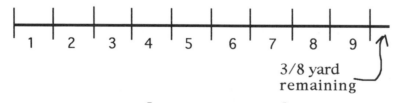

3/8 yard remaining

Nine boys can cut their $\frac{5}{8}$-yard pieces, and $\frac{3}{8}$ yard will be left over.

This type of division question is not asked as frequently as the partitive division question. Consequently, many people have a hard time identifying the unit in this type of fraction problem. In a quotitive division problem, whatever unit you were given is reinterpreted in terms of the divisor. The divisor becomes the new unit of measure. The answer is frequently stated in terms of the divisor.

Example. How many pieces of rope could be cut?

What part of $\frac{5}{8}$ of a yard is $\frac{3}{8}$ of a yard?

$$\frac{\frac{3}{8}}{\frac{5}{8}} = \frac{3}{5} \text{ of a piece. So we have } 9\frac{3}{5} \text{ pieces of rope.}$$

Notice that neither 9 pieces nor 10 pieces is the answer to this question. The question is answered by a mixed number, a whole piece and a fractional part of a piece. Also notice that the original length of rope, the 6 yards, becomes less important and all of the measuring is done in terms of the $\frac{5}{8}$-yard pieces. This means that the remaining piece (the leftover portion of rope) must also be reinterpreted in terms of the new unit, the $\frac{5}{8}$-yard piece, to determine what part of a piece remains.

Example. When you buy a slice of pie at Delaney's Pie Shop you get $\frac{1}{3}$ of a pie. If Mr. Delaney has $4\frac{1}{2}$ pies in his refrigerator, how many slices does he have?

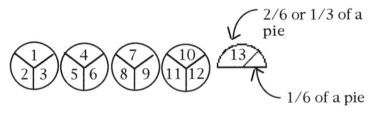

2/6 or 1/3 of a pie

1/6 of a pie

$\frac{1}{6}$ of a pie is $\frac{1}{2}$ of $\frac{1}{3}$ of a pie, so Delaney has $13\frac{1}{2}$ slices.

In the case of quotitive division, the quotient question is: How many equal shares are there? The part—whole comparison, however, is implicit in the quotient question: What part of a share is the remainder? The critical understanding is that the divisor is the unit to which the remainder is compared.

Increasing Problem Difficulty

Partitioning should not be viewed as an introductory fraction activity and restricted to the lower elementary grades. If students are not readily able to answer the quotient and the part—whole questions, they need more partitioning experiences. There are many middle school students who cannot answer these questions. Even when students appear to understand quotients when using familiar contexts, such as sharing like pizzas, they may have difficulty if given a composite unit, such as a pack of gum or a 6-pack of cola. Continue to increase the difficulty by using more complex units and by asking questions whose fractional answers move away from the fractions with which students are most comfortable—halves, thirds, and fourths. Similarly, with quotitive division questions, students need experiences with many different kinds of units and fractional amounts. Here are some guidelines for encouraging students' development in partitioning:

• Ask how much is in each share.
• Do not accept answers that fail to answer "how much," such as those that answer how many pieces are in a share.
• Ask what part of the original amount one share is.
• In quotitive division, ask how many shares there are.
• Elicit different partitions and encourage students to look for equivalent fractions.
• Encourage the partitioning of different kinds of units: continuous, discrete, arrays, composite units such as packaged items, different-shaped items, and so forth.
• Do not always use "nice" or familiar fractions.

STOP   Before going to the next chapter, try the following activities.

Activities

In each picture, look for one share. Do not use your pencil. Try to do these visually.

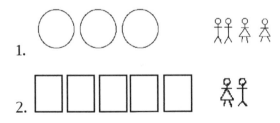

1.

2.

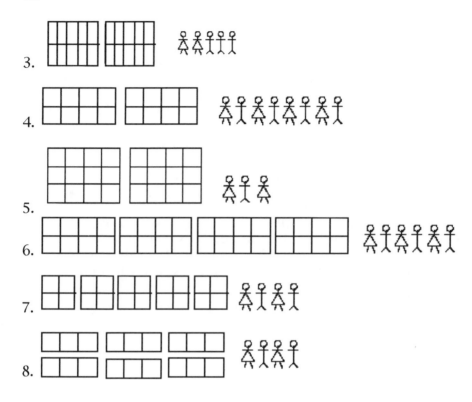

3.

4.

5.

6.

7.

8.

9. a. Ask and answer the quotient question about #8.
   b. Ask and answer the part—whole question about #8.

10. The numerator of a part—whole comparison is a counting number.
Does it count
a. the number of pieces in a share?
b. the total number of shares?
c. the total number of pieces in the designated shares?
d. the number of objects in the unit?
e. a designated number of shares?

11. The denominator of a part—whole comparison tells what is being
counted. Does it refer to
a. the number of pieces in a share?
b. the total number of shares?
c. the total number of pieces in the designated shares?
d. the number of objects in the unit?
e. a designated number of shares?

12. Does the numerator of a quotient represent
a. the number of pieces in a share?
b. the total number of shares?
c. the total number of pieces in the designated shares?
d. the number of objects in the unit?
e. a designated number of shares?

13. Does the denominator of a quotient represent
a. the number of pieces in a share?
b. the total number of shares?
c. the total number of pieces in the designated shares?
d. the number of objects in the unit?
e. a designated number of shares?

14. Some children drew pictures to show how much each person would get if 3 people shared 4 candy bars. Their partitions are shown. For each picture, write the fractions denoting each piece of a share and determine all of the equivalent parts that you would like the children to discover as they compare these partitions.

15. If 5 people share 4 pancakes, how much will each person eat? How much of the pancakes will each person eat?

16. If 4 people share 2(6-packs) of cola, how much will one share be? What part of the unit is one share?

17. Three people shared 8(6-packs) of cola. Students A, B, and C drew pictures to show one share of the cola. Rank the students' strategies according to their sophistication.

A.

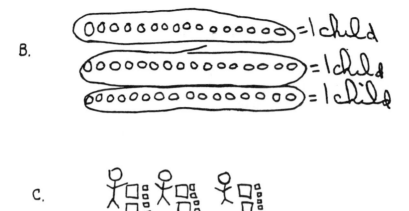

B.

C.

18. Students A and B showed how much each person would get if 3 people shared 4 pizzas. What is the difference in their strategies and which is more sophisticated?

A.

B.

19. Students A and B showed how much each person would get if 3 people shared 4 pizzas.
a. Partition the pizzas using a more sophisticated strategy than either of the children used.
b. Partition the pizzas using a strategy that is more sophisticated than student A's strategy and less sophisticated than student B's strategy.

A.

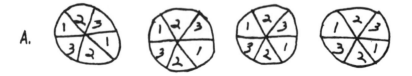

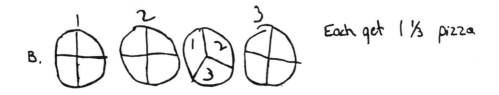

B.   Each get 1 ⅓ pizza

20. Five people shared two prepartitioned candy bars. Students A, B, C, and D showed how much each person would receive. Analyze the students' work.

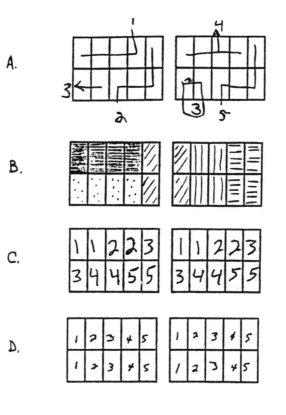

A.

B.

C.

D.

* * * * * * * * * * * * * * * * * * * *

STOP   Think, discuss, then write.

Reflection

1. For naming fractional parts, the unit is divided into equal or fair shares. Do those shares need to be the same size? Do they need to be congruent (the same shape)?

2. The fraction bar is sometimes used to represent the division operation. That is, some people write $\frac{3}{4}$ when they mean $4\overline{)3}$ or $3 \div 4$. This means that $\frac{3}{4}$ designates an operation rather than a number. Justify this use of fraction notation.

3. Find as many connections as you can between the part—whole and the quotient interpretations of rational numbers.

Chapter 7
Rational Numbers as Operators

STOP

Children's Strategies

Three sixth grade children tried to solve the following problem. Stop and solve the problem yourself. Then describe what happened when each child went to the computer and carried out his or her plan. Tell what size picture (as a fraction of the original) each child produced.

You had a picture on your computer and you made it $\frac{3}{4}$ (or 75%) of its original size. You changed your mind and now you want it back to its original size again. What fraction of its present size should you tell the computer to make it in order to restore its original size?

After solving the problem, the children were given a picture $\frac{3}{4}$ of its original size on a drawing program that allowed them to scale pictures up and down, and they carried out their plans. (The program allowed for scaling any percent from 10% to 1000% of the original dimensions.)

Brigit

Just I would make it 4 times bigger than it is now. I would get a picture 3 times its size. This is how I figured it out

Then I would divide by 3 to get its regular size.

1. 400%
2. 33%

Do these steps.

Take $\frac{1}{3}$ of it.

Elliot

To get it to 3/4 you had to do 75% of the original. So that means you took off 25% of its size. To get it back, you could enlarge it 25% by setting the number at 125%.

Stella R.

If I put this strip of paper in, it
will be

12 in.

[strip drawing]

$\frac{3}{4}$ will be

9 in.

[strip drawing] (It will get

skinny too.)

So I have to do   9 in. × ? = 12 in.

9 × 1 = 9   100 %

$9 \times \frac{1}{3} = 3$ 33.333 %

So I will do | 133.33 % |

* *

Operators and Operations

In the operator subconstruct of rational numbers, we think of rational numbers as functions. In this role, rational numbers act as mappings, taking some set or region and mapping it onto another set or region. More simply put, the operator notion of rational numbers is about shrinking and enlarging, contracting and expanding, enlarging and reducing, or multiplying and dividing. Operators are "transformers" that
• lengthen or shorten line segments,
• increase or decrease the number of items in a set of discrete objects, or
• take a figure in the geometric plane, such as triangle or a rectangle, and map it onto a larger or smaller figure of the same shape.

An operator is a set of instructions for carrying out a process. For example, "$\frac{2}{3}$ of" is an operator that instructs you to multiply by 2 and divide the result by 3. To apply the process "$\frac{2}{3}$ of," we perform familiar operations such as multiplication and division. The operations of multiplication and division may be viewed as individual operations or, when one is performed on the result of the other, may be regarded as a single operation. For example, multiplication by $\frac{2}{3}$ may be viewed as a single operation on a quantity Q, or it may be viewed as a multiplication performed on a division on quantity Q, or it may be viewed as a division performed on a multiplication on quantity Q:

$$\frac{2}{3}(Q) = 2\left(\frac{Q}{3}\right) = \frac{2(Q)}{3}$$

In the process of applying an operator, both shrinking and enlarging (contracting and expanding, enlarging and reducing) may take place. The end result of the process is shrinking or enlarging, depending on which has dominated the process: the end result of a "$\frac{4}{3}$ of" operator will be enlarging because it specifies more enlarging than reduction. It enlarges by a factor of 4 and reduces by a factor of 3.

Representing the Effects of Operators

The effects of rational numbers acting as operators can be pictured in various ways. In the first two examples, we consider the effect of two different interpretations of the operator "$\frac{3}{5}$ of. "

Example. "$\frac{3}{5}$ of" means to take 3 copies of a quantity and divide the result by 5

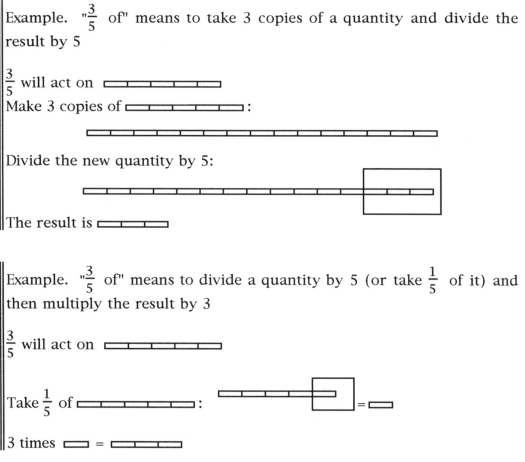

Example. "$\frac{3}{5}$ of" means to divide a quantity by 5 (or take $\frac{1}{5}$ of it) and then multiply the result by 3

In these examples, the operator acted on a given length. In   the classroom, you will find that it is easier for children to use linking cubes to perform these operations, , or to measure and draw lengths with a ruler.

Example. Show how the operator "$1\frac{1}{4}$ of" acts on the rectangle ☐ .

It will make the rectangle 5 times larger, then reduce it to $\frac{1}{4}$ of that size.

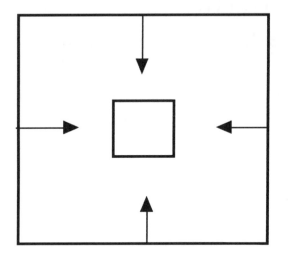

Example. Another way:

"$1\frac{1}{4}$ of" acting on the rectangle ☐ might first reduce the size to $\frac{1}{4}$ of its original size, then enlarge the resulting rectangle to 5 times its size.

Notice that regardless of the model we were using, the result was the same whether we did the enlarging first and the reducing second, or the reducing first and the enlarging second.

In the classroom, two dimensional objects are easily scaled on a computer. Because scale transformations may be performed so quickly and easily, children can perform lots of experiments in sizing in a short period of time, and learn to anticipate the effects of a sequence of scaling operations.

Another slightly different representation, one which represents fractional parts geometrically, is a flow distribution. The following example shows $\frac{2}{3}$ of 18 candies. In this model, the pipe representing $\frac{2}{3}$ has twice the diameter of the pipe representing $\frac{1}{3}$ and some of the original items get thrown away or go down the drain when the operator has the effect of reducing the size of some input quantity. This model does not work for operators that enlarge input quantities.

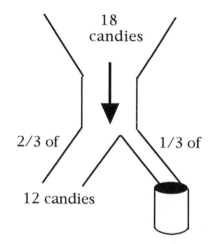

In all of the examples, note that the operator interpretation of rational numbers is different from the part—whole comparison. In the operator interpretation, the significant relationship is the comparison between the quantity resulting from an operation and the quantity that is acted on. The operator defines the relationship $\frac{\text{quantity out}}{\text{quantity in}}$.

Example. 12 candies and 18 candies related to each other in a "two-to-three" way when the operator "$\frac{2}{3}$ of" acted on a set of 18 candies to produce 12 candies.

Example. 35 candies relate to 20 candies in a "seven-to-four" way when the operator "$1\frac{3}{4}$ of" acts on a set of 20 candies to produce a set of 35 candies.

Another representation, the function table, situated either vertically or horizontally, may be used to list various input and output values. Then students may be asked to find the rule that relates the input and the output. The operator "$\frac{2}{3}$ of," for example, explains the relationship between the sets given in the tables.

Example.

input	6	9	60	150
output	4	6	40	100

input	output
6	4
9	6
60	40
150	100

$$\text{output} = \frac{2}{3}\,\text{input}$$

Composition

The examples we have been discussing involve a process called *composition*. When you perform some operation, then perform another operation on the result of the first operation, it is possible to "compose" operations, or do a single operation that is some combination of the two. We saw that the operator "$\frac{3}{5}$ of" defined a composition of multiplication (an enlargement, making something three times its size) with division (a reduction, making something $\frac{1}{5}$ of its size, or dividing by 5). The individual operations that are composed are simply multiplication and division by natural numbers (1,2,3,4,...). These operations call into play the same knowledge and strategies that children developed in their experiences with whole numbers before they ever encountered fractions. The only difference is that fraction symbolism is used. Division by 5 is written as multiplication by $\frac{1}{5}$. Performing one operation after the other is written as a multiplication: (3 times something) divided by 5 is the same as $\frac{3}{1} \cdot \frac{1}{5}$ or $\frac{3}{5}$ of something. While interpreting operators as multiplication followed by division and then again as divisions followed by multiplication, children build on their whole number knowledge, but to understand operators, more than that is necessary. Students must come to view the composition as a single operation, and, in time, interpret compositions of compositions.

Increasing Complexity

After children become accustomed to the composition of the operations of multiplication and division, the exchange model for an operator such as "$\frac{2}{3}$ of" can help them to see the result of the composed operations as a single operation by examining only the input and the output, and making explicit the two constituent operations.

Example. The "$\frac{2}{3}$ of" operator may be interpreted as an exchanger. It will trade 2 items for every 3 it is given. For example, for every three quarters that you put into a machine, it might given you 2 bus tokens.

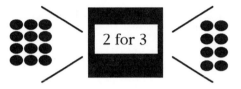

The operator interpretation of rational numbers also lends itself well to a machine representation. We can think of the machine as a box in which some input is transformed according to some rule and then ejected from the machine. There are three elements involved: the input, the transformation (undifferentiated into it parts) and the output. If we know two of these elements, we can determine the third.

Example. I have a "1 for 4" machine and it outputs 12 items. How many must have gone into the machine?

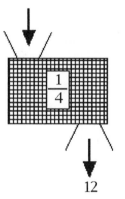

48 must have gone in because the machine puts out 1 item for every 4 items that were put into it.

Example. If I put 12 items into a machine and saw 8 items come out, what kind of operation did the machine perform?

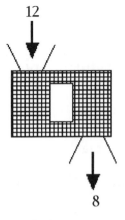

It output 8 on 12, so it must be an 8 for 12 machine, or a $\frac{2}{3}$ machine.

The problem solved by the children at the start of the chapter involves a composition of operators that may be characterized as two connected function machines. The first operator was given; it can be represented as a $\frac{3}{4}$ machine. It acted on the unit and produced an output $\frac{3}{4}$ of its size. The output from this operation became the input for another machine whose operation is unknown, from which we would like to receive the original unit as output. We could picture it like this:

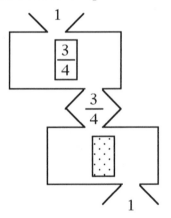

We have seen that shrinking and enlarging are multiplicative processes, rather than additive ones. Elliot's solution, typical of many children's solutions, is an additive one. He thinks that shrinking the picture involved subtracting something from its size, so he proposes to "ellarge" by adding 25%. When he set the computer's scaling control at 125%, the computer produced a picture that was $\frac{375}{400}$ ($\frac{3}{4} \cdot \frac{125}{100}$) of its original size. Brigid was very close. She proposed to enlarge the $\frac{3}{4}$ -size picture to 400% then reduce that version to $\frac{1}{3}$ its size. When she entered 400%, the computer produced a version of the picture that was 3 times the original size, and when she entered 33%, she got a version that was $\frac{99}{100}$ of the original size. The small discrepancy is due to her failure to use a precise enough percentage for $\frac{1}{3}$ ($33\frac{1}{3}$% or 33.33%). Stella entered a more accurate figure, 133.33%, and the computer produced a figure that was virtually indistinguishable from the original.

This problem calls for an "undoing" of the original reduction. The opposite process to multiplying by $\frac{3}{4}$ is multiplying by $\frac{4}{3}$. Notice that $\frac{3}{4} \cdot \frac{4}{3} = 1$. This means that multiplying by $\frac{4}{3}$ is the opposite process of multiplying by $\frac{3}{4}$, and thus returns the unit, the full-size picture. $\frac{4}{3} = 1\frac{1}{3} = 133.33\%$.

Operators as a Foundation for Fraction Multiplication and Division

The composition of operators leads very naturally to fraction multiplication. For example, $\frac{2}{3}(\frac{3}{4})$ means "take $\frac{2}{3}$ of $\frac{3}{4}$ of a unit" and it is equivalent to "take $\frac{6}{12}$ or $\frac{1}{2}$ of the unit." We can think of this as a composition of the operator "$\frac{3}{4}$ of" and the operator "$\frac{2}{3}$ of." This is a complex idea for children because it is several times removed from the whole number knowledge that they could employ when first introduced to a single operator, such as "$\frac{2}{3}$ of."

"$\frac{2}{3}$ of" is a rule for composing the operations of multiplication and division.

"$\frac{3}{4}$ of" is a rule for composing the operations of multiplication and division.

"$\frac{2}{3}$ of ($\frac{3}{4}$ of)" is a composition of operators, defined by a composition of a composition of operations.

An area model is a convenient way to illustrate these compositions and to lay a foundation for future operations with fractions. In this case, the operator maps a region onto another region.

Let 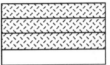 represent the unit and shade $\frac{3}{4}$ of it.

Without explicit attention to the individual operations of multiplication and division underlying the " $\frac{3}{4}$ of" operator, $\frac{3}{4}$ operated on 1 unit. The shaded result is $\frac{3}{4}$ of 1.

Now, the operator " $\frac{2}{3}$ of " will operate on the result obtained by applying the operator " $\frac{3}{4}$ of." That is, we will take $\frac{2}{3}$ of ($\frac{3}{4}$ of 1).

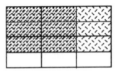

We used horizontal divisions to show the first operator. Now use vertical lines to divide the area into thirds. The darker shaded region is $\frac{2}{3}$ of ($\frac{3}{4}$ of 1). To read the result, notice that the unit consists of 12 small rectangles, so the darker shaded region is $\frac{6}{12}$.

Example. $2\frac{1}{3} \times \frac{1}{2}$

If 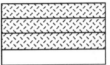 is 1, then $2\frac{1}{3}$ of 1 is

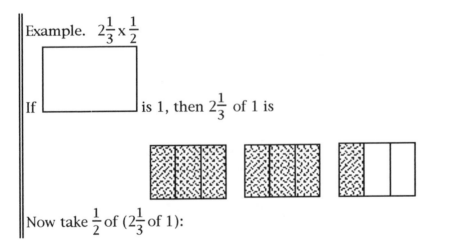

Now take $\frac{1}{2}$ of ($2\frac{1}{3}$ of 1):

The unit is 6 squares and we have 7 darker shaded squares. The result is $\frac{7}{6}$.

The darker shaded pieces may be reorganized to create a mixed number. For example, if we collect all of the darker shaded squares in our previous above, we can see that we get $1\frac{1}{6}$.

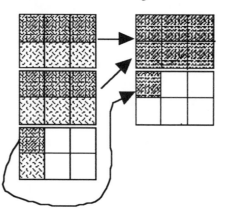

Division may also be interpreted as the composition of two operators and may be modeled using an area model.

Example. $\frac{3}{4} \div \frac{2}{3}$.

This division answers the question: "How many $\frac{2}{3}$ of 1 are there in $\frac{3}{4}$ of 1?"

= 1

Reunitize the unit rectangle, marking fourths in one direction and thirds in the other

How much is $\frac{2}{3}$ of 1? Notice that it is the area of 8 squares.

Shade $\frac{3}{4}$ of 1 and see how many times you can measure out ($\frac{2}{3}$ of 1) or 8 squares.

1.	2.	3.	
4.	5.	6.	
7.	8.	1.	

Out of the area ($\frac{3}{4}$ of 1), we can measure the area ($\frac{2}{3}$ of 1) $1\frac{1}{8}$ times.

Notice that the unit was used to determine $\frac{3}{4}$ and $\frac{2}{3}$, but that the divisor, $\frac{2}{3}$, became the new unit in terms of which the remainder was interpreted.

Compositions and Paper Folding

Paper folding activities also provide models for compositions and prepare students for understanding fraction multiplication.

Take an $8\frac{1}{2}$" by 11" sheet of paper as your unit. Again you are using an area model. The unit area is the area of the sheet of paper. Fold it in half by bringing the $8\frac{1}{2}$" edges together. You have in front of you the result of taking $\frac{1}{2}$ of 1. We can write it this way:

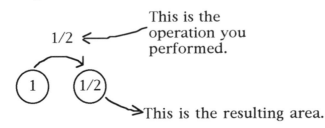

This is the operation you performed.

This is the resulting area.

Now fold in half again. With your second fold, you have taken $\frac{1}{2}$ of ($\frac{1}{2}$ of 1). Record the result this way:

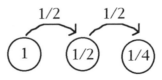

Shade the rectangle that faces you. Now open up the paper and see what part of it is shaded. You should be able to see that the shaded region is $\frac{1}{4}$.

$\frac{1}{2}$ of ($\frac{1}{2}$ of 1) = $\frac{1}{4}$.

Example. Use paper folding to show the result of these operations: $\frac{1}{4}$ of $\frac{2}{3}$

First fold a paper into thirds. (Bend the paper into a "z" shape

and make the edges even.) Open the paper, shade $\frac{2}{3}$, and refold it so that only the shaded area is facing you.

You have done this: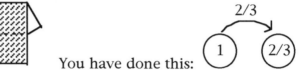

Now fold into fourths. With a different color, shade the area that is facing you. Open the paper and determine what part of the unit area your shaded area represents.

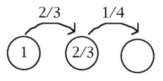

You should be able to see that it is $\frac{2}{12}$.

Paper folding helps to convey the sense that an operator is a rule describing the result of an action performed on the result of a previous action. It also helps build a base of understanding for fraction multiplication, and is particularly effective in demonstrating that a product is not always larger than its factors. For example, it is quite clear to children that the result of taking $\frac{1}{4}$ of $\frac{2}{3}$ is not something larger than $\frac{2}{3}$.

Understanding Operators

To say that a student understands rational numbers as operators means that
1) the student can interpret a fractional multiplier in a variety of ways:
a. $\frac{3}{4}$ means $3 \cdot (\frac{1}{4}$ of a unit);
b. $\frac{3}{4}$ means $\frac{1}{4}$ of (3 times a unit).

2) when two operations (multiplication and division) are performed one

on the result of the other, the student can name a single fraction to describe the composite:

a. multiplying a unit by 3 and then dividing that result by 4 is the same as multiplying the unit by $\frac{3}{4}$;

b. dividing a unit by 4 and then multiplying that result by 3 is the same as multiplying the unit by $\frac{3}{4}$.

3) the student can identify the effect of an operator and can state a rule relating inputs and outputs:

a. an input of 9 and an output of 15 results from a 15 for 9 operator (an operator that enlarges), symbolized as $\frac{15}{9}$;

b. the output $= \frac{15}{9}$ of the input.

4) the student can use models to identify a single composition that characterizes a composition of compositions:

$\frac{2}{3}$ of ($\frac{3}{4}$ of a unit) $= \frac{1}{2}$ of a unit.

STOP   Before going to the next chapter, try the following activities.

Activities

1. Which operators will produce an enlargement and which operators will produce a reduction?

2. Every operator both enlarges and reduces. Does a "$\frac{5}{3}$ of" operator do more enlarging or more reducing?

3. Name an operator that does more reducing than it does enlarging.

4. Taking $\frac{1}{3}$ of the result of taking $\frac{3}{4}$ of something is equivalent to multiplying by _____ .

5. In a certain school, $\frac{5}{9}$ of the teachers are female, $\frac{3}{8}$ of the male teachers are single, and $\frac{1}{3}$ of the single males are over 50. What

fraction of the teachers are single males under 50?

6. Describe in symbols what happens in the pictures:

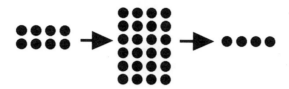

7. Use symbols to explain the process shown:

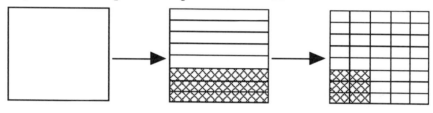

8. Use pictures to show 2 different interpretations of $\frac{2}{3}$ of a set of 9 dots.

9. Draw conclusions about the relative size of the fractions represented by the machines in the following diagrams:

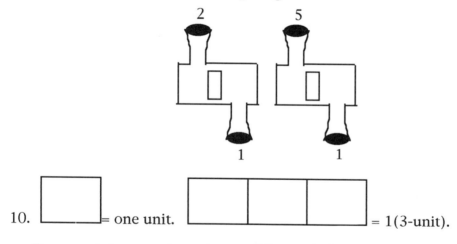

10. ☐ = one unit.   ☐☐☐ = 1(3-unit).

a. Draw a picture to show 1 out of 5 equal shares of a 3-unit and name the result.

b. Draw a picture to show 3 copies of $\frac{1}{5}$ of a unit and name the result.

c. Draw a picture to show $\frac{1}{5}$ of 3 (1-units) name the result.

11. Use symbols to say what this picture says:

12. Using pictures, show what happens to a set of 12 objects when a "$\frac{5}{6}$ of" operator acts on the results of a "$\frac{3}{4}$ of" operator.   Also, show what happens when a "$\frac{3}{4}$ of" operator acts on the results of a "$\frac{5}{6}$ of" operator.

13. State three different meanings for the operator "$\frac{2}{9}$ of."

14. Use an area model to do the following multiplications:

a. $\frac{3}{4} \times \frac{1}{2}$

b. $1\frac{1}{3} \times \frac{3}{5}$

c. $1\frac{1}{2} \times \frac{1}{3}$

15. Use an area model to do the following divisions:

a. $\frac{5}{7} \div \frac{1}{3}$

b. $\frac{2}{3} \div \frac{5}{8}$

c. $1\frac{3}{4} \div \frac{2}{5}$

d. $1\frac{5}{6} \div 1\frac{1}{3}$

16. Find the number of men and the number of women if you know that there are 16 children.

17. Fold a unit into sixths and shade $\frac{5}{6}$. Fold another unit into ninths and shade $\frac{4}{9}$. Refold both units. Continue the folding process on each unit until the denominators of the resulting units are the same.

Rename $\frac{5}{6}$ in terms of the new denominator.

Rename $\frac{4}{9}$ in terms of the same denominator.

18. Use paper folding to perform the following composition that results in $\frac{1}{24}$. Write the notation for two more compositions that result in $\frac{1}{24}$, each having a different number of steps.

* * * * * * * * * * * * * * * * * * * *

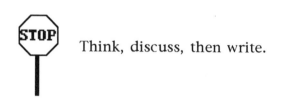 Think, discuss, then write.

Reflection

1. Design a lesson in which fraction equivalence may be investigated through paper folding.

2. Do operators add the way part—whole comparisons do? Justify your answer.

Chapter 8
Rational Numbers as Measures

Children's Strategies

The following interview with Martin was conducted in June, at the end of fifth grade. Martin had worked extensively on number lines for 2 years and he developed some sophisticated techniques for thinking about rational numbers. Martin was asked to find two fractions between $\frac{1}{8}$ and $\frac{1}{9}$. Before going on, read the following protocol from the interview and try to understand how Martin was thinking about rational numbers.

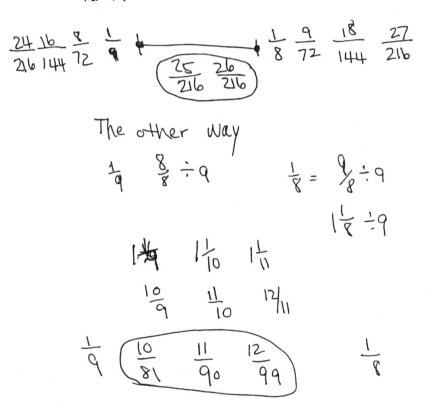

I: Martin, tell me how you thought about this problem and came up with these answers.

M: Well, first the numbers are backwards. If you want to arrange them the way they would be on the number line, you should say between $\frac{1}{9}$ and $\frac{1}{8}$ since $\frac{1}{9}$ is smaller.

I: Good point. What did you do after you rearranged those fractions?

M: Well, I thought about how I could hit both of them on the number line. If I keep breaking down my units, I can't hit both fractions until I get to seventy-twos. Then I would have $\frac{8}{72}$ and $\frac{9}{72}$. Now if I split each space in half, I will get 144s, but then I would get only one fraction between them. That means I need to split into three equal parts to get 216s. That's how I got $\frac{24}{216}$ and $\frac{27}{216}$. Then it is easy to see that $\frac{25}{216}$ and $\frac{26}{216}$ are between them.

I: Yes, good. I understand how you thought about that. But what are these other fractions you have written?

M: The teacher didn't say if she wanted them equally spaced or not. So I did it both ways.

I: Tell me what you mean by "both ways."

M: Well, if you don't care if all the fractions are equally spaced, I could find lots of other fractions between $\frac{1}{9}$ and $\frac{1}{8}$.

I: How do you do that?

M: I go back to the $\frac{1}{9}$—that's one unit divided by 9 or you could say $\frac{8}{8}$ divided into 9 equal parts. Then $\frac{1}{8}$ is what you get when you divide $\frac{9}{8}$ into 9 equal parts. So if I pick something less than $1\frac{1}{8}$ and divide it into 9 equal parts, it will be between those two fractions. Like I could pick $1\frac{1}{9}, 1\frac{1}{10}, 1\frac{1}{11}, 1\frac{1}{12}$, or as many as I want and they'll all be bigger than 1 and less than $1\frac{1}{8}$. Then $1\frac{1}{9}$ or $\frac{10}{9}$ divided into 9 equal parts would be $\frac{10}{81}$. $1\frac{1}{10}$ or $\frac{11}{10}$ divided into 9 equal parts would be $\frac{11}{90}$. $1\frac{1}{11}$ or $\frac{12}{11}$ divided into 9 equal parts would be $\frac{12}{99}$. And you can keep going and they'll all be between there.

* * * * * * * * * * * * * * * * * * *

Measurement

Imagine timing a swim meet. If you time a 100-meter backstroke race to the nearest hour, you would not be able to distinguish one swimmer's time from another. If you refine your timing by using minutes, you may still not be able to tell the swimmers apart. If the swimmers are all well trained, you may not be able to decide on a winner even if you measure in seconds. In high-stakes competitions among well-trained athletes (the Olympics, for example), it is necessary to measure in tenths and hundredths of seconds.

Suppose you are working on a project that requires some precision. You need to determine the exact length of a strip of metal in inches. You put it up to your ruler with one end at 0 and the other end of it lying between 4 and 5 inches. (Note that only the right end is shown.) What would you say its length is?

You might think to yourself: "The length is between $4\frac{9}{16}$ and $4\frac{10}{16}$, so I'll call it $4\frac{19}{32}$."

These situations convey the nature of the measurement interpretation of rational number. A unit of measure can always be divided up into finer and finer subunits so that you may take as accurate a reading as you need. On a number line, on a graduated beaker, on a ruler or yardstick or meter stick, on a measuring cup, on a dial, or on a thermometer, some subdivisions of the unit are marked. The marks on these common measuring tools allow readings that are accurate enough for most general purposes, but if the amount of stuff that you are measuring does not exactly meet one of the provided hash marks, it certainly does not mean that it cannot be measured. The rational numbers provide us with a means to measure any amount of stuff. If meters will not do, we can partition into decimeters; when decimeters will not do, we can partition into centimeters, or millimeters.

When we talk about rational numbers as measures, the focus is on successively partitioning the unit. Certainly partitioning plays an important role in other models and interpretations of rational numbers, but there is a difference. There is a dynamic aspect in measurement. Instead of comparing the number of equal parts you have to a fixed number of equal parts in a unit, the number of equal parts in the unit can vary, and what you name your fractional amount depends on how many times you are willing to keep up the partitioning process.

Rational numbers measure directed distances of certain points from zero in terms of some unit distance. (We say "directed" because rational numbers may be negative, as on a thermometer, and we say "certain" points because there are other points on a number line whose distance from zero cannot be measured with rational numbers.) The rational numbers become strongly associated with those points and we speak of them as if they *are* points, but they are, in fact, measures of distance. With this caveat, we continue to refer to rational numbers as points on the number line, and we restrict ourselves to the positive rationals in this chapter.

In the measure subconstruct, a rational number is usually the measure assigned to some interval or region, depending on whether one is using a one- or two-dimensional model. In a one-dimensional space, a rational number measures the distance of a certain point on the number line from zero. In a two-dimensional space, a rational number measures area. The unit is always an interval of length 1 if you are working on a number line.

Lots of Connections

The measure interpretation of rational numbers shares many ideas and mechanisms with the part—whole comparisons, quotients, and operators that we have studied so far. Experiences with part—whole comparisons provide the language and symbols used in measure contexts. Partitioning, the mechanism that provided the experiences for understanding quotients plays a major role in naming distances from zero on the number line. In particular, an understanding of the composition of operators plays a leading role in determining the outcome of successive partitions of an interval.

To identify a point on the number line with a rational number that describes how far it is from zero, we may begin by partitioning the unit interval into an arbitrary number of equal parts. Each of those parts may be partitioned into an arbitrary number of equal parts, and these, in turn, may be partitioned again. This process is actually a composition of operations. We can keep a record of our partitioning actions, as well as the size of the subintervals being produced, using the same arrow notation we used in our paper folding activities (Chapter 7).

Example. If we begin by marking $\frac{1}{2}$ of the unit interval, then we partition each piece into 3 equal parts, then each piece into 4 equal parts, we can keep track of the operations we have performed using arrow notation:

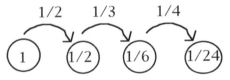

This means that the subintervals that result from our composition of operations each measure $\frac{1}{24}$ of the unit interval.

$$\frac{1}{24} = \frac{1}{4} \text{ of } (\frac{1}{3} \text{ of } (\frac{1}{2} \text{ of } 1)).$$

Example. Locate $\frac{17}{48}$ on the given number line.

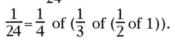

Because we have choices as to the size of subunit we can use to measure a distance from zero, the compensatory principle and the idea of fraction equivalence also come into play. The smaller the subunit used to measure the distance, the more of those subunits will be needed; the larger the subunit, the fewer that will be needed to cover the distance. When two different subunits cover the same distance, different fraction names result. There is only one rational number associated with a specific distance from zero, so the fractions are equivalent.

Example. The unit is invariant, and so is the distance of any point from zero, but because the unit may be subdivided into any number of congruent parts, a point may be identified by different names.

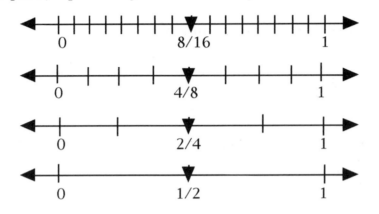

In part—whole comparisons, we are given the unit in a problem's context, (either implicitly or explicitly). If it is given implicitly, we can reason up or down to determine the unit. Likewise, when using rational numbers to measure distances on the number line, we must have the unit interval marked, or else we need information to tell us the size of the subintervals represented by the hash marks. Once we know the size of the subintervals, we can determine the unit interval.

Example. Given the point $\frac{2}{3}$, determine point X.

If $\frac{2}{3}$ consists of 10 subintervals, then $\frac{1}{3}$ must consist of 5. The unit, or $\frac{3}{3}$, must consist of 15. If each subinterval represents $\frac{1}{15}$, then the distance of X from 0 must be $\frac{6}{15}$.

But if 1 is 15 subintervals in length, then $\frac{1}{5}$ must be 3, and $\frac{2}{5}$ must be 6.

This means that $\frac{6}{15} = \frac{2}{5}$.

Even before introducing any algorithms for addition and subtraction of fractions, rational numbers viewed as measures on a number line provide a good model for these operations. It anticipates the use of a common denominator in the standard algorithm and provides a basis for later work with vectors.

Example. What is the sum of $\frac{2}{3}$ and $\frac{1}{4}$?

For example, given two number lines with the same unit interval located on each, identify the points $\frac{2}{3}$ and $\frac{1}{4}$.

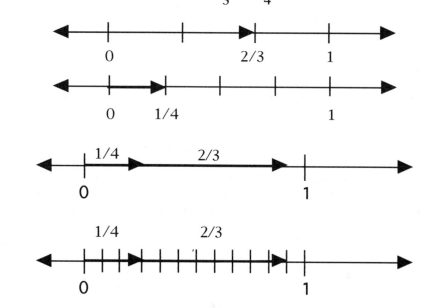

Each of these fractions represents a distance, so putting the arrows end-to-end is like adding one distance on to the other. The total distance may be found through the successive partitioning process. Because the unit can be divided into any number of congruent parts, we can find a subdivision that will "work" in the sense that when we place the arrows end to end, the tip will fall on the end of an interval for which we have a fraction name. For example, the unit interval in this problem is partitioned into fourths, but if we further refine each fourth by dividing it into three equal parts, the unit will be divided into twelfths. Because one of the hash marks representing twelfths coincides with the tip of the arrow, we can read the distance, $\frac{11}{12}$.

Teaching Problems

Current instruction overlooks the essential nature of rational numbers as measures. Number lines are used in the same way that other continuous units are used in part—whole comparisons. For example, there is essentially no difference between using a number line and using a pizza or a cake if the task is to locate $\frac{3}{4}$ on this number line.

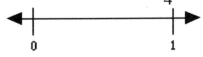

Using different markings on the number line, such as

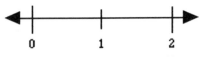

may make the task slightly different, but still does not address critical aspects of understanding.

Commercially available products such as fraction strips, rods, and pattern blocks (length and area models) provide students some experience with different units and subunits of measure, but they have severe limitations. They do not allow students the freedom to break down the unit into any number of subdivisions. The subdivisions available to the user are restricted by the sizes of the pieces supplied, while on the number line, a given unit can be divided into any number of congruent parts. After using certain predetermined subunits in manipulative products, most students fail to recognize the infinite number of subdivisons allowable on the number line. Often when they no longer have lengths or areas to provide visual means of making comparisons, we discover that they have not developed any reasoning or strategies or even any intuitions about how to compare two fractions in size. It is unlikely that any other embodiment can come close to the power of the number line for conveying the measurement interpretation of rational numbers.

An obvious obstacle to providing children with successive partitioning experiences is their inability to accomplish the partitioning with enough accuracy. Decent hand-eye coordination and accuracy is required. Most fourth graders are not able to do the tasks, but only a small number of fifth and sixth graders have difficulty. This seems to suggest that this interpretation of rational numbers should not be one of the first in the instructional sequence. When children in fifth and sixth grades were introduced to successive partitioning on a number line, they enjoyed the activities very much and, in no time at all, they had developed efficient partitioning strategies. Martin and the group of students he worked with in class, soon abandoned the physical act of partitioning and were able to reason about size and order of fractions with ease. It was clear that the partitioning experience had enhanced their rational number sense, their understanding of fraction equivalence, and other notions as well.

The Density of Rational Numbers

Simply stated, the *density property of rational numbers* says that between any two fractions there is an infinite number of fractions and that you can always get as close as you like to any point with a fraction. Successive partitioning helps us to name other fractions between two given fractions.

Example.   Name three fractions between $\frac{1}{3}$ and $\frac{1}{4}$.

We know that when we have partitioned the unit interval into twelfths, $\frac{1}{4}$ is renamed as $\frac{3}{12}$, and $\frac{1}{3}$ is equivalent to $\frac{4}{12}$.

If we partition the interval between $\frac{3}{12}$ and $\frac{4}{12}$ again, this time dividing it into two equal parts, then our new subunits will be twenty-fourths and $\frac{3}{12}$ and $\frac{4}{12}$ will be named $\frac{6}{24}$ and $\frac{8}{24}$, respectively.

If instead, we partition the interval between $\frac{3}{12}$ and $\frac{4}{12}$ again by dividing each subunit into three equal parts, then our subunits will each be $\frac{1}{36}$ of the unit and our given fractions will be renamed $\frac{9}{36}$ and $\frac{12}{36}$. Then it is easy to see that $\frac{10}{36}$ and $\frac{11}{36}$ lie between them.

This is a common method, and as Martin observed in his interview at the beginning of the chapter, it results in fractions that are equally spaced: $\frac{9}{36}$ $\frac{10}{36}$ $\frac{11}{36}$ $\frac{12}{36}$. Martin had also invented his own method, which allowed him to name as many fractions as he liked between two given fractions. How would Martin find some fractions between $\frac{1}{4}$ and $\frac{1}{3}$? First he would write all of his fractions so that they had the same denominator. Let's say that he was going to use fourths. $\frac{1}{3} = \frac{?}{4}$ Because he knew that $\frac{1}{3}$ is $\frac{4}{3}$ divided by 4, so he would write:

$$\frac{1}{4} \quad \overline{}_4 \quad \overline{}_4 \quad \overline{}_4 \quad \overline{}_4 \quad \overline{}_4 \quad \overline{}_4 \quad \frac{\frac{4}{3}}{4}$$

All of the fractions between $\frac{1}{4}$ and $\frac{1}{3}$ would then have denominators of 4

and numerators between 1 and $1\frac{1}{3}$: $\frac{1\frac{1}{4}}{4}, \frac{1\frac{1}{5}}{4}, \frac{1\frac{1}{6}}{4}, \frac{1\frac{1}{7}}{4}, \frac{1\frac{1}{8}}{4}$,....meet the requirements.

Understanding Rationals as Measures

Although the measure interpretation of rational numbers is closely related to the other interpretations that we have discussed so far, it deserves special attention because it highlights different aspects of the rational numbers than the other interpretations do. Experience with the measure personality of the rational numbers entails a dynamic movement among an infinite number of stopping-off places along the number line, and helps students to build a sense of the density of the rational numbers, a sense of order and relative magnitudes of rational numbers, and a richer understanding of the degrees of accuracy in measurement. In short, this fluidity, flexibility, and comfort in navigating among the rational numbers is called rational number sense.

    In summary, it may be said that students understand the measure personality of rational numbers when they (a) are comfortable performing partitions other than halving; (b) are able to find any number of fractions between two given fractions; and (c) are able to use a given unit interval to measure any distance from the origin.

STOP   Try some successive partitioning activities for yourself.

Activities

In each case, find the rational number represented by "X."

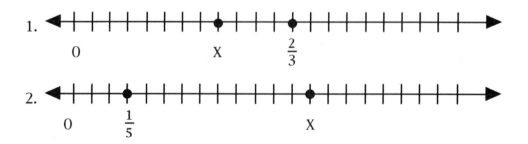

1.

    0   X $\frac{2}{3}$

2.

    0       $\frac{1}{5}$ X

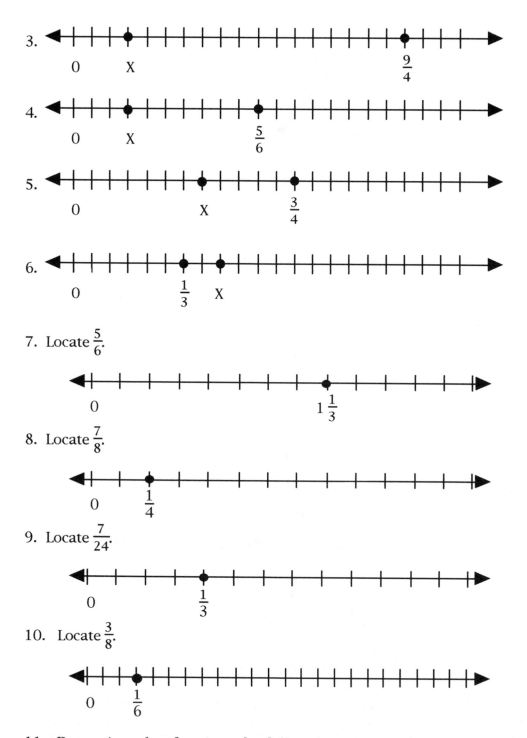

3.

0   X $\frac{9}{4}$

4.

0   X $\frac{5}{6}$

5.

0   X $\frac{3}{4}$

6.

0              $\frac{1}{3}$ X

7. Locate $\frac{5}{6}$.

0                              $1\frac{1}{3}$

8. Locate $\frac{7}{8}$.

0    $\frac{1}{4}$

9. Locate $\frac{7}{24}$.

0              $\frac{1}{3}$

10. Locate $\frac{3}{8}$.

0    $\frac{1}{6}$

11. Determine what fraction of a full tank remains in each gas tank.

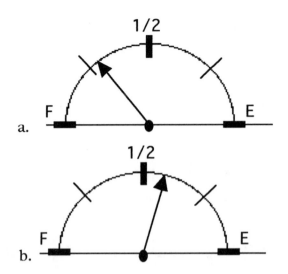

12. a. Put an arrow on the following gas gauge to show how much gas you would have left in your tank if you filled it up and then took a drive that used 6 gallons. A full tank holds 16 gallons.

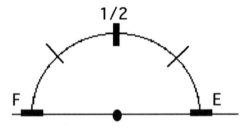

b. Your gas tank was reading "empty," but you were low on cash. You used your last $4.00 to buy gas at a station where you paid 1.13^9 per gallon. If a full tank holds 14 gallons, put an arrow on the gas gauge to show how much gas you had in your tank after your purchase.

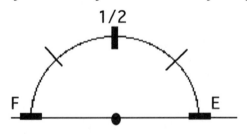

c. You filled up your tank this morning and then took a drive in the country to enjoy the fall color. Your odometer said that you had gone 340 miles and you have been averaging about 31 miles per gallon. If your gas gauge looked like this when you got home, how much does your gas tank hold when it is full?

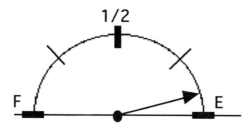

13. Two candles are made of different kinds of wax. They are of equal length and they are lighted at the same time, but one candle takes 9 hours to burn out and the other takes 6 hours to burn out. After how much time will the slower-burning candle be exactly twice as long as the faster-burning candle?

14. Write each of these fractions as a sum of unit fractions all with different denominators. A unit fraction is a fraction whose numerator is 1 (for example, $\frac{3}{4} = \frac{1}{2} + \frac{1}{4}$).

a. $\frac{2}{3}$

d. $\frac{7}{9}$

b. $\frac{3}{5}$

e. $\frac{13}{14}$

c. $\frac{5}{6}$

f. $\frac{23}{24}$

15. I buy motor oil in plastic bottles that have a clear view strip in one side so that it is possible to read how much oil is in the container. There is a quart of oil in each bottle and the scale on the view strip indicates the amount in ounces.

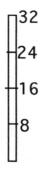

What fraction of a bottle remains in each of these partially used bottles that I found in the garage?

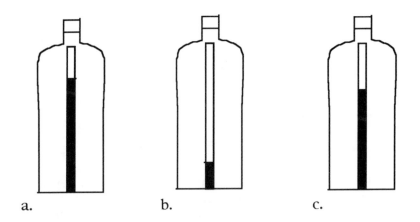

a.   b.   c.

16. If you paid to park for 25 minutes on the following meter, draw an arrow to show how your time would register on this meter.

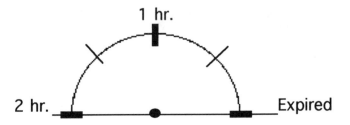

17. Name two numbers between each pair of points.

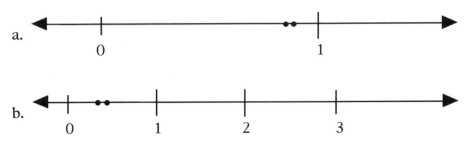

18. Try this investigation.

a. On each of the following number lines, you will successively partition the interval until you can name the rational number corresponding to the point marked on the number line. Keep track of the size of your subintervals using the arrow notation we used in paper folding.

b. On the first number line, begin by partitioning the unit interval into two equal parts. On the second number line, begin by partitioning the interval into three equal parts. On the third number line, begin by partitioning the interval into 10 equal parts. In each case, continue the process until you have achieved enough accuracy to name the point.

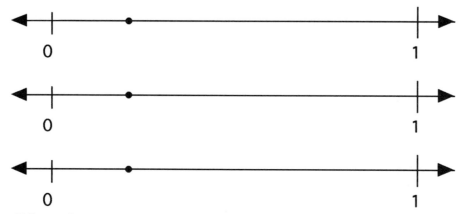

c. When the partitioning process has been completed on each number line, use your calculator to obtain a decimal representation for the fraction you named.

d. Next, using a metric ruler, read the location of the point, correct to two decimal places. (Note that the interval is 10 cm. long and you can read the point's location in millimeters.)

e. Compare the accuracy of your results with the reading from the metric ruler. If you were not correct to two decimal places, try again, this time using the metric ruler to help you accurately size your subintervals.

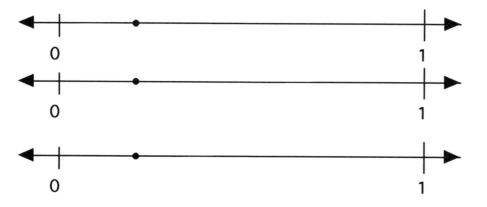

19. In each case, use a number line to order these fractions from smallest to largest.

a. $\dfrac{11}{12}, \dfrac{5}{6}, \dfrac{21}{24}$

b. $\dfrac{3}{9}, \dfrac{5}{6}, \dfrac{1}{2}$

c. $\dfrac{13}{14}, \dfrac{6}{7}, \dfrac{27}{28}$

20. By partitioning the interval between the given fractions, find two fractions between them.

a. $\dfrac{1}{6}$ and $\dfrac{1}{5}$

b. $\dfrac{9}{10}$ and 1

21. Maurice and his two friends shared a long licorice stick. Just after they cut it fairly and before anyone ate the candy, another friend came along. How can the boys give the fourth person a fair share?

22. Determine three fractions between $\dfrac{1}{5}$ and $\dfrac{1}{6}$ using Martin's method.

* * * * * * * * * * * * * * * * * * * *

STOP

Think about the following questions, discuss them with others, and then record your thinking.

Reflection

1. If you have a unit interval that was partitioned into 18 equal subintervals, what rational numbers would you be able to locate without further partitioning?

2. When $\dfrac{7}{8}$ is a measure, what is the meaning of the numerator? What is the meaning of the denominator?

3. Explain why different names emerge for the same distance from zero.

4. What role does the compensatory principle play in unitizing? Consider this reunitizing scheme as you think about your response.

$$\frac{1(1\text{-unit})}{3(1\text{-units})} = \frac{2(\frac{1}{2}\text{-units})}{6(\frac{1}{2}\text{-units})} = \frac{6(\frac{1}{6}\text{-units})}{18(\frac{1}{6}\text{-units})}$$

Chapter 9
Quantitative Relationships:
Visual and Verbal

Children's Strategies

The following interview was part of a teaching experiment with middle school children, grades 6 through 8. These children needed to do a lot more thinking about quantities and their relationships. It made little sense to teach them to set up the equation $\frac{a}{b} = \frac{c}{d}$, cross multiply, and divide until they had some sense of what a proportion is and is not. Instruction was designed to build on some everyday phenomena and to help them to build on what they know about themselves and proportions in the human body. The children were asked, "If your arms were 6 feet long, how tall would you be?" Kevin, a sixth grader, became so involved with this question that he spent several days thinking about it. Stop and answer this question for yourself. With a colleague or partner, discuss (a) the relationships that might be important for solving the problem and (b) some of the vocabulary you need to talk about the problem. Analyze the following excerpt of Kevin's discussion to determine whether his answer is correct and in which directions his thinking needs to develop.

I: If your arms were six feet long, how tall would you be?
K: (Long pause.) Six feet one.
I: Why do you say that?
K. 'Cause you don't want your fingers to drag on the ground.
I: Show me with your thumb and your pointer finger how long an inch is.
K: (Shows a length of approximately two inches.)
I: Seems to me, if your fingers were only an inch off the ground, you would bump them on every stone you passed.
K: Yeah, I guess you would.
I: Well what do you think about that?
K: I guess you better have them up a few more inches. Probably five or six.
I: Draw me a picture. What would you look like then?
K: (Long pause.) Nah. I can't do that. My arms would be coming out my head. Now wait a minute. My arms are as long as my head plus the rest of me down to my stomach. My waist is half of me. My waist is about the middle of my body and my arm is about half my body. So I would say that if I had arms six feet long, I would have to be about 12 feet tall.

(The next day, Kevin reported that he had had a doctor's appointment for a physical and this caused him to return to the question we had been discussing.)

K: I just had a physical after school yesterday, so I found out I am
    exactly five feet tall. (K extended his arm in front of him.) My arm is
    about two feet long I would say. So if I grew twice as tall, my arms
    would be twice as long. That would be four feet. Somebody with arms
    six feet long would be about two feet taller than that, or 12 feet tall.
    So the answer I got yesterday must be about right.

                    *

Quantitative Reasoning

All of the interpretations of rational numbers we have looked at so far,
as well as ratios and proportions, are all about mathematical
relationships.   Before we introduce symbols, it is important to get
children to discuss the relationships among quantities in real-world
situations. The study of relationships begins on a visual level and may
be clarified and extended when children develop a vocabulary, talk
about those relationships, and analyze them. Visually and verbally
analyzing relationships also teaches children to go beyond obvious,
surface-level observations and to think more about why things work
the way they do. It is important that reasoning about relationships
occur long before symbolic instruction so that children learn that there
is more to do when they first confront a situation than to merely extract
the numbers and operate blindly with them. It can help them to realize
that there are good reasons for the operations we perform on quantities.
        This chapter explores some of the situations that may be used to
build quantitative reasoning with young children. Quantitative
reasoning may or may not involve numbers. In addition to reasoning
with quantities in standard form, that is, as numbers and their
associated units of measure (e.g., 5 square feet, 24 milliliters), we can
also make qualitative judgments (more, less, fewer, greater, farther,
nearer, etc.) without actually having a quantity. For example, you can
compare the heights of two people in your family without having to
measure them. When one is standing beside or near the other, you can
tell which is taller. If you are in New York, you can safely say that
Philadelphia is closer than Los Angeles without checking a distance
table to get the miles between the cities. Even when a problem gives
quantities in their usual form, reasoning about relationships can
replace lots of computation.
        To give you a better idea of what is entailed in quantitative
reasoning, here are a few questions that require no work.

STOP Stop and answer these questions before going on. Do not use a
          calculator. Do not even use a pencil and paper!

1. You have 6^4 pennies and you arrange them in a square array. How many pennies will be in each row and column?

2. How much does package weigh if it weighs 9 pounds plus half its own weight?

3. The return on Jason's investments has been fluctuating rapidly during the last month. After the first week, he had twice $654,321, but by the end of the month had lost half of it. How much money did he have at the end of the month?

* * * * * * * * * * * * * * * * * * *

If you have not solved them, here are some clues. Use the clues and try the questions again. Do not reach for your calculator.

1. Clue: Think about the relationship between the given quantity and a square (a number multiplied by itself).
2. Clue: Two halves make a whole.
3. Clue: What is the relationship between doubling and halving?

* * * * * * * * * * * * * * * * * * *

Were you able to answer the questions without calculating? To answer the first question, ask yourself, "In the quantity 6^4 pennies, what square number do you have? Since $6^4 = (6^2)^2$, there must be 6^2 pennies in each row and column. Answering the second question simply relies on the fact halves of the same quantity are always identical. (Or else they would not be called halves!) If the package weighs 9 pounds plus half its weight, 9 pounds must be half its weight. The package weighs 18 pounds. The third question is answered by realizing that doubling then halving the same quantity results in the same quantity that you had in the beginning. If you take twice $654,321 and then half of that amount, you end up with $654,321.

In Proportion

Our earliest understanding of proportionality occurs on a visual level even before we learn to walk. We rely on visual data to give us information about such things as scale, degree of faithfulness of models, perspective, and so forth. During their early elementary years, we can help children to build on this intuitive knowledge by making it more explicit and open to analysis.

We use the word proportion in several different ways, and it is important that students understand all of its uses. For example, if someone asks "What proportion of the class is women?" they are really asking what fraction or part of the class is women. Or if it is said that the number of cases of a disease has reached epidemic proportions what is meant is merely that it has grown to a great size.

This discussion, uses two types of comparisons to decide questions of proportionality. The first compares the picture of an object to a real object. That is, it compares the picture of an object to something external, usually the real object. When we say that an object is drawn "in proportion," we mean that there is a relationship between a real object and the sketch of that object such that for all of the corresponding dimensions of the object, the ratios between drawn size and real size are equal. If a real person is five feet tall and has arms 2.2 feet long and in a portrait, the person is painted three feet tall, then his arms should not be 2.2 feet long or the portrait will be out of proportion. Technically speaking, to be in proportion, the comparison between every measurement on the real person and every corresponding measurement on the portrait should be the same.

A second important sense of the word refers to relations within a single object—an internal proportion, For example, suppose you are asked to judge the proportion of this rectangle:

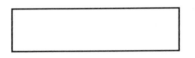

That means to judge the way in which the dimensions of the rectangle relate to each other. Without taking any actual measurements, you would take the width of the rectangle and visually lay it out against the length, making the judgment that there are about 4 of the widths in the length. You could say that the rectangle is about four times as long as it is wide, or you would say that

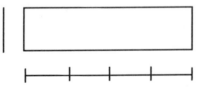

the ratio of its width to its length is 1:4.

In high school, we use a more precise mathematical definition of proportionality, but with elementary and middle school children, visual and verbal activities provide a good introduction to the idea of proportionality. We often rely on built-in capabilities, rather than on measuring and comparing. We judge internal and external ratios visually. Even as children, we have a good sense of whether something looks right or not. We can immediately detect when some feature is exaggerated as compared to the rest of a face, or whether a hand is too small compared to the rest of a person's body. Discussions of proportionality arise naturally when we make conscious and try to describe some of these tacit processes that guide our intuition.

If we agree to rely on this sense, we must also agree that we will tolerate some inaccuracy. Things may look "about" right, or "close enough," but without taking exact measurements, we might not realize when there are some subtle distortions that our eyes cannot detect. But when the amount of distortion reaches a certain level, our internal sensors kick in and tell us that something does not look right. For example, look at the following picture. This rabbit is drawn on different scales in different directions, so it does not closely resemble a rabbit. It is drawn "out of proportion."

By the time children come to school, they have several well-developed visual proportional detectors. For example, children are not fooled by the juxtaposition of two sketches such as that of the rabbit and the bear shown below. They know that the sizes of the animals are not their real sizes, nor do the sketches portray their relative sizes. Children understand implicitly that each drawing in itself is a faithful model of the real animal it represents, but taken together, the pair of drawings is not representative of a scene in which the real animals are standing next to each other. Both animals are scaled down, but they are drawn on different scales.

When we talk to children about situations involving proportional relationships, we start on a visual level so that they can make use of their internal sensing devices, but our goals should take them well beyond noticing or perceiving whether things look right or not.
We need to encourage children to:
• identify measurable characteristics
• build a language to talk about the phenomenon under consideration
• describe regularities, relationships, or structure
• connect to other real world or mathematical phenomena
• to connect situations to each other: " this is like the _____ problem"
• to use visualization to change static pictures: "what would happen if..."
• use informal notation systems to describe relationships and change

Discussing Quantitative Relationships

Most children need help to get beyond their intuitive understandings. They do not always have appropriate words to talk about size relationships. Most children understand comparison in an additive sense. For example:

> John has 3 cookies and Mary has 7 cookies.
> How many more cookies does Mary have?

In this case, subtraction provides a way to compare Mary's cookies and John's, but when talking about scale and proportion, we need the language to compare things multiplicatively. Observe the relationships of the sizes of objects to each other and help students to verbalize these relationships with the words "relative to" and "compared to."

Examples

Compared to a real bear, the picture of the bear is smaller.
Compared to a real rabbit, the picture of the rabbit is smaller.
Relative to the bear picture, the rabbit picture is too large.
But is it too large relative to a real bear?

We also need to encourage students to make verbal statements about changing relationships, and then to use arrow notation to describe the quantity structure.

Example. We have a picture of a child watching a balloon rise into the sky.

Verbal statement of the quantitative relationships:
The higher the balloon floats into the sky, the smaller it looks.

Arrow notation: height of the balloon ↑ apparent size ↓

Example. We have a picture of three children with candy bars. Two other children are standing close by.

What will happen if the 3 children decide to share their candy?
Verbal statement: The more children who share it, the less candy there is for each child.

What quantities are changing?
The number of children and the amount of candy per child.

Arrow notation: number of children ↑ amount of candy per child ↓

Students quickly adopt the habit of referring to up—up situations, up—down situations, down—up situations, and so on. Later, this language and notation can be extended into more powerful ideas and the categories can be refined (for example, all up—up situations are not the same).

While, on the surface, it seems that a teacher would have no trouble discussing these situations with children, in reality, it turns out to be difficult. The reason is that children (and even many adults) have trouble distinguishing a quantity (a measurable characteristic) from a physical description.

Example. Water is running from a faucet into a bathtub. What is changing?

Physical description: The bathtub is filling up.
An appropriate quantity: amount of water (volume)

Example. You have a picture of Jack standing next to the giant at the top of the beanstalk.

Physical Description: The giant is much bigger than Jack.
An appropriate quantity: height

The point is that merely asking children to provide descriptions of a picture will not promote quantitative reasoning. Although they are not attempting to take any measurements, discussing quantities entails knowing what the measurable characteristics are. Noting the distinction between description and quantity identification is a necessary step in mathematizing a problem situation. Anyone can look at the picture and see that the giant is taller than Jack is. Measuring the heights of the two characters uses mathematics to prove that assertion.

Classroom discussion also needs to address ideas such as stretching, shrinking, distortion, being in proportion, and being out of proportion. It is not so important to make the scales explicit. It is more important to develop language and ideas. For example, there are several different conditions under which two objects appear to be out of proportion.

In the picture of the rabbit and the bear shown earlier, each is drawn on a different scale. That means that the bear might be sketched at $\frac{1}{30}$ its normal size and the rabbit might be $\frac{1}{10}$ its normal size. So when you put them side by side, the rabbit appears much larger than the bear. The pictures are out of proportion in relation to each other. If both had been drawn at $\frac{1}{30}$ their normal size, they would appear to be correct in size relative to each other. Children's first explanation for this might be that "they were shrunk by different amounts."

Sometimes within the same picture different parts are drawn out of proportion. A good example is a caricature. In a caricature, different parts of the same face are drawn on different scales. The artist chooses some facial feature and deliberately intensifies it by sketching it larger than it should be in relation to the rest of the face. We notice the distortion immediately because it conflicts with the image that we have in our memory. We are still able to identify the subject, but something about the picture does not look "normal." Have students look at some caricatures and discuss why certain facial features are out of proportion and what statement the artist might be trying to make with the distortion.

A third type of distortion occurs when two dimensions of a single object are drawn on different scales. For example, the distorted rabbit was about twice as wide as he was high. On a computer it is easy to change the vertical and horizontal scales so that students can experiment with scales and observe the effects. Although it is very time-consuming to draw pictures in different scales, the computer provides a convenient medium in which to make many trials in a short period of time. Have students produce drawings in which length and width are on different scales, judge the proportion of the picture, and use multiplicative language to describe it.

More Abstract Activities

As children are preparing to study fractions, they need to be able to think more abstractly. Several kinds of activities are useful. Using the imagination or transforming a situation in the mind's eye is more difficult than using pictures or objects. The level of abstraction may also be increased by investigating below-the-surface relationships in verbal analogies and in activities with centimeter strips.

Activities that require pure visualization are more demanding for children because all of the relevant information and relationships are stored and manipulated in their heads. The situation Kevin discussed at the beginning of this chapter is a good example of the difficulty of visualization. It was difficult enough when he had to imagine what he might look like if he had arms that were six feet long, and even more difficult to test his conjecture that he would be 6 feet and 1 inch tall. The remarkable progress Kevin made in his thinking about the problem is a good argument for encouraging students to reason in situations where visualization is required. It was a problem that he could take with him, and he continued to think about it, even outside of the school day. In time, Kevin revised his original conjecture and adopted a more sophisticated strategy, a building up strategy involving a doubling process. Unfortunately, he resorted to additive thinking when it was impossible to double again. His strategy showed that he is still an additive thinker, rather than a multiplicative thinker. Even worse, the fact that he arrived at the same answer twice convinced him of the goodness of his additive model. Nevertheless, within a short period of time and within a single context, he showed good progress in moving away from nonsensical toward more mathematical thinking. Given more situations to think about and discuss, he will continue to revise his thinking.

Another way to encourage younger children to think about relational similarities is through the use of pictorial and verbal analogies. You may have encountered these on intelligence tests, college entrance examinations, or other standardized tests.

Examples

(1) dog is to fur as bird is to _____
This is often written dog : fur :: bird : _____

(2) eyes : television :: ears : ?

(3)

(4) fire : ashes :: special occasion : ?

(5) bee : honey :: snake : ?

Analyzing analogies provides an alternate and more abstract means of studying relationships. In analogies, there is a relationship between the first pair of terms and the goal is to supply the missing term in the second pair so that it conveys a similar relationship. Historically, both psychologists and mathematicians have contended that there is a close connection between analogical reasoning and proportional reasoning. Some have argued that proportions involve a more complex system of relationships than pictorial and verbal analogies, and, if this is the case, then it is likely that a child will be unable to understand all of the relations in a proportion if he or she cannot apprehend the relational similarity in analogies.

In discussing analogies, children should be encouraged to give more than simple answers. They should also explain the relationship that led to their response. This is because it is often possible to complete an analogy merely by making associations and without even thinking about relational similarity. For example, in the third problem stated above, a child might say "hair" because we typically associate hair with our heads. This response might be made without even considering the relationship between hand and glove. The relationship that explains the connection between hand and glove and between head and hand is that the first member of each pair is "protected and kept warm by" the second member. Encourage children to make complete statements: "Bee is to honey as snake is to venom, and the relationship is that the first member of each pair "produces a liquid called" the second.

If the child is asked to explain the reason for the response, you gain two valuable pieces of information about the child's thinking.

First, you can tell whether or not the child's response is based on relational similarity. If the child says "Hair because hair grows on a head," then the child has made an association and has not considered the relationship between hands and gloves. "Grows on" does not describe the relationship between hand and glove. If the child says "Hair because gloves cover up our hands and hair covers up our head," then you know that the child is considering relational similarity. The child detects the relationship "covers up." Another child might give the same response by considering the relationship "keeps warm."

From a child's response, it is also possible to obtain information about the depth of the relationships the child is perceiving. For example, if the child says "Hat because a hat protects our head just like gloves protect our hands," the child detects a deeper relationship than one who focused on observable characteristics, such as a hat "goes on" a head and a glove "goes on" a hand. Example 4 involves a less obvious, analogy that calls for deeper reasoning. Ashes are all that remain after a fire and memories are all that remain after a special occasion. This is a higher order relationship because it is not directly observable or able to be directly experienced. In proportions, the comparison of two quantities yields a third new quantity that is often not able to be directly experienced, so the ability to answer higher order analogies suggests some relationship to the ability to understand higher order relationships such as ratios and rates.

One problem with analogies is that they may be stretched to the breaking point, thus making it difficult or impossible to determine the relational similarity. If you are constructing your own higher order analogies, it might be a good idea to discuss them with someone else before trying them with your class, just to be sure that others perceive the same relationships as you do.

In addition to pictures, other concrete materials such as centimeter strips or Cuisenaire rods may be used to discuss relationships.

Example. Is the relationship between purple and blue strips the same as the relationship between red and yellow strips?

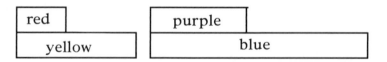

Align the colored strips with white strips, which are one unit in length, in order to determine the relationships:

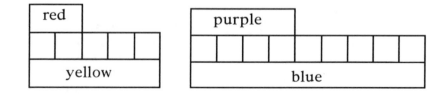

Red covers $\frac{2}{5}$ of yellow and purple covers $\frac{4}{9}$ of blue. So "the red strip does not cover the same proportion (fraction) of the yellow as the purple does of the blue."

Example. Another answer.

The purple strip (or rod) is twice as long as the red, but blue is not twice the length of yellow.

Although this problem is presented in a concrete form, it involves higher order multiplicative thinking. The relationships in the problem closely resemble those in a proportion. Notice that the explanation used in the first example examined the relationship within each pair of strips, and the second explanation examined the relationship between corresponding members of the pairs (first to first and second to second). In a proportion, the within and the between relationships must be the same.

Seeing Fraction Operations

The conceptual benefits of expressing relationships visually and verbally continue to accrue well into the beginning of fraction instruction. In the following activities, all of the fractional operations are available to students long before they are taught formal algorithms. These visual and verbal reasoning activities can play a large role in helping students to build conceptual understanding out of informal knowledge.   In reading through the following example, answer the questions, but also pay attention to the way in which the questions are asked.

Example. Look at this Big Stix candy bar.

Half the candy bar = _____ sticks.

2 sticks = _____ of the candy bar.

If you have $\frac{1}{2}$ the candy bar and I have $\frac{1}{3}$ of the candy bar, how much do we have together?

What part of the candy bar remains for someone else?

If you have $\frac{1}{2}$ the candy bar and I have $\frac{1}{3}$ of the candy bar, who has more?

How much more?

$\frac{1}{2} - \frac{1}{3} = $ _____ of a bar

How much of the candy bar is half of a third?

$\frac{1}{2} \times \frac{1}{3} = $ _____ of a bar

How many times will $\frac{1}{3}$ fit into $\frac{1}{2}$?

By skillfully asking questions of children, you can help them to reason through simple fraction operations. Notice that, without knowing any more than the meaning of a part—whole fraction, children can answer all of the questions, and that in the process, they are actually performing these operations:

$$\frac{1}{2} + \frac{1}{3} = \frac{5}{6}$$
$$1 - \frac{5}{6} = \frac{1}{6}$$
$$\frac{1}{2} - \frac{1}{3} = \frac{1}{6}$$
$$\frac{1}{2} \times \frac{1}{3} = \frac{1}{6}$$
$$\frac{1}{2} \div \frac{1}{3} = 1\frac{1}{2}$$

At first, just have the children look at the picture and answer questions about it. Later, go back and write the symbols for the operations.

Here is another visual approach to fraction operations. Look at the following figure and try to answer each of the following questions for yourself before reading the explanation.

Example. Can you see $\frac{3}{7}$?

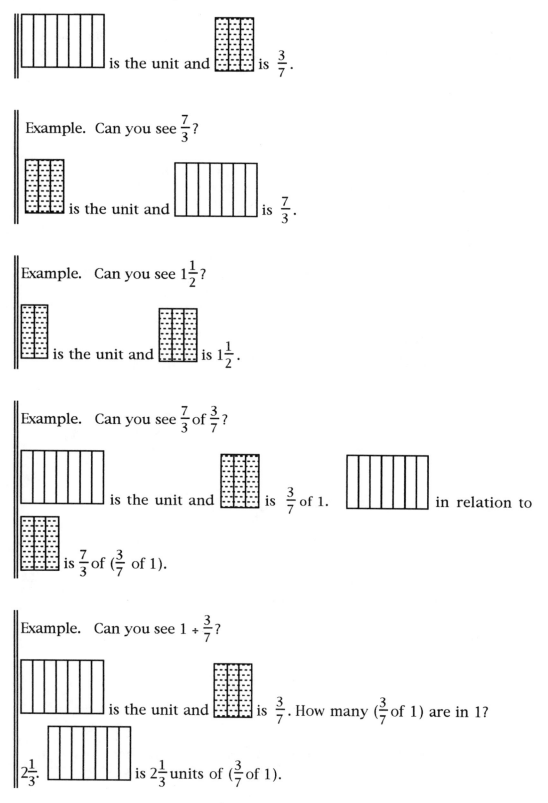

is the unit and [   ] is $\frac{3}{7}$.

Example. Can you see $\frac{7}{3}$?

[   ] is the unit and [   ] is $\frac{7}{3}$.

Example. Can you see $1\frac{1}{2}$?

[   ] is the unit and [   ] is $1\frac{1}{2}$.

Example. Can you see $\frac{7}{3}$ of $\frac{3}{7}$?

[   ] is the unit and [   ] is $\frac{3}{7}$ of 1. [   ] in relation to

[   ] is $\frac{7}{3}$ of ($\frac{3}{7}$ of 1).

Example. Can you see $1 \div \frac{3}{7}$?

[   ] is the unit and [   ] is $\frac{3}{7}$. How many ($\frac{3}{7}$ of 1) are in 1?

$2\frac{1}{3}$. [   ] is $2\frac{1}{3}$ units of ($\frac{3}{7}$ of 1).

STOP As you think about the following activities, remember that the goal is to use terminology correctly in describing important relationships.

Activities

1. Draw a knife, fork, and spoon in their proper positions next to the dinner plate represented here. To make an accurate drawing, what are all of the relationships that must be taken into consideration?

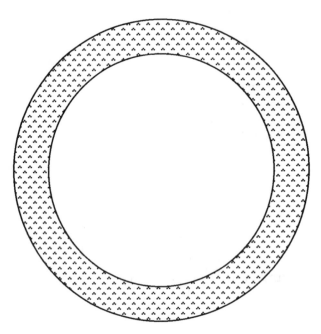

2. If you were to draw a sketch of Mrs. Jones standing next to her car, how tall would you make her? How did you decide?

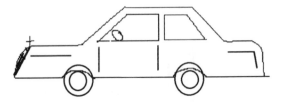

3. Describe each of these caricatures. What is the difference between a caricature and an ordinary drawing? Make some conjectures

concerning the reason why the artist may have drawn certain features out of proportion.

4. To advertise our go-to-school night, a local pizzeria made a 3-foot pizza in the gymnasium and served it to parents, teachers, and students. The three people who served the pizza estimated that each group was served the portion indicated in the picture. What can you say about the way they distributed the pizza?

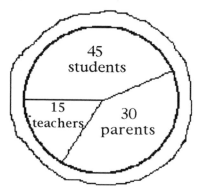

5. Suppose the first cat in the following picture went through a shrinking machine. Would he look like the second cat?

6. If this boy drives the tractor from one end of the field to the other, will both wheels cover the same distance? How do you know?

7. In each case, discuss possible responses and the relation on which they are based.

a. picture : frame :: yard : ?

b. giraffe : neck :: porcupine : ?

c. food : body :: rain : ?

d. car : gasoline :: sail : ?

e. sap: tree :: blood: ?

f. sandwich : boy :: carrot : ?

g. pear : tree :: potato : ?

h. tree: leaves :: book : ?

i. conductor : train :: captain : ?

j. wedding: bride :: funeral : ?

8. The small cookie shown below is covered with sprinkles and chocolate chips. The large cookie is not yet decorated. Without counting numbers of pieces, decorate the large cookie with sprinkles and chocolate chips so that both cookies are decorated similarly.

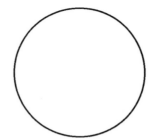

a. Name two different visual judgments that children need to make to be able to decorate the large cookie.

b. How could you check whether your visual judgments were accurate or not?

9. The following questions refer to this candy bar:

a. How many pieces in half the candy bar?

b. How many pieces in $\frac{1}{5}$ of the candy bar?

c. How many pieces in $\frac{1}{2} + \frac{1}{5}$ of the candy bar?

d. How much of the candy bar is $\frac{1}{2} + \frac{1}{5}$?

e. If I had half the candy bar and I ate $\frac{1}{5}$ of it, how much would I have left?

f. Write the symbols for the operation you performed in part e.

g. How many pieces in $\frac{1}{5}$ of $\frac{1}{2}$ the candy bar?

h. What conclusion can you draw from g?

i. How many times does $\frac{2}{5}$ of the candy bar fit into my half?

j. Write the symbols for the operation you performed in i.

10. Judge the proportions of width to length of these rectangles.

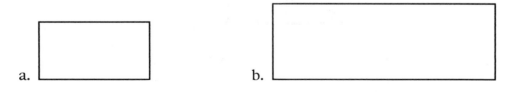

a.   b.

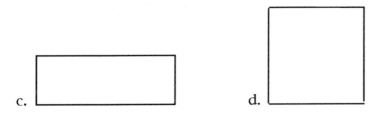

c.   d.

11. Pretend you have a little dog who is as high as your knee when he is standing on all four feet. If you were a giant, 8 feet tall, how high would your dog be if he still came up to your knee?

12. In each of the pictures, the first two blocks define a relationship. Does the second pair show the same relationship as the first pair? If not, replace one of the blocks in the second pair so that you get the same relationship as in the first pair.

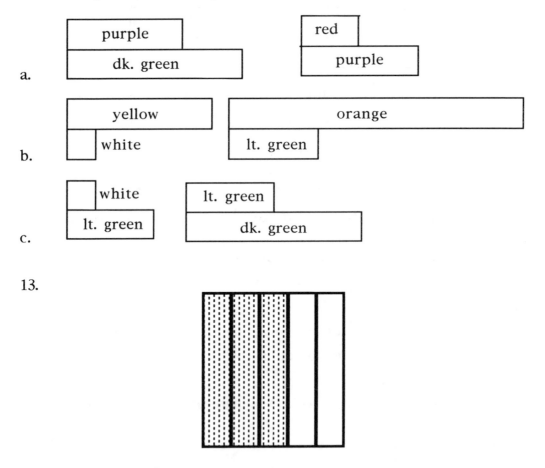

a.

| purple |
| dk. green |

| red |
| purple |

b.

| yellow |
| white |

| orange |
| lt. green |

c.

| white |
| lt. green |

| lt. green |
| dk. green |

13.

a. Can you can see $\frac{3}{5}$ of something? What is the unit?

b. Can you see $\frac{5}{3}$ of something? What is the unit?

c. Can you see $\frac{2}{3}$ of $\frac{3}{5}$? Draw the unit. Draw $\frac{3}{5}$. Indicate $\frac{2}{3}$ of it.

d. Can you see $\frac{5}{3}$ of $\frac{3}{5}$?

e. Can you see $1 \div \frac{3}{5}$?

f. Can you see $\frac{3}{5} \div 2$?

g. Can you see $\frac{5}{4} \div \frac{3}{4}$?

14. Dianne runs laps every day. Given each statement below (a—d), draw a conclusion about her running speed today.
a. She ran the same number of laps in less time than she did yesterday.
b. She ran fewer laps in the same amount of time as she did yesterday.
c. She ran more laps in less time than she did yesterday.
d. She ran more laps in the same time as she ran yesterday.
e. Under what conditions would you not be able to compare Dianne's speed today with her speed yesterday?

15. Use this carton of eggs as a visual prop, and write some questions that children can answer by looking at the picture. Model your questions after those used in the Big Stix problem. Write the appropriate number sentence that goes with each.

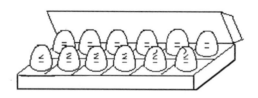

* * * * * * * * * * * * * * * * * * *

STOP   Take some time to think about the ideas in this chapter.

Reflection

1. Using a picture from a magazine, list all of the questions you could ask children in order to help them reason about multiplicative quantitative relationships.

2. What are scale drawings? What sorts of statements (using appropriate language about relationships) would you expect children to be able to make after a lesson involving scale drawings?

3. Think of some contexts, not mentioned in this chapter, that involve proportional relationships.

Chapter 10
Reasoning With Fractions

STOP *Children's Strategies*

Some children were asked to think about this problem:

$$1 \div \frac{2}{3}$$

Troy, Carson, Grace, and Lindsay, the fifth graders who produced the following work, had been building meaning for fractions for two full years without ever mentioning algorithms or doing formal computation. Each of them thought about the problem in a different way. Analyze their solutions, paying special attention to the various interpretations of fractions they used.

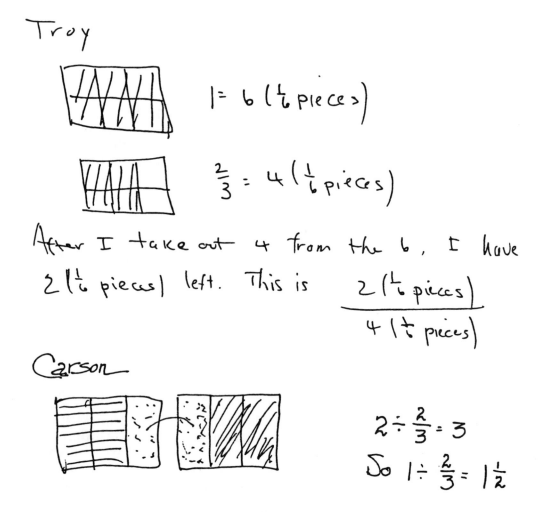

Troy

$1 = 6 \ (\frac{1}{6} \text{ pieces})$

$\frac{2}{3} = 4 \ (\frac{1}{6} \text{ pieces})$

After I take out 4 from the 6, I have 2 ($\frac{1}{6}$ pieces) left. This is $\dfrac{2 \ (\frac{1}{6} \text{ pieces})}{4 \ (\frac{1}{6} \text{ pieces})}$

Carson

$2 \div \frac{2}{3} = 3$

So $1 \div \frac{2}{3} = 1\frac{1}{2}$

Grace

$\frac{2}{3}$ is twice as big as $\frac{1}{3}$ and I know $\frac{1}{3}$ goes into 1 three time. So $\frac{2}{3}$ can go in only half as many times.

Lindsay R

$$1 = 3\left(\tfrac{1}{3}\text{'s}\right) = 1\tfrac{1}{2}\left(\tfrac{2}{3}\text{'s}\right)$$

* * * * * * * * * * * * * * * * * * * *

Ordering Fractions

Children need lots of informal experiences with fractions before proceeding to formal fraction operations because they need to build up some fraction sense. This means that students should develop an intuition that helps them make appropriate connections, determine size, order, and equivalence, and judge whether answers are or are not reasonable. Such fluid and flexible thinking is just as important for teachers who need to distinguish appropriate student strategies from those based on faulty reasoning.

It is not too difficult to think about the relative sizes of two fractions when their denominators are the same. For example, which is larger, $\frac{3}{5}$ or $\frac{2}{5}$? This is similar to a whole number situation because it is like asking, "If all the pieces are the same size, do you have more if you have 2 of them or 3 of them?"

Similarly, if both numerators are the same, then the size of the pieces becomes the only critical issue. For example, which is larger, $\frac{3}{7}$ or $\frac{3}{5}$? In this case, we think, " If a pie has been cut into sevenths, the pieces are smaller than those from a pie that has been cut into fifths."

It can be more difficult to compare fractions if the numerators and the denominators are different, because then you are comparing different numbers of different-sized pieces. For example, "Would you rather have 3 pieces from a pie that has been cut into 5 equal-sized pieces ($\frac{3}{5}$) or 4 pieces from a pie that has been cut into 9 equal-sized pieces ($\frac{4}{9}$)? You need to decide which option gives you more: fewer pieces when the pieces are larger or more pieces when the pieces are smaller.

Another way to think about the size of two fractions is to picture a number line with some familiar landmarks on it. If you can decide that one of the fractions you are comparing lies to the left of $\frac{1}{2}$, for example, and that the other lies to the right of $\frac{1}{2}$, then it is easy to tell which it larger.

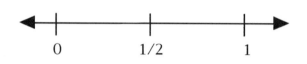

$$0 \qquad 1/2 \qquad 1$$

Example. Compare $\frac{3}{4}$ and $\frac{1}{5}$.

$\frac{3}{4} > \frac{1}{2}$ and $\frac{1}{5} < \frac{1}{2}$.

So $\frac{3}{4} > \frac{1}{5}$.

It is often useful to enhance this strategy by using fractional parts of the denominator.

Example.

The fraction $\frac{2}{3}$ is larger than half because $\frac{1\frac{1}{2}}{3} = \frac{1}{2}$.

$\frac{5}{11}$ is less than $\frac{1}{2}$ because $\frac{5\frac{1}{2}}{11} = \frac{1}{2}$.

$\frac{5}{11}$ is greater than $\frac{1}{4}$ because $\frac{2\frac{1}{4}}{11} = \frac{1}{4}$.

Example. Which is larger, $\frac{3}{5}$ or $\frac{4}{9}$?

We have a pie cut into 5 equivalent slices. Exactly half the pie would consist of $2\frac{1}{2}$ slices, so 3 slices is more than half the pie and $\frac{3}{5}$ lies somewhere to the right of $\frac{1}{2}$.

Now think of a pie cut into 9 equivalent slices.   Exactly half the pie would consist of $4\frac{1}{2}$ slices. But we have only 4 slices, so $\frac{4}{9}$ lies somewhere to the left of $\frac{1}{2}$.

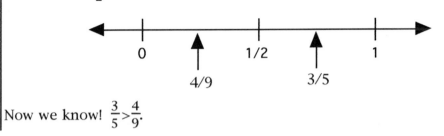

Now we know! $\frac{3}{5} > \frac{4}{9}$.

   When the fractions you are comparing lie on opposites sides of your reference point, this method works, but when you find that both fractions lie on the same side of your reference point, you need another method of comparison. At this point, a commonly used strategy asks "how far away from" the chosen reference point the fractions are. You may hear children say that $\frac{3}{5}$ is only 2 parts away from the unit and $\frac{4}{9}$ is 5 parts away, so $\frac{3}{5}$ must represent the larger amount. Beware of this faulty reasoning, Right answer! Wrong reason!   The parts that are being compared here are of different sizes, just as they were in the fractions $\frac{4}{9}$ and $\frac{3}{5}$. It is true in some other cases that 2 of the larger parts represent a distance farther from 1 than 5 of the smaller parts. For example, $\frac{2}{4}$ is smaller than $\frac{6}{11}$ although $\frac{2}{4}$ is only 2 parts from the whole and $\frac{6}{11}$ is 6 part away from the whole. The size of the parts matters!

Example. Which is larger, $\frac{2}{3}$ or $\frac{3}{5}$?

$\frac{2}{3} > \frac{1}{2}$ and $\frac{3}{5} > \frac{1}{2}$

How much larger than $\frac{1}{2}$ is $\frac{2}{3}$? $1\frac{1}{2}$ parts is half of 3, so 2 parts out of 3 is larger than half by $\frac{\frac{1}{2}}{3}$.

How much larger is $\frac{3}{5}$? $2\frac{1}{2}$ parts is half of 5, so 3 parts out of 5 is larger than half by $\frac{\frac{1}{2}}{5}$.

Now which is larger, $\dfrac{\frac{1}{2}}{3}$ or $\dfrac{\frac{1}{2}}{5}$? Because the pie cut into thirds has larger pieces than the pie cut into fifths, a half of a piece from the pie cut into thirds is larger than half of a piece from the pie cut into fifths.

So, $\dfrac{2}{3} > \dfrac{3}{5}$.

Example. Compare $\dfrac{5}{11}$ and $\dfrac{1}{4}$.

$$\dfrac{5\frac{1}{2}}{11} = \dfrac{1}{2} \quad \text{and} \quad \dfrac{2\frac{1}{4}}{11} = \dfrac{1}{4}$$

So, $\dfrac{5}{11} > \dfrac{1}{4}$

The ordering strategies we have discussed so far may be summarized as follows:

1. Same-Size Parts (SSP). When comparing same-size parts, the fraction with the greater numerator has the greater value.

$$\dfrac{5}{8} < \dfrac{7}{8}$$

2. Same Number of Parts (SNP). When comparing fractions in which the numerators are alike (that is, you have the same number of parts in each), but the denominators are different (that is, the pieces are of different sizes) the larger number denominator indicates the smaller fraction.

$$\dfrac{3}{5} > \dfrac{3}{7}$$

3. Compare to Reference Point (CRP). When comparing fractions with different numerators and denominators, compare them to some reference point (e.g., $\dfrac{1}{2}, \dfrac{1}{4}, 1$).

$$\dfrac{4}{5} > \dfrac{2}{7} \quad \text{because} \quad \dfrac{4}{5} > \dfrac{1}{2} \text{ and } \dfrac{2}{7} < \dfrac{1}{2}$$

$\dfrac{9}{10} > \dfrac{8}{9}$ because $\dfrac{9}{10}$ is only $\dfrac{1}{10}$ away from 1, while $\dfrac{8}{9}$ is $\dfrac{1}{9}$ away from 1.

Sometimes younger children need visual models to help support their thinking as they compare fractions. The following area model is useful.

Example. Compare $\frac{3}{8}$ and $\frac{4}{9}$.

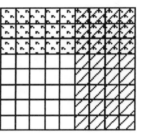

Represent $\frac{3}{8}$ by slicing and shading a rectangle horizontally and $\frac{4}{9}$ by slicing and shading vertically.
$\frac{3}{8} = \frac{27}{72}$ and $\frac{4}{9} = \frac{32}{72}$.
$\frac{4}{9} > \frac{3}{8}$

Notice that this process generates a common denominator. However, that denominator may not always be the lowest common denominator. After using this area model, you might ask children if they can see a way to add the fractions. Some children can immediately use the fractions with common denominators to add, but sometimes they invent other clever techniques, such as this one used by a third grader.

Example. $\frac{3}{8} + \frac{4}{9}$

Represent the fractions as shown, then notice that if you count the total number of squares shaded (i.e., you add), the ones in the overlapping area will get counted only once. So move a copy of that area into some unmarked squares before counting all marked squares.

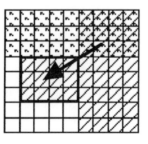

$$\frac{3}{8} + \frac{4}{9} = \frac{59}{72}$$

Another popular method of comparing fractions is to represent each fraction using a different copy of the same unit. Young children are less successful with this method   When the fractions are different enough in size and children can partition accurately enough, this model works. However, when the fractions are very close in size, it becomes less dependable. The following example is from a third grader's work.

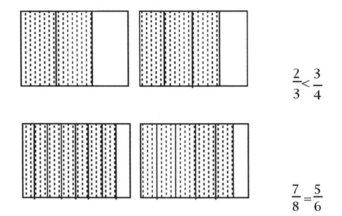

$$\frac{2}{3} < \frac{3}{4}$$

$$\frac{7}{8} = \frac{5}{6}$$

As you can see, the student reached a correct conclusion in the first case, but inaccurate partitioning caused the student to draw the wrong conclusion in the second case. Students who are taught equivalence and order primarily through the use of this area model are slow to develop any ability to reason because they become overly dependent on the way fractions look. Because we want to help students develop sound methods of reasoning, as opposed to making purely visual judgments, instruction should not rely heavily on any one visual model.

Other Useful Ways of Thinking

Martin's method (see chap. 8) for determining a number of fractions between two given fractions relied on the use of equivalent fractions.   By rewriting a fraction using an equivalent expression, namely, a fraction within a fraction, he was able to name many fractions between the two he was given. In addition to Martin's method, there are other ways to produce equivalent forms that can help you to reason about fractions. The next two examples suggest rewriting a fraction as the sum of other fractions.

Example. Find three fractions between $\frac{3}{5}$ and $\frac{4}{5}$.

$\frac{4}{5} = \frac{3}{5} + \frac{1}{5}$, so if we add something less than $\frac{1}{5}$ to $\frac{3}{5}$, we will name a fraction less than $\frac{4}{5}$: $\frac{3}{5} + \frac{1}{6} = \frac{23}{30}$, $\frac{3}{5} + \frac{1}{7} = \frac{26}{35}$, $\frac{3}{5} + \frac{1}{8} = \frac{29}{40}$

Example. Compare $\frac{7}{8}$ and $\frac{9}{10}$.

Write each fraction as a sum of unit fractions:

$$\frac{7}{8}=\frac{1}{2}+\frac{1}{4}+\frac{1}{8} \qquad \frac{9}{10}=\frac{1}{2}+\frac{1}{4}+\frac{1}{10}+\frac{1}{20}$$

Then it can be seen that $\frac{7}{8}$ is greater by comparing the unlike portions of the two fractions: $\frac{1}{8}$ or $\frac{3}{24}$ is less than $\frac{1}{10}+\frac{1}{20}=\frac{3}{20}$.

Example. Find two fractions between $\frac{7}{8}$ and $\frac{9}{10}$.

From the sums of unit fractions, it can also be seen that $\frac{9}{10}$ is $\frac{3}{20}-\frac{1}{8}=\frac{1}{40}$ greater than $\frac{7}{8}$. Divide the difference, $\frac{1}{40}$ into 3 equal parts. Each part is $\frac{1}{120}$.

$$\frac{7}{8}+\frac{1}{120}=\frac{106}{120} \qquad \frac{7}{8}+\frac{2}{120}=\frac{107}{120} \qquad \frac{7}{8}+\frac{3}{120}=\frac{108}{120}=\frac{9}{10}$$

Therefore, fractions in between are $\frac{106}{120}$ and $\frac{107}{120}$.

Flexible Use of Interpretations

Another useful technique in working with fractions, especially when they are out of context, or not situated in a story problem, is to rely on the various interpretations you have studied: part—whole comparisons, quotients, measures, and operators. The children who answered the question at the beginning of this chapter were flexible thinkers. They had developed multiple interpretations for fractional numbers and had a good sense of the way things "work" in the fraction world. Some of them were so competent in reasoning about fractional quantities that if they never learned any formal algorithms for fraction operations, they had sufficient knowledge to solve any fraction problem they might encounter. Grace knew that $\frac{2}{3}$ is twice the size of $\frac{1}{3}$. She also knew that if she measured with a unit that was twice as big, she would get only half as many copies of it. Essentially, she told us that if there are three $\frac{1}{3}$s in 1, then there can be only be one and a half $\frac{2}{3}$s in 1. Lindsay simply unitized the unit into chunks of size ($\frac{2}{3}$-unit). Troy unitized both the

unit and the divisor into chunks of size ($\frac{1}{6}$-unit), then measured the

unit with the divisor.   Underlying Carson's strategy was an

understanding of a fraction as a quotient. He understood $\frac{2}{3}$ as the result

of dividing 1(2-unit) or 2 (1-units) into 3 equal shares. So he first
looked at two copies of a rectangle unitized into thirds so that he could
measure out 3 shares. He then claimed that starting with only 1
rectangle would yield half as much.

 As you think about the following activities, remember that the
goal is to use terminology correctly in describing important
relationships.

Activities

1. Compare by shading: $\frac{4}{5}$ and $\frac{5}{6}$.

2. Compare the fractions in each pair. Justify your answer using SNP,
SSP, or CRP.

a. $\frac{8}{14}, \frac{4}{9}$

b. $\frac{3}{17}, \frac{3}{19}$

c. $\frac{5}{13}, \frac{8}{13}$

d. $\frac{3}{2}, \frac{4}{3}$

3. Use Martin's method to find three fractions between the given
fractions.

a. $\frac{7}{13}, \frac{7}{14}$

b. $\frac{6}{8}, \frac{7}{8}$

4. If $\frac{2}{3}$ of the people at the picnic are adults, then

a. are there more children or more adults?
b. how many times the number of children are adults?
c. how many times the number of adults are children?

5. Using each of the numbers 5, 6, 7, and 8 only once, construct a sum with the given properties:

a. the smallest possible sum
b. the largest possible sum

c. the smallest possible positive difference
d. the largest possible positive difference

e. the smallest possible product
f. the largest possible product

g. the smallest possible quotient
h. the largest possible quotient

6. H means "holds the same amount as "

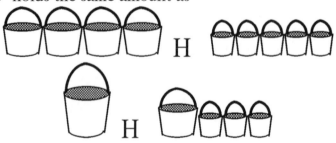

Which holds more:

7. How much does each bucket hold?

8. How much does each bucket hold?

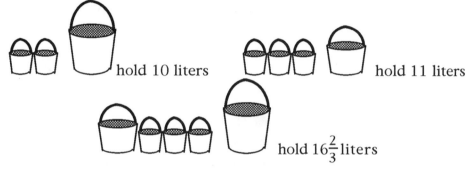

9. How much does each bucket hold?

10. If $\frac{5}{8}$ of the people in Aggieville are students, then

a. are there more students or nonstudents?
b. how many times the number of nonstudents are students?
c. how many times the number of students are nonstudents?

11. What happens to the size of a positive fraction when the following changes are made:
a. the numerator is increased
b. the numerator is increasing and the denominator is increasing
c. the denominator is increased
d. the numerator and the denominator are both multiplied by the same number
e. the numerator and the denominator are both increasing but the denominator increases faster than the numerator

12.   In Mrs. Brown's class, there are $\frac{5}{3}$ as many students as in Mrs. Henderson's class.
a.   Which teacher has more students?
b.   If you know the number of students in Mrs. Henderson's class, how do you find the number of students in Mrs. Brown's class?
c.   If you know the number of students in Mrs. Brown's class, how do you find the number of students in Mrs. Henderson's class?
d.   If Mrs. Henderson has 27 students, how many does Mrs. Brown have?
e.   If Mrs. Brown has 30 students, how many does Mrs. Henderson have?

13.   Construct a fraction very close to 1.   Construct another fraction even closer to 1.

14. Mrs. Holt asked the children in her class what a clone is. Jimmy said that it is an exact copy. She then went on to explain :

Here is $\frac{2}{3}$: ● ● ○. $\frac{2}{3}$ has many clones. Here is one of them. He is made of three copies of $\frac{2}{3}$.

What do you suppose its name is?
A clone is made by making exact copies of $\frac{2}{3}$.   The clones have different names, but they all look alike and they behave just like $\frac{2}{3}$.

$\frac{2}{3}$ has 2 parts out of 3 shaded and $\frac{6}{9}$ has 2 parts out of 3 shaded:

a.   What concept is Mrs. Holt discussing with her students?
b.   What is the name of this fraction?   ● ● ● ○ ○
c.   Make a clone by taking two copies of the fraction in b.   Make another clone by making three copies of the same fraction. Name both clones.
d.   Suppose you want to know whether or not each of the following fractions is a clone of the fraction in b. How can you find out?

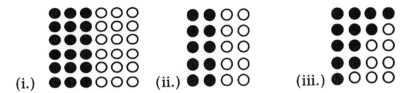

15. Later, Mrs. Holt asked her students to figure out which fraction was larger, $\frac{4}{6}$ or $\frac{7}{9}$. Jimmy told Mrs. Holt that he could use clones to help decide which fraction was larger. Here is the work he produced. How did he do it?

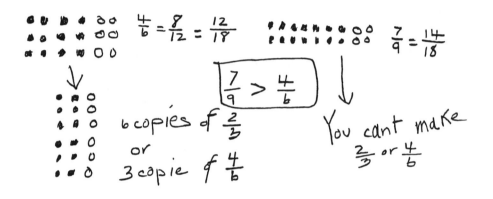

16. Use Jimmy's method to determine which fraction in each pair is larger.

a. $\frac{5}{6}, \frac{13}{18}$ b. $\frac{11}{12}, \frac{7}{8}$ c. $\frac{3}{5}, \frac{5}{6}$

17. A pound of cheese cost \$3.85. Will $\frac{9}{10}$ lb. cost more or less? How much more or how much less?

18. Decide which of the two fractions in each pair represents a larger amount using reasoning only. Use reasoning to justify your answer. Common denominators and cross multiplying strategies are not to be used here.

a. $\frac{3}{7}, \frac{5}{8}$ c. $\frac{4}{9}, \frac{5}{11}$ e. $\frac{3}{8}, \frac{5}{9}$ g. $\frac{6}{11}, \frac{7}{12}$

b. $\frac{3}{7}, \frac{2}{5}$ d. $\frac{2}{5}, \frac{5}{9}$ f. $\frac{3}{7}, \frac{5}{12}$

19. A man was stranded on a desert island with enough water to last him 27 days. After 3 days, he saved a woman on a small life raft. If they can keep their water supply from evaporating, they figure that they can share their water equally for 18 days. What portion of the man's original daily ration was allotted to the woman?

20. Who has more pizza, the girls or the boys?

21. In a certain scout troop. 70% of the scouts had a compass, 75% had matches, 85% had a knife, and 85% had a watch. What percent of the scouts had all four pieces of equipment?

22. The distributive property can help you to multiply fractions without doing written computation. Mentally add each product:

$$3\tfrac{1}{2} \times 1\tfrac{1}{4} = (3 \times 1) + (3 \times \tfrac{1}{4}) + (\tfrac{1}{2} \times 1) + (\tfrac{1}{2} \times \tfrac{1}{4}) = 4\tfrac{3}{8}.$$

Use this method to mentally multiply these fractions:

a. $1\tfrac{1}{2} \times \tfrac{1}{4} =$

b. $2\tfrac{1}{4} \times 4 =$

c. $3 \times 2\tfrac{1}{8} =$

d. $2\tfrac{2}{3} \times 6\tfrac{1}{2} =$

e. $1\tfrac{1}{5} \times 2\tfrac{1}{2} =$

f. $2\tfrac{1}{3} \times 4\tfrac{1}{2} =$

* * * * * * * * * * * * * * * * * * * *

STOP Take some time to connect this chapter to previous chapters.

Reflection

1. Represent the fraction $\frac{1}{3}$ using as many different models as you can (pie, paper folding, rods, machine, number line, 3 chips, 9 chips, etc.). Discuss what might be the strengths and weaknesses of each model.

2. How do you know that $\frac{4}{6} = \frac{6}{9}$? Give as many different explanations as you can.

Chapter 11
Ratios

STOP *Children's Strategies*

Josh and Kristin are seventh grade students. They solved the following problem. Look at their work, arranged in the form of ratio tables, and see if you can figure out what each is doing. See if you can account for the discrepancy in their answers. Correct any errors and carry out the calculations to the correct solution.

For every 50 people who attend the school fair, about 37 of them will purchase a raffle ticket in addition to paying the entrance fee. After buying the prizes for the raffle, the school makes a profit of $1.25 for each raffle ticket sold. 723 people have purchased tickets to the fair. How much money can the school expect to make on the raffle?

Josh

Attend	50	100	700	5	1	3	20	723
Raffle	37	64	448	3.7	.75	2.25	14.8	448 + 14.8 + 2.25 =

×2   ×7   ÷5   ×3   ÷10   ×4

465 tickets

$1.25 on every ticket = $581.25

Kristin

people who go	50	200	600	100	20	1	3
people who get raffle tickets	37	148	444	74	148	.74	2.22

×4   ×3   ÷5   ÷20   ×3   ×2

$$723 = 444 + 74 + 14.8 + 2.22 = 535.02$$

535 tickets $1.25 each = $668.75

* * * * * * * * * * * * * * * * * * * *

What Is a Ratio?

A *ratio* is a comparison of any two quantities. A ratio may be used to convey an idea that cannot be expressed as a single number. Consider this example:

> Harvest festivals in towns A and B drew visitors from all of the surrounding areas. Town A reported a ratio of 4,000 cars to its 3 square miles. Town B reported a ratio of 3,000 cars to its 2 square miles.

Why was the information reported in this way? By comparing the number of cars to the size of the town, we get a sense of how crowded each town was with cars, of how difficult it may have been to drive around and to find parking. This information is different from either of the pieces of information that were combined to create it. It answers the question "Which town was more congested during the festival?"

Sometimes, ratios are used to compare two quantities that refer to a single situation or to a very limited range of similar cases. For example, the ratio of 4,000 cars to 3 square miles refers only to town A and only during the harvest festival. It would not be useful to apply that ratio to another town or in another season.

Ratios sometimes compare measures of the same type. There are two types of ratios that compare measures of the same type: part—whole: comparisons and part—part comparisons. Part—whole comparisons are ratios that compare the measure of part of a set to the measure of the whole set. Part—part comparisons compare the measure of part of a set to the measure of another part of the set. For example, in a carton of eggs containing 5 brown and 7 white eggs, all of the following ratios apply: 5 to 7 (brown to white part—part comparison), 7 to 5 (white to brown part—part comparison), 5 to 12 (brown part—whole comparison), 7 to 12 (white part—whole comparison).

Ratios may also compare measures of different types. A ratio that compares measures of different types is usually called a *rate*. But implicit in the use of the word "rate" is the additional assumption that the comparison describes a quality that is common to many situations. For example, $3 per yard is a rate that describes the relationship between cost in dollars and number of yards in all of the following instances: $6 for 2 yards, $24 for 8 yards, $54 for 18 yards, and so on. It involves two different measures: number of dollars and number of yards. The diagram on the next page summarizes the different types of ratio.

In some ways, ratios are like the other interpretations of rational number, but in some ways, they are very different. Ratios are not always rational numbers, but part—whole, operator, measure, and quotient fractions are always rational numbers. Consider the ratio of the circumference of a circle to its diameter: $C:d = \pi$. Pi (π) is not a

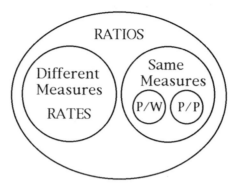

rational number because it cannot be expressed as the quotient of two integers. Another example is the ratio of the side of a square to its diagonal: $1:\sqrt{2}$. $\sqrt{2}$ is an irrational number. Ratios may have a zero as their second component, but fractions are not defined for a denominator of zero. For example, if you report the ratio of men to women at a meeting attended by 10 males and no females, you could write 10:0.

Our attempt to define and distinguish ratios and rates gives us some rough ideas with which to start. However, when we consider the many ways in which the words are used in both mathematical and nonmathematical circles, definitions can prove unsatisfactory. Part of the difficulty is that for instructional purposes, everyday language and usage of rates and ratios is out of control. The media have long employed ratios and rates and the language appropriate to ratios and rates in many different ways, sometimes inconsistently, sometimes interchangeably. Students are exposed to less-than-correct usage and terminology, and it is no easy task to reconcile precise mathematical ideas with informal, colloquial usage.

Even if we could precisely define ratios and rates and the difference between them, definitions do not discharge the full meaning of the idea being defined. The nature and meaning of rates and ratios come from problem situations. An exploration of the contexts that provide the sources of meaning and the applications of ratios and rates exposes the critical understandings that we would like children to develop about ratios and rates. In order to help children encounter all of the nuances in meaning, teachers must be prepared to help children analyze each situation individually. This chapter and chapter 12 are designed to give teachers some ideas about what to look for and what to talk about with children. In addition to comparing, ordering, and judging the equivalence of ratios, many new ideas emerge as we discuss connections with the other interpretations of rational numbers. In particular, we analyze ratios within contexts and ask whether they are extendible, reducible, reversible, homogeneous, and divisible.

Notation and Terminology

A ratio is sometimes written in fraction form, but not always; part—whole comparisons, operators, measures, and quotients are most often written in the fraction form $\frac{a}{b}$.

The ratio of a things to b things may be written in several ways:

1. $\frac{a}{b}$ or a/b
2. a → b
3. a : b
4. (a)b

In different countries different notations are favored. In the United States, we use the colon notation and fraction notation alternately, depending on which characteristics of ratios we wish to highlight. Fraction notation is used when referring to those aspects in which ratios behave like other interpretations of rational number written in fraction form (part—whole comparisons, operators, measures, and quotient), while the colon notation is favored by those who like to emphasize the ways in which ratios do not act like other fractions. If the fraction notation is used, care should be taken to use quantities, and not merely numbers. That is, a ratio of 5 girls to 7 boys should not be written $\frac{5}{7}$, but rather, as $\frac{5 \text{ girls}}{7 \text{ boys}}$. When people are not careful to label quantities and they write $\frac{5}{7}$ in the fraction form devoid of context, the conceptual and operational differences between ratios and part—whole fractions can become fuzzy or lost. When children are trying to build up meaning for fractions and ratios, it is probably a good idea to use different notations for each. Regardless of the notation used, any of the following may serve as a verbal interpretation of the symbols:

1. a to b
2. a per b
3. a for b
4. a for each b
5. for every b there are a
6. the ratio of a to b
7. a is to b

Many statements may be translated into ratio language and symbolism. Often, ratio language is used as an alternate way of expressing a multiplicative relationship.

Example. There were $\frac{2}{3}$ as many men as women at the concert.

This says that the number of men was $\frac{2}{3}$ the number of women. Let m represent the number of men and w represent the number of women. then:

$m = \frac{2}{3} w$ or $\frac{m}{w} = \frac{2}{3}$

This can be written as m:w = 2:3
The ratio of men to women is 2 to 3.

Although most mathematics curricula introduce ratios late in the elementary years, for some children, from the beginning of fraction instruction, the ratio interpretation of rational numbers is more natural than the part—whole comparison. These children identify

●● ○ ○ ○ and

as $\frac{2}{3}$. There is some research evidence that when children prefer the ratio interpretation and classroom instruction builds on their intuitive knowledge of comparisons, they develop a richer understanding of rational numbers and employ proportional reasoning sooner than children whose curriculum used the part—whole comparison as the primary interpretation of rational numbers. These children favored discrete sets of coins or colored chips to represent ratios. Our discussion of equivalence and comparison uses strategies that they developed to help explain their thinking.

Equivalence and Comparison of Ratios

Chips or other discrete objects provide a useful way to talk about the differences between part—whole comparisons and ratios.

● ● ○

The usual part—whole interpretation of this picture is $\frac{2}{3}$. The ratio interpretation is 2: 1 or $\frac{2}{1}$. To keep things straight, we use the colon notation when we mean a ratio. We look at equivalence and order under both the part—whole and the ratio interpretations in order to see differences and similarities.

Example. Is $\frac{6}{9}$ equivalent to $\frac{2}{3}$?

See if the chips in $\frac{6}{9}$ can be rearranged to show $\frac{2}{3}$.

The chips show $\frac{2}{3}$ because there are 2 shaded columns out of a total of 3 columns.

Example. Is 6:9 equivalent to 2:3?

We can see that 6:9 is a 3-clone of 2:3.

Note that although the way we read the dots was different in each example, the process was the same.

One way to compare fractions is to represent each with chips and clone them until both sets contain the same number of chips. Equalizing the denominators is just like finding a common denominator.

Example. Compare $\frac{3}{4}$ and $\frac{5}{8}$.

Two copies of $\frac{3}{4}$ is $\frac{6}{8}$, so $\frac{3}{4}$ is larger.

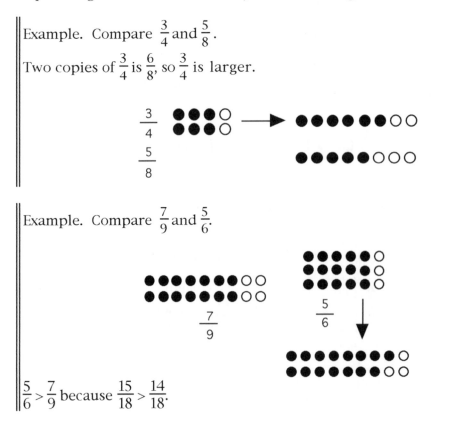

Example. Compare $\frac{7}{9}$ and $\frac{5}{6}$.

$\frac{5}{6} > \frac{7}{9}$ because $\frac{15}{18} > \frac{14}{18}$.

Another way to compare fractions is to clone them until their numerators are the same.

Example

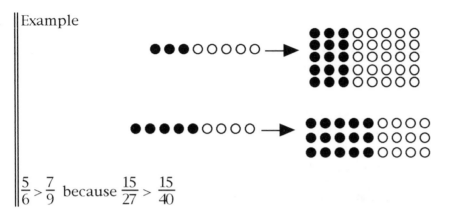

$\frac{5}{6} > \frac{7}{9}$ because $\frac{15}{27} > \frac{15}{40}$

Ratios may be compared in several different ways, but it is the interpretation that is tricky.   Ratios have a for—against, positive—negative interpretation. Comparing ratios is similar to asking which is better odds, 5 for and 6 against, or 2 for and 3 against?

Example. Compare 5:6 and 2:3.

If we begin by representing 2:3, we can clone it and remove copies of 5:6 until one of the colors is exhausted.

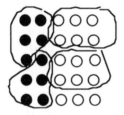

Essentially, this process has equated the fors. We cloned 2:3 until we had 10 for, 15 against. We compared this to a 2-clone of 5:6, or 10 for and 12 against. In the 2:3 clone, we have more against us. Thus we conclude that 5:6 is greater or 5:6 is the better odds. This process is like equalizing the numerators in fractions.

Example. Another way.

Beginning with the 5:6 ratio, remove as many copies as you can of the 2:3 ratio. Then the 5:6 ratio shows more fors and we conclude that (5:6) > (2:3). This process is like equalizing the denominators in fractions.

When the odds interpretation is not feasible, another useful technique in interpreting ratios involves their duality. Every ratio has a *dual*. This means that a ratio such as 3 girls to 4 boys gives us the same information as 4 boys to 3 girls.

Example

In Mrs. Jones class there are 3 girls for every 4 boys. In Mrs. Smith's class, there are 5 girls for every 8 boys. Which class has the larger ratio of girls to boys?

We can begin with Mrs. Smith's class, cloning it and removing the 3:4 ratio as many times as possible.

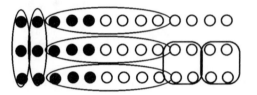

Then there are 4 boys left in Mrs. Smith's class. This means that in Smith's class, the ratio of boys to girls is larger. So the ratio of girls to boys is larger in Jones' class.

Whether the ratio interpretation is students' initial model for understanding equivalence and comparison, or it is introduced after they have had experience with other interpretations, students need ample time to develop operations using chips or dot representations. When they are given the time to develop a way to think about ratios, they make the same kinds of observations that arise from part—whole orientations. They notice that you can compare by equalizing numerators (for numbers), or by equalizing denominators (against numbers). They notice that in the dot drawing, 15 girls:20 boys represents Jones class and 15:24 represents Smith's class and they can reason that there are relatively more girls in Jones' class. They begin to notice shortcuts such as the following: Mrs. Jones class has 3 girls to every 4 boys, or 6 girls to 8 boys, but Mrs. Smith has only 5 girls to every 8 boys. Instruction should allow enough time for these insights to occur so that students can form meaningful connections with the other rational number interpretations.

Connecting Ratios to Part-Whole Comparisons

Ratios and part—whole fractions are both comparisons, but a part—whole comparison is a more restricted type of comparison than a ratio is. In a part—whole comparison, the numerator is part of the same object or set of objects referred to in the denominator, so both are measured with the same units. If we have $\frac{5}{6}$ of a pizza, we have 5 slices out of 6 slices, where the 5 slices and the 6 slices are all equal in size. However, a ratio compares virtually any two quantities. Those quantities may or may not be alike in some characteristic. For example, the ratio 5:60 may mean that 5 people out of 60 got tickets, or that it took 5 gallons of gas to drive 60 miles, or that it takes $5.00 to buy 60 candies.

Given some part—whole information, you can construct relevant ratios, and given some ratio information, you can construct some part—whole information.

Example. You have a dozen eggs, 5 of which are brown.

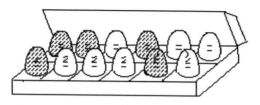

What part of the whole carton are the 5 brown eggs?
$$\frac{5 \text{ eggs}}{1 \text{ carton}} = \frac{5 \text{ eggs}}{12 \text{ eggs}} = \frac{5}{12} \text{ of a carton}$$

The ratio of brown to white eggs is 5:7.

Example. You have a dozen eggs in which the ratio of brown to white eggs is 3:9.

The brown eggs make up $\frac{3}{12}$ of the carton.

The white eggs make up $\frac{9}{12}$ of the carton.

Now suppose that you were blindfolded and you took 4 eggs out of the carton. Could you predict how many of them are brown? No! Both the ratio 3:9 and the fractions $\frac{3}{12}$ and $\frac{9}{12}$ refer only to the entire carton. They do not refer to any subset of the carton. If you grab 4 eggs at random, you have no guarantee of getting 1 brown and 3 white.

If you are told that the ratio of girls to boys in a class is 3:4, can you construct any relevant part—whole comparisons? The ratio tells us that for every three girls, there are 4 boys. In the whole class, there must be some multiple of 7 students. We cannot tell if there are 14, 21, or more students in the whole class, but if we could put the total number of girls over the number of students in the whole class, that fraction would reduce to $\frac{3}{7}$. That is, the class is $\frac{3}{7}$ girls and $\frac{4}{7}$ boys.

Connecting Ratios to Operators: Extendibility and Reducibility

There are several ways in which ratios are not like other rational number interpretations. Ratios are **not** reversible the way operators are. They cannot be inverted and used to return a quantity to its original size. Although fraction numerators and denominators cannot be interchanged without changing the meaning of the fraction, ratios have dual interpretations. 3 candies:4 children is a different ratio than 4 candies:3 children. However, if we preserve the quantities (i.e., keep the numbers and their labels together), 3 candies:4 children and 4 children:3 candies give us similar information about the same situation. Another example is the rate 5 miles per hour. Its dual is 1 hour per 5 miles. Depending on the question we are considering, it may be more useful to choose one form of the ratio over the other.

The operator stretches a quantity if it is a number greater than 1, or it shrinks a quantity if it is a number less than 1. When we analyze ratios to determine whether or not they are extendible and reducible, we are really trying to decide how closely they relate to the operator interpretation of rational numbers (chap. 8). Sometimes a ratio may be sensibly extended, but in other situations, it does not make as much sense to do so. Children should be encouraged to think about every situation, not merely to mechanically generate additional ratios.

Example. Oranges are sold 3 for $.69.

The ratio 3:69 may be meaningfully extended to 6:138.
That is, if we saw the price of oranges advertised as 3 for $.69, we might reasonably assume that we could purchase 6 for $1.38.

Example. John is 25 years old and his son is 5 years old.

The ratio $\frac{25}{5} = \frac{5}{1}$ compares the father's age to son's age right now. Next year it will not be true that the father is five times as old as his son, nor will it be true at any time in the future. The ratio $\frac{5}{1}$ describes the age relationship only in the present situation. It is not extendible over any other years and has no predictive capacity.

Ratios are sometimes meaningfully reducible, even though information is lost. However, they are not **always** meaningfully reducible.

Example. John is 25 years old and his son is 5 years old.

The ratio 25:5 is reducible to 5:1 In reducing the ratio, the present ages of the boy and his father are lost, but the information that the father is five times as old as his son is retained.

Example. This season, our team had a record (ratio) of 4 wins:2 losses.

A ratio of 2 wins:1 loss is not the same as a ratio of 4 wins:2 losses. In reducing the ratio, information about the total number of games is lost. The given ratio, 4 wins:2 losses, a season record, tells us that the team played 6 games. The ratio 2 wins:1 loss no longer describes the team's season record because it refers to only 3 games. Furthermore, we cannot assume that the season record is a multiple of the ratio 2 wins:1 loss. That ratio does not refer to either the first half or the second half of the team's season because there are many different ways in which they could have had a season of 4 wins and 2 losses. Try listing them.

Connecting Ratios to Measures: Homogeneity

Another aspect of understanding ratios entails determining whether or not they refer to a characteristic that is homogeneous or uniformly spread out in a given context. When we discuss the homogeneity of ratios, we are relating them to measures. Essentially, if we are asking whether a ratio is evenly spread out over a certain domain, we are asking if it exists in any smaller piece of the domain that we may choose to consider. In the measure interpretation of rational numbers, the one-ness of the unit was homogeneous or equally spread out over an interval on the number line (or over an area) so that we could break down that interval into smaller and smaller parts and still be able to tell their fractional names by comparing them to the unit interval. Also, given any subinterval, no matter how minute, we can construct the unit interval. Sometimes a ratio is evenly spread out over a domain, but sometimes it is not.

Example. There is a ratio of 3 girls to 4 boys in a class. If you chose 7 students at random, will you get 3 girls and 4 boys?

Not necessarily. The ratio 3 girls:4 boys or, similarly, the fractions $\frac{3}{7}$ girls and $\frac{4}{7}$ boys, refer to the total girls and total boys as compared to the total number of students in the class. They do not apply to portions of the class.   This means that the ratio of girls to boys in the class is not homogeneous throughout the class.

Example. You have a 30% concentration of alcohol in water.

The amounts of the elements that compose this mixture exist in constant ratio to one another no matter what size sample we choose to inspect. This mixture is composed of 3 parts alcohol to 7 parts water. No matter what size sample is taken from the mixture—3 cups, 3 drops, or 3 gallons— it will consist of alcohol and water in a ratio of 3 parts to 7 parts.

Connecting Ratios to Quotients: Indices and Divided Ratios

Single-number ratios are those resulting from the division of the two quantities of which they were originally composed. A divided ratio may be an index, meaning that it indicates some sort of condition, or it may be more like a prescription. The divisibility of ratios connect them to the quotient interpretation of rational numbers.

Example. John's batting average is .368.

The batting average is not an average in the sense of being an arithmetical mean, and unlike average speed, it is not reported as a comparison of two quantities. A batting average is the divided ratio of the number of hits to the total number of times at bat (where "hits" and "at bat" have technical definitions). A baseball batting average is an indicator of the ability of a batter.

Examples of divided ratios

π = 3.14159...(approximately 3.14) is the ratio of the circumference of a circle to its diameter.
1: $\sqrt{2}$) (approximately 1.4) is the ratio of the diagonal of a square to it side.
ϕ = 1.61803...is the golden ratio.
1.9 is the ratio of the length to the width of the American flag.

These ratios are reported in their divided form rather than being reported as comparisons. This is because of their dual nature as descriptions and prescriptions. They describe very special properties of circles, squares, some rectangles, and the American flag. However, flags, rectangles, circles, and squares come in many different sizes. Reporting their special properties as divided ratios gives us a formula for reproducing them in many different sizes. For example, if π were reported as $\frac{15.708}{5}$, then it would refer to the circumference and diameter of a specific circle, the one with a diameter of 5 units. However, π = 3.14159 identifies the special relationship of the circumference to the diameter in all circles.

The interpretation of divided ratios always requires some special attention. Consider the ratio 5 cookies:2 children. If we write 5:2 in fraction form, $\frac{5}{2}$, and obtain the indicated quotient, do we get something meaningful?

$$5 \text{ cookies} \div 2 \text{ children} = 2\frac{1}{2} \text{ cookies per child}$$

We can accept that.   However, if you divide 4 textbooks:5 children, you get $\frac{4}{5}$ book per child.   Taken at face value, this quotient is awkward. Nevertheless,   you   hear   such   things   as   1.5   children   per household—another divided ratio.   These divided ratios convey information as averages.   On the average, there are $2\frac{1}{2}$ cookies per child; every child does not necessarily h a v e $2\frac{1}{2}$ cookies.   Every child in the classroom does not have $\frac{4}{5}$ book.   Rather, the information tells us how close a particular class is to having enough books to go around.

In other cases, interpretation may be complicated by the interaction of ratio properties, for example, extendibility and divisibility. Suppose John had a good day at bat, and hit 5 times out of his 6 times at bat. As a divided ratio, his average could be reported as .833. It would be nearly impossible for John to extend such an exceptional record. He could not keep up such a performance over 40 times at bat, and yet, 3 out of 4 and 30 out of 40 are both .833. Thus, the divided ratio obscures that fact that 3:4 and 30:40 are very different phenomena.

Ratio Operations

The greatest difference between ratios and the other interpretations of rational numbers is in the way they combine through the arithmetic operations.   The other interpretations of rational numbers are all different conceptually, but they are indistinguishable once they are written symbolically. They add, subtract, multiply, and divide according to the same rules. However, we do not operate on ratios in the same way that we do on fractions.

Example. Yesterday Mary had 3 hits in 5 turns at bat. Today she had 2 hits in six times at bat. How many hits did she have for a two-day total?

Mary had 3:5 + 2:6 = 5:11 or 5 hits in 11 times at bat. If we were adding fractions, we could not write $\frac{3}{5}+\frac{2}{6}=\frac{5}{11}$!

Example. An entire day's food supply for 3 aliens consists of 5 food pellets. Suppose they plan to travel to earth for a day. They want to send 12 creatures to earth, and their current food supply consists of 22 pellets. Can they send 12 creatures?

One way to answer the questions is to ask: How many times can we divide (3c:5p) out of (12c:22p)? We model the division by repeated subtraction. If we use the label c as a shorthand notation for creatures and p for pellets, we get

$$(12c{:}22p) - (3c{:}5p) = (9c{:}17p)$$
$$(9c{:}17p) - (3c{:}5p) = (6c{:}12p)$$
$$(6c{:}12p) - (3c{:}5p) = (3c{:}7p)$$
$$(3c{:}7p) - (3c{:}5p) = (0c{:}2p).$$

This shows that $(12c{:}22p) \div (3c{:}5p) = 4$ groups with $(0c{:}2p)$ remaining. That is, if you divide 12 creatures to 22 food pellets by 3 creatures to 5 food pellets, you find that you can send 4 groups of aliens (12 creatures) and have 2 food pellets left over. If we write the ratios in fraction form, here is what we just did:

$$\frac{12}{22} \div \frac{3}{5} = \frac{12 \div 3}{22 \div 5} = 4\,\text{r.}\,(0{:}2)$$

But when we perform the division using the standard division algorithm for fractions we get:

$$\frac{12}{22} \div \frac{3}{5} = \frac{20}{22},$$

a fraction which is useless in answering the original question.

Ratio Tables and Children's Primitive Strategies

Ratio tables (also called proportion tables) can be useful in facilitating proportional reasoning. If used properly, they can be tools that facilitate powerful ways of thinking. However, when they are presented as convenient devices for keeping work organized, they fail to facilitate any kind of reasoning at all.

Example. How much pizza should I buy if there will be 50 people at my party? The planning guide says that I should figure that 3 pizzas will serve about 10 people.

A student used the following table to solve the problem:

pizzas	3	6	9	12	15
people	10	20	30	40	50

This student used an additive strategy. If the student were really multiplying, he or she would have thought, "5 times as many pizzas will serve 5 times as many people." This student built up to the required number of pizzas by successively adding 3 on the top row of the chart and successively adding 10 on the bottom row. The building up strategy is one that children use spontaneously and it has been used to achieve a correct solution. However, there is a question as to whether some children see multiplicative relations when they persist in using additive strategies that give correct answers. Do they focus on the relationship between pizza and people? Do they realize that the numbers of pizzas and the number of people in each column have the same relationship? Most often, interviews with the students reveal that they do not. Successes with additive strategies do not necessarily encourage the exploration and adoption of more efficient strategies and should not be interpreted as proportional reasoning.

Students are also very adept at halving and doubling. When we pose problems whose solutions may be achieved only by halving or doubling, we are not encouraging the student to engage in serious reasoning.

Example

For every 400 fans, the concession stand at the stadium sells about 30 baseball caps. At that rate, how many caps should they have on hand when the attendance is expected to be 6,400 people?

fans	400	800	1600	3200	6400
caps	30	60	120	240	480

Without ever thinking about the ratio relationships at all, a student can successively double the top number, successively double the bottom number, and achieve a correct solution.

An obvious instructional tactic is to vary the kinds of questions, quantity structures, and numbers so that students are forced beyond their comfort zone, so that they must think about relationships and adopt increasingly efficient solutions. This may be done in several ways:

• give problems whose quantities both decrease;
• give problems whose quantities both increase;
• give problems involving inversely proportional relationships;
• give problems that necessarily involve numbers other than whole numbers;
• give problems whose solutions allow for combinations of multiplication/division and addition/subtraction operations;
• give problems not solvable by halving or doubling;
• give problems that allow the use of shortcuts.

Example

A party planning guide says that 3 pizzas will serve about 7 people. How much pizza is needed for 350 people?

Two different and correct tables are given.

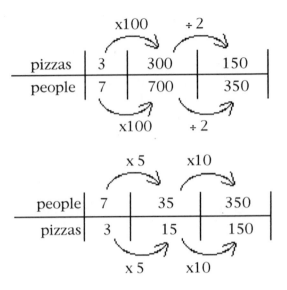

Example

Grandma has some special plant food that comes in powder form. The directions say to mix 2.5 teaspoons with 8 ounces of water. There are 8 teaspoonfuls left and I am going to mix it all up. How much water should I add?

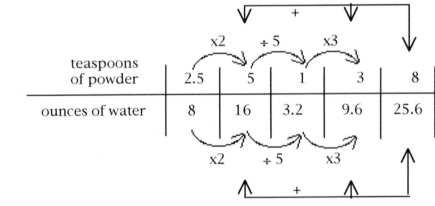

Example

Mark had 38 hours of free time last week, and he spent 24 hours working at his dad's store. He always gives his dad the same portion of his free time. This week, he worked only $17\frac{1}{2}$ hours at the store. How much free time did Mark have this week?

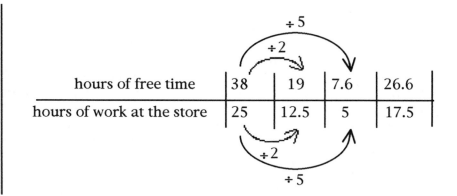

Of course, there is always more than one correct way to build a ratio table. When students produce different tables, it is a good idea to have them present and discuss their strategies. If you are unsure about whether any operation has been performed correctly, remember that you can always check to ensure that all ratios in the table are equivalent. In the last problem, for example,

$$\frac{38}{25} = \frac{19}{12.5} = \frac{7.6}{5} = \frac{26.6}{17.5}$$

The appropriate use of the ratio table is to systematically organize one's work as the operations of multiplication, division, addition, and subtraction are combined to produce equivalent ratios until some target quantity is achieved. However, this is not a trial and error process. Analyze the quantities before starting the table to work out your plan. Suppose you begin with a ratio involving the quantity 35 pounds and you wish to end up with an equivalent ratio involving the quantity 18 pounds. Think about how you might obtain the 18 pounds:

35 ÷ 5 = 7
7 + 7 = 14, but I still need another 4 pounds
7 ÷ 7 = 1
1 x 4 = 4
7 + 7 + 4 = 18

This gives the following scheme for half of the ratio table. The same operations would then be performed on the other component of the ratio.

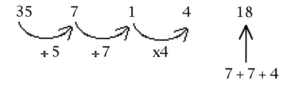

Instruction must play some role in encouraging students to build strategic tables. Students spontaneously produce ratio tables that use building up strategies or halving or doubling, but they do not readily produce tables using the strategies just illustrated. However, these cannot be taught directly; ratio tables are individual constructions that record personal thought processes. The teacher might model efficient processes so that students see the benefit of shortcuts and jumps, but students need time to incorporate them into their own ways of thinking. Because ratio tables provide a written record of student processes, they are good assessment tools. The length of students' ratio tables corresponds to the sophistication of their reasoning. As they learn to combine quantities using a variety of operations, their efficiency increases and their work contains fewer unnecessary steps.

Josh and Kristin, the children whose work you analyzed at the start of the chapter, were not beginners with ratio tables. They had considerable experience in using the tables to solve problems. They both used efficient strategies and they were not afraid of fractional (decimal) numbers when they occurred. Their answers did not agree because Josh made a computation error. When he multiplied 37 raffle tickets by 2, he got 64 instead of 74.

STOP Do the following activities before going on to the next chapter.

Activities

1. Translate these statements into ratio notation:
a. There are 2 boys for every 3 girls.

b. Farmer Jones has $\frac{4}{5}$ as many cows as pigs.

c. Mary is $\frac{2}{3}$ as tall as her mom.

d. Dan is $2\frac{1}{2}$ times as heavy as Becky.

2. Interpret the following picture as a) a part—whole comparison, and b) a ratio.

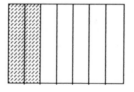

3. There are 100 seats in the theater, with 30 in the balcony and 70 on the main floor. 80 tickets were sold for the matinee performance, including all of the seats on the main floor.
a. What fraction of the seats were sold?
b. What is the ratio of balcony seats to seats on the floor?
c. What is the ratio of empty seats to occupied seats?
d. What is the ratio of empty seats to occupied seats in the balcony?

4.

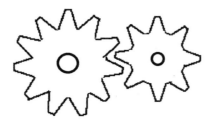

a. If the large gear makes one complete turn, how many turns will the small gear make?
b. If the small gear makes 5 turns, how many turns will the large gear make?

c. How many teeth would the large gear need in order to make $1\frac{1}{3}$ turns in the time that the small gear makes 4 turns?

d. How many teeth would the smaller gear need in order to turn $3\frac{2}{3}$ times to 4 turns of the large gear?

5. Kim compared 3:4 and 5:9 and her picture is shown here.

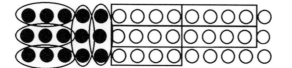

a. What could she conclude?
b. What do the 7 empty circles outside of the boxes mean?
c. Reinterpret the picture in terms of a ratio subtraction expressed symbolically.

6. Make dot pictures comparing these ratios or fractions and write the operations symbolically:
a. 5:6 and 11:12
b. 12:16 and 3:4
c. 5:8 and 7:9
d. $\frac{7}{8}$ and $\frac{9}{10}$
e. 7:8 and 9:10

f. $\frac{4}{9}$ and $\frac{3}{10}$

g. 4:5 and 8:15

7. Some fifth graders were asked to compare the fractions $\frac{3}{4}$ and $\frac{5}{8}$. Here is Jennifer's work. Analyze her strategy.

Dear Mrs.L,

    I can do it two ways.

If I start with $\frac{3}{4}$ I make clones until I can get $\frac{5}{8}$ out of it.

$\frac{3}{4}$ is bigger. There is money left and all the people got in.

If I start with $\frac{5}{8}$ I make clones until I can get $\frac{3}{4}$ out of it.

$\frac{5}{8}$ is smaller. There is no money left and 4 people still need to get in.

I go until I use up one of the numbers.

Jennifer

8. Draw the dot picture that explains what is happening in the following ratio arithmetic:
a. 2(4:3) - 7:6 = 1:0
b. 4(5:3) - 5(4:2) = 0:2
c. 5(6:8) - 4(4:10) = 14:0

9. For each of the following situations, determine if the ratios are extendible to more general situations and reducible without loss of information.
a. For every 3 adults in a theater there are 6 children.
b. A small gear on a machine has 30 teeth and a large gear has 45 teeth.
c. In a certain classroom, the ratio of children with pets to those without is 12:14.

d. The ratio of the perimeter to the area of a square is 12:9.
e. In a bag of candies, the ratio of red pieces to green pieces is 3: 6.
f. The ratio of my age to my mother's is 4:6.
g. Dave's height is 6 feet and his baby son is 24 inches long. The ratio of their height's is 6:2.
h. The Latte House sells coffee for $2.60 for 4 ounces.
i. The Wilsons have 6 children. The ratio of boys to girls in the Wilson family is 4:2.

10. In each situation given, discuss the divisibility of the ratio and interpret all quotients.

a. Because of the different schedules and work habits of the faculty members on a certain university campus, there is sufficient parking for everyone when the ratio of parking places to faculty members is 3:4.
b. A survey in a small town reported a ratio of 124 children to its 80 families.
c. The ratio of John's age to his son's age is 5:1.
d. Based on the vacation schedules of the participating families, the manager of a time-share condo maintains a ratio of 3 condos to 8 families.
e. Based on the number of students and the teachers' reports on computer assignments, a school estimated that it would need a ratio of 4 computers to 10 students.

11. A school system reported that they had a student—teacher ratio of 30:1. How many more teachers would they need to hire to reduce the ratio to 25:1?

12. Build a ratio table for each of the following situations:
a. In class today, Amy, who weighs 160 lb., found out that she would weigh 416 pounds on the planet Jupiter. How much would Jess weigh, if her weight on earth is 120 lb?
b. If I want to allow $\frac{3}{5}$ of a pizza for each person who attends my party, how much pizza will I need for 14 people?
c. If 5 out of every 8 seniors at Marquette University live in apartments, how many of the 30 students in my math class are likely to live in the dorm or at home?
d. I paid $1.12 tax on a $20 purchase. How much tax will I be charged if I spend $45.50?
e. $4.50 U.S. is the equivalent of $6 Australian. How much is $17.50 Australian in U.S. dollars?

13. As children gain some facility with ratios, they begin to take shortcuts and to invent their own strategies for comparing. Sometimes they are good strategies; sometimes their strategies are flawed and need revision. Study the way each of these students reached his or her conclusion and determine which strategies are good ones.

Student A compares 3:4 and 5:8.

3:4   5:8

"My picshure shows that 3:4 > 5:8."

Student B compares 3:4 and 5:6.

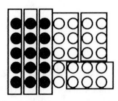

"3:4 > 5:6 because there are 5 copies of 3:4 and only 3 copies of 5:6."

Student C compares 5:8 and 7:9.

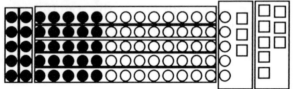

"I got 0:-11. This means that 7:9 is smaller than 5:8."

* * * * * * * * * * * * * * * * * * * *

   Think, discuss, and write.

Reflection

1. Give supporting arguments for·your answers to the following questions:
a. Are divided ratios homogeneous?
b. Is a probability a part—whole comparison? Is a probability a ratio?
c. Are all part—whole comparisons ratios?
d. Are all ratios part—whole comparisons?
e. Are all ratios fractions?
f. Are ratios rational numbers?

2. List as many ways as you can in which 3:5 is not like $\frac{3}{5}$.

Chapter 12
Analyzing Change

STOP

Student Strategies

Dena is a high school student who was asked to think about the
following problem. Her work is shown here. First use the
data to make your own conjecture. Then analyze Dena's work and try to
explain why she was not able to say much about the given data.

A ball is dropped from various heights and each time, someone
measures the height it reaches after one bounce. What
conjecture can you make based on the following data?

Trial	Drop Height in Meters	Bounce Height in Meters
1	1.5	1.2
2	1.2	1
3	3	2.4
4	.9	.7

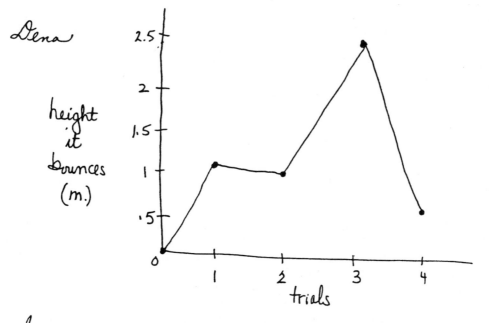

Dena

height
it
bounces
(m.)

trials

It appears that most bounces will be between
0 and 1 m. (about). Someone might have not
measured accurately on the third trial.

* * * * * * * * * * * * * * * * * * * *

Quantities and Change

Situations involving change are complex, but they are also pervasive in the mathematics encountered beyond elementary school. In their early years, children need to develop some understanding of quantities that result from counting or measuring, such as 6 candy bars, 3 pizzas, 25 miles, or 10 square feet, but in order to develop real mathematical power, they need to study the behavior of related quantities under change.

There are many reasons why students should encounter change in their elementary and middle school mathematics curricula. Change is an unavoidable part of life; we are all faced with change in our lives, families, and careers, in economics, in weather, in politics, and so on. We would have no control over our lives, environment, and experiences without some knowledge of the different types of change that affect us and the ability to detect patterns in those changes. Calculus, the mathematics of change, and all of higher mathematics depends on the ability to understand and represent change.

Most of a student's knowledge of change and rates is intuitive and built on personal experience. There has been minimal treatment of change and rates in the mathematics curriculum; therefore, students have gaps and misconceptions in their knowledge of change. Before students study algebra, they need to encounter change in their mathematics classes, to develop a language for describing and talking about change, to begin to categorize change according to its general types, and to develop some representations for the types of change they encounter. This chapter examines some situations that may be used to facilitate classroom discussion about change. What do you talk about when you discuss change? Finally, we will discuss several ways to represent change at the presymbolic level.

What is Changing?

One of the biggest problems that students have in high school and at the university level is that they fail to recognize and coordinate all of the quantities that are relevant in a given situation. A related problem is that students often have a limited conception of a variable. They see a variable as an unknown with some static value, and have trouble conceptualizing a variable as a quantity that changes. Their problems are often traceable to two sources. First, students of middle school age and lower tend to focus on the physical properties of objects and situations, rather than on their measurable characteristics. Second, in spite of the fact that change occurs over time, time is often ignored as a relevant factor in a change situation. Consider a very simple situation:

You ride your bicycle down the street. What changes?

Some typical responses from middle school students include:
> a. I moved away from where I started.
> b. My bicycle pedals went up and down.
> c. My wheels went around.

These responses indicate that many students do automatically mathematize a situation. They make surface-level observations and do not analyze a situation in terms of quantities. The characteristics of the situation that may be quantified are distance from the starting point, height of the pedals from the ground, elapsed time, and speed. There is little chance of students comparing quantities if they are not attending to quantifiable characteristics of the situation.

A second troublesome issue is students' understanding of time. Time is a quantity that either explicitly or implicitly operates in change situations. Time makes situations dynamic; it adds flow and/or connectivity. The passage of time is explicit in situations where the number of bacteria is doubling every 4 hours, or you are driving 174 miles in 3 hours. It is implicit in situations such as riding your bike down the street, or organizing trials in an experiment.

The bouncing ball problem Dena considered at the beginning of this chapter is often used as an introduction to functions in high school or university-level mathematics courses. For at least two reasons, Dena could not make sense of the problem. She did not focus on a measurable characteristic of the situation, but rather, she focused on the trials. In addition, in Dena's mind, each trial remained an independent snapshot of what was happening. Before we can use the data to build a relationship between drop height and bounce height, it is necessary to first "see" height as a quantity that is changing over time. In other words, as time passes, we can think of the drop height as starting from a certain point and decreasing to zero, or starting at zero and gradually increasing. This perspective on the situation would allow us to order the data in a certain way, rather than graphing it in the order it is recorded. It would also allow us to "fill in" information between the data points, extend the data (imagine what would happen if more data were collected with higher and lower drop heights, and other heights in between those given), and then make a conjecture about the relationship between drop height and bounce height. If Dena had arranged her data according to increasing or decreasing drop heights, she might have been able to see that bounce height for this particular ball was about 80% of the drop height.

Change and Invariation in the Same Situation

In the midst of change, important relationships can remain constant. For example, whether you are mixing a quart of lemonade or a gallon, the ratio of scoopfuls of drink mix to pints of water is the same. If you buy grapes, although the amount you pay increases if you buy 3 pounds instead of 2 pounds, the rate $1.19 per pound remains constant.

Elementary school children can have considerable difficulty detecting a constant relationship, especially in situations that do not involve money. This does not necessarily mean that the children have a problem or that the relationships are inherently difficult. Sometimes students have never thought about anything except the given facts and it has not occurred to them to examine tacit relationships. They have never been asked the question "What is not changing?" Even after they have had considerably experience with fraction equivalence—situations in which two numbers are changing together but their relationship to each other remains the same—children can have trouble detecting a constant relationship in a real context where other quantities are changing. This phenomenon suggests that it is more likely that analysis of real contexts is likely to help them understand what is happening in the more abstract world of fractions, but not vice versa. There is no replacement for examining quantitative relationships in real contexts.

When Things Depend

When two quantities are changing, sometimes the change in one of them depends on the change in the other. For example, the price you pay for a pizza depends on the diameter of the pizza; the amount of sales tax you pay depends on the amount of your purchase; how long it takes to run a mile depends on how fast you are running. When we say that one thing depends on another, we are not necessarily saying that other factors do not affect the situation. For example, how long it takes to run a mile depends on how fast you can run, but there may be other important factors as well, such as opposing wind speed and whether it is raining or not. When we make that statement about dependency, we are merely saying that your running speed is one of the things on which your time for the mile run depends, not the only thing.

In the examples just used, we can see that dependency is not always a two-way street. One changing quantity does not always depend on the other. For example, the diameter of a pizza does not depend on the price the customer pays. The amount a person purchases does not depend on the sales tax that will be charged. Sometimes things do not depend on other things at all! How many lights are turned on in Milwaukee at night has nothing to do with how many people in the city wear glasses!

Direction of Change

Another important consideration is the direction in which change is occurring. Children have a tendency to say that if two quantities are related and one is increasing, so is the other, or if one is decreasing, so is the other. In fact, two quantities can depend on each other and change in the same direction (both go up or both go down), or they may change in different directions (one up, one down).

Arrow notation is useful in helping children to analyze quantities and their relationships under change and to make sense of a situation before starting to do any graphing or computation. Children call the following activity "In, Out, Up, and Down." They are given a short story in which two quantities are changing. One quantity goes inside a circle, and one outside. Arrow notation is used to designate the direction of change for each quantity, then the student reasons up or down to fill in the blank.

Example.   3 cupcakes inside 1 package
___ cupcakes inside 5 packages

cupcakes ↑

packages ↑   1   5

Example.   8 people clean a house in $1\frac{1}{3}$ hours
3 people clean it in _____ hours

people ↓   ⑧ ① ③

hours   ↑ $1\frac{1}{3}$ $10\frac{2}{3}$ $3\frac{5}{9}$

Later, after children have become accustomed to analyzing relationships, dependency can be taken into account. Consider these familiar situations.

If you have more people working on a job, the time it takes to finish the job is less than if you have fewer people working on the job (assuming, of course, that they are all working and not messing around). This is a dependency relationship. Time to finish the job depends on number of people working. We can use arrow notation to record the directions of change in the relationships:

number of people ↑ time ↓

As the number of people goes up, time to do the job goes down. We note the direction of change for the independent variable first (number of people), and then the direction of change in time since time depends on the number of people. You have to know how the number of people changes before you can tell how the time changes.

Suppose you have bagged candies. If you have more candies in the bag, the weight of the bag will be greater than if you have fewer.

This is a dependency relationship. The weight of the bag depends on the number of candies in the bag. Using arrow notation, we could record the directions of change this way:

number of candies ↑   weight of the bag ↑

All situations that we might characterize as ↑↑ situations are not the same. ↑↑ and ↓↓ are large categories, each encompassing different subtypes of change.   By the time they are in middle school, students should be able to detect differences within these major categories. We examine some methods for finer analyses of change relationships in chapter 14.

The Shape of Change

Change happens in many different ways, sometimes according to patterns, and sometimes irregularly. We can think of change in terms of its shape. For example, think about the way the moon changes over a long period of time.

full   full

Think about the way that the number of passengers on a bus changes between the time the bus begins and ends its route. Finally, think about how intense the light is if you move the book you are reading farther and farther away from a lamp. You probably have a sense that each of these is a different kind of change. If we were to sketch the shapes of these changes, we would see very different pictures. Here are some of the general shapes of change.

increasing
The first curve shows a rapid increase in the beginning that later slows down. The second shows a steady or constant increase. The third shows an increase that starts off slowly and later picks up speed.

decreasing
The first curve shows a rapid decrease that later slows down. The second shows a steady or constant decrease. The third curve shows a decrease that happens slowly at first and then becomes more rapid.

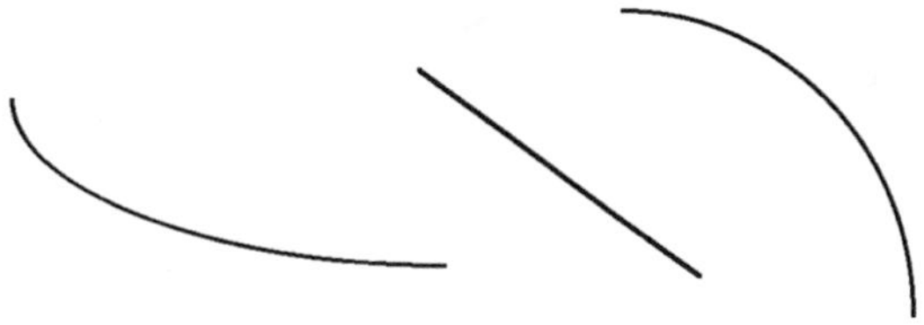

periodic or cyclic

irregular

stepped

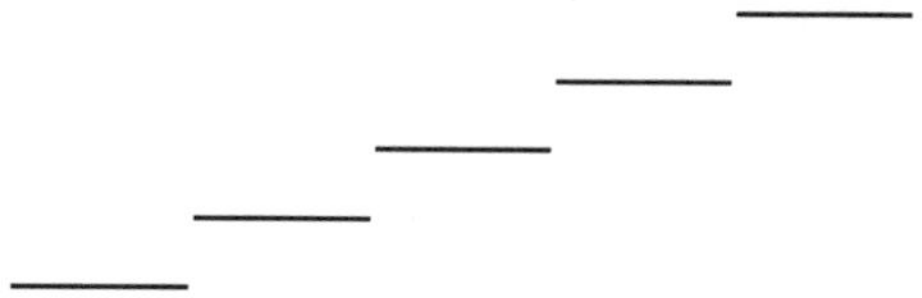

The shape of change in a sketch or graph is related to how quickly one quantity is changing in relation to another.

The Rate of Change

Change occurs at different speeds, and when we speak of "rate of change," we are referring to the speed at which some quantity is changing.   Sometimes when two quantities are changing in the same situation, one changes faster than the other changes.   An important part of analyzing change is determine how quickly one quantity changes in relation to the other. A quantity might be changing in relation to the passage of time. In this case, we refer to "change over time." However, we can also determine rate of change in relation to a changing quantity other than time.

Example. Your pulse changes, depending on the kind of activity in which you are engaged. To get your heart rate, you count your pulse beats over a certain period of time, say 15 seconds, then multiply by 4 to get the number of beats in a minute. In this case,

$$\text{heart rate} = \frac{\text{number of pulse beats}}{\text{time in minutes}}.$$

Your heart rate will be different during different time intervals. If you are resting, it will be slower; if you are exercising, it will be faster.

Example. If you were traveling up a mountain, you would find that the air temperature changes. If you want to know how quickly it is changing, you would take the temperature, move higher up the mountain, and take another reading. In this case,

$$\text{rate of change in temperature} = \frac{\text{change in temperature}}{\text{change in height}}.$$

Sometimes the rate of change is constant. This means that every time the independent variable changes by the same amount, x, the dependent variable changes by a certain amount, y. For example, for every 5 minutes, the temperature rises 1 degree. Sometimes the rate of change is not constant. That means that every time the independent variable changes by the same amount, the dependent variable changes by a different amount. For example, in the first 5 minutes, the temperature rose 2 degrees, in the next 5 minutes, the temperature rose 3 degrees, in the next 5 minutes, the temperature rose 5 degrees, etc. In the following example we have both kinds of change.

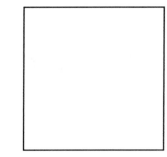

P = 4 inches   P = 6 inches
A = 1 square inch   A = 2.25 square inches

Suppose a square has dimensions 1 inch by 1 inch. What is its perimeter? (Remember: Perimeter is the distance measured along its boundary.) The perimeter of a 1 inch square is 4 inches. For a square that measures 1.5 inches on a side, the perimeter is 6 inches.

In each case, what is the area? (Remember: area is a measure of the space the figure takes up on a flat surface.) First cut a piece of cardboard 1 inch long and 1 inch wide; the piece of cardboard is a square inch. See how many times it can be used to cover your figure and you will have the area of the figure in square inches. For a one inch square, the area is 1 square inch. For the 1.5 inch square, the area is 2.25 square inches.

If we consider squares whose sides are longer and figure out their perimeters and areas, we can complete the following table:

length of side	perimeter in inches	area in square inches
1	4	1
1.5	6	2.25
2	8	4
2.5	10	6.25
3	12	9
3.5	14	12.25
4	16	16
4.5	18	20.25
5	20	25
5.5	22	30.25
6	24	36

Clearly both measurements, perimeter and area, are increasing as the squares get larger. That is, as the length of the side of the square increases, perimeter increases ($\uparrow\uparrow$). As the length of the side of the square increases, area also increases ($\uparrow\uparrow$). However, both increasing quantities are not increasing in the same way. Look at the perimeter column in the previous table. The perimeter keeps increasing by 2 inches. Note that this is absolute change. But when we talk about rate of change, we want change in perimeter in relation to the change in length of side. We get a change of 2 inches in the perimeter for each increase of half an inch in the length of the side. We can write this as $\frac{2}{.5}$. Similarly, the perimeter increased by 6 inches (14 - 8 = 6) when the side increased by 1.5 inches (3.5 - 2 = 1.5). Thus, we can write the rate of change as $\frac{6}{1.5}$. We can say that the rate of growth in the perimeter, that is, the growth in the perimeter relative to the increase in the length of a side, is $\frac{2}{.5} = \frac{6}{1.5} = 4$. The rate of growth in the perimeter is constant (always the same), and when we graph it, we get a straight line.

How does the area change as the side length increases? The area is changing in a different way. It is not the same for each increase in the side of the square. In fact, each time the length of the side increases by another half inch, the area takes a larger jump than it did with the previous increase. If we graph the area on the same graph with the perimeter, we can see that the area curve increases slowly until we have a square of side 4, where its rate of change is equal to that of the perimeter. After 4, it surpasses the perimeter curve and continues to increase more rapidly.

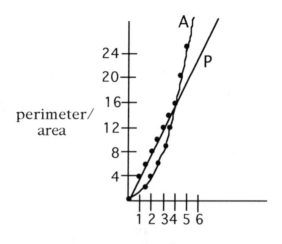

side of square

Students need to be able to discuss not only change, but rate of change, that is, how fast some quantity is changing in relation to some other quantity. A graph tells at a glance how fast one quantity is changing with respect to another. Move your finger along the curve for a certain distance. Look at the interval corresponding to that distance on the horizontal axis as well as the corresponding distance on the vertical axis. If the horizontal interval is greater than the vertical, then the independent variable is changing more quickly. If the vertical change is greater than the horizontal, then the dependent variable is changing more quickly.

Sketching Change

Sketching graphs of change situations helps students to better understand how quantities are related to each other and gain further insight into the nature of change. *Sketching* means indicating the general shape of the graph of one quantity's relationship to another. It does not mean that scales must be attached to the graph and that precise points must be plotted. Certain rules do apply, however, to both sketching and graphing. Here is an easy way to do it. We will use this example:

The faster you run, the less time it will take to get there. (↑↓)

1. Decide which variable depends on which. Which value do you have to know before you can decide the other? That one is called the independent variable. Label the horizontal axis with the name of the independent variable. Put the dependent variable on the vertical axis.

In our example, does time depend on running speed or does running speed depend of time? Time depends on running speed. So we label the axes like this:

time

running speed

2. Now pick some reference point on each axis so that you can determine what more or less time means and what a faster or slower speed means.

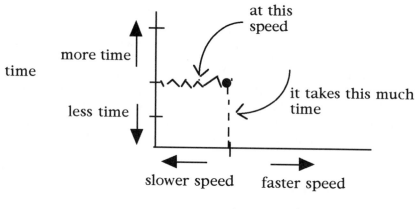

time

more time

less time

at this speed

it takes this much time

slower speed   faster speed

running speed

3. Think about what happens to time as speed varies. (a) When you run faster, the time is shorter. (b) When you run slower, the time is longer. Points a and b correspond to these two statements.

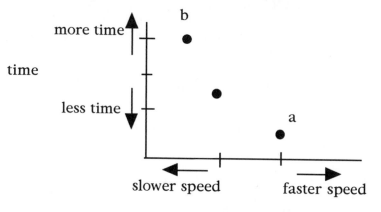

time

more time

less time

b

a

slower speed   faster speed

running speed

4. Now you can sketch the general shape of the relationship between running speed and time.

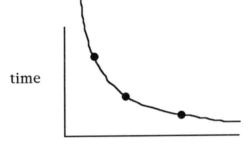

time

running speed

Remember: there is no substitute for thinking. You must think about the relationships before you can decide where to put the points that give the general shape of the sketch. Also, you want to think about a few other details. For example, it will always take you some amount of time to get to your destination, no matter how fast you are running. This means that your graph will never touch the horizontal axis. Similarly, you would never get to your destination if your speed were zero, so the graph will never touch the vertical axis either. A line that the graph gets close to but will never touch is called an *asymptote*. You should be careful to include asymptotes in your sketches whenever they are appropriate.

Discussing Change

Students need to discuss all types of change situations so that eventually they recognize what is special about proportional relationships. In discussing change, the following questions are most important:

1. Which quantities are changing?
2. Does the change in one quantity depend on the change in the other?
3. Are there any relationships that remains invariant (unchanging?)
4. If two quantities are changing, in which directions are they changing?
5. Can you represent the change using arrow notation?
6. Is one quantity changing more quickly than another? How can you tell?
7. Can you sketch the relationship between the two changing quantities?

These questions should be part of a teacher's line of questioning whenever students are solving problems. They encourage students to engage in an essential type of mathematical thinking.

Work the following problems before going to the next chapter.

Activities

1. For each situation, list the changing quantities.
a. you are filling your car's gas tank
b. you travel by car from Milwaukee to Chicago
c. you make several credit card purchases
d. you are scuba diving
e. you are draining the water in your bathtub

In each scenario described below (2—4), tell which quantities change and which do not change.

2. While I was waiting for the bus, I was standing next to a change machine and two people came up and used it.   A man inserted a quarter and received 2 dimes and 1 nickel.   Then a woman inserted a dollar bill and received 8 dimes and 4 nickels.

3.   Sarah was playing with some poker chips.   She had the following arrangement in front of her:

The next time I looked, she had another arrangement:

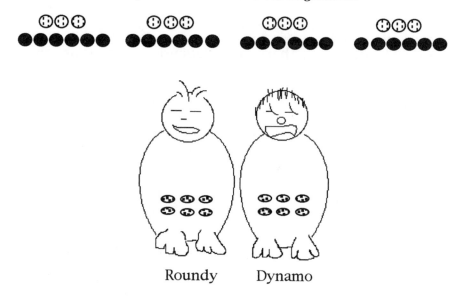

Roundy   Dynamo

4. Roundy and Dynamo are two extraterrestrials visiting earth for a couple of days. They brought their own food supply with them. Roundy eats three food pellets and Dynamo eats two food pellets for each meal. In this picture taken on the first day of their visit, you can see the food pellets each one had eaten. On the second day of their visit, they each ate only two meals.

5. Head shrinkers? Between the first picture and the second, what changes? What does not change?

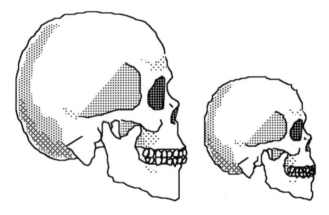

6. Mr. Trent and his students were working all morning in the science lab, where students sit three to a table. For mid-morning break, Mr. Trent put two candy bars on each table and told the students to share them. "Before you start your snacks though, I would like you to push four tables into a group." Suppose you are in that science class and you love candy. If you had your choice, would you rather get your share of the candy before or after the tables are pushed together? Explain your answer.

7. Two variable quantities are given in each example. Tell whether one depends on the other. If there is a dependency relationship, which depends on which?

a. Cost of getting into the amusement park; the number of people in your family.
b. The reading on you car's odometer; how fast the car is moving.
c. How long it takes you to travel; the distance you travel.
d. Attendance at a Brewers game; how many seats are in the stadium.

8. Use "In, Out, Up, and Down" notation to analyze these short stories and then find the missing component.

a. $30 for 15 games

_____ for 3 games

b. $3\frac{1}{4}$ hours to play one game of golf

_____ hours to play 3 games

c. 18 candies for 6 people
    _____ for 15 people

d. 3 people clean the yard in $4\frac{1}{4}$ hours
    2 people clean it in _____ hours

e. read 2 pages in 3 minutes
    read _____ pages in 20 minutes

f. run 14 laps in 24 minutes
    run _____ laps in 4 minutes

g.   6 people rake a yard in 3 hours
        _____ for 4 people to do it

9. Some of the statements given below are correct; others are not.
Is there a dependency relationship between the important quantities in
the situation? If so, use arrow notation to denote the direction of
change in each variable. If the statement is incorrect (does not make
sense), change one number in the statement so that it is correct. If you
cannot fix the statement, tell why.

a. If 1 bag of salt weighs 40 pounds, 3 bags should weigh 120 pounds.
b. If a cruise ship takes 30 people on a tour, it takes 2 hours to complete
the tour, but if only 15 people go on the same tour, it will take only 1
hour.
c. If it takes 6 people 1 hour to clean a house, then it would probably
take 3 people about $1\frac{1}{2}$ hours to clean it.
d. If 1 boy can mow the lawn in 3 hours, 2 boys could mow the lawn in 6
hours.
e. If 1 boy has 3 sisters, 2 boys probably have 6 sisters.
f. If it takes 3 boys 2 hours to deliver papers on a certain route, then 6
boys could probably do the route together in 1 hour.
g. If 1 orchestra can play a symphony in 1 hour, 2 orchestras can
probably play it together in 1/2 hour.

10. Identify each of the following kinds of change with one of the
general categories: increasing, decreasing, periodic, irregular, or
stepped. Do not sketch.
a. The number of leaves on a maple tree changes over the course of
several seasons.
b. How loud the music sounds to you changes as you move farther away
from your stereo.
c. The height of a tree changes in relation to the number of years that
have passed since you planted it.
d. The number of people in a movie theater changes over 10
consecutive showings of a movie.
e. The amount of air in your lungs changes as you breathe in and out
over the course of a day.
f. The amount of water in a glass changes according to how long the
water has been running into it.

11. As a fund-raising project, a club decided to print and sell calendars. There is a fixed cost for every order of $850 for photography, typesetting, and printing. In addition, there is a cost of $3.25 for each calendar printed.

a. Write an equation that represents the cost of printing some number of calendars, say x.
b. What is the average cost of printing 10 calendars? 100 calendars? 500 calendars?
c. What is the relationship between the average cost and the number of calendars printed? Express the relationship in words and in arrow notation.
d. Is one quantity changing more quickly than the other? How can you tell?

12. Sketch a graph that shows your activity.

a. You run as fast as you can for 5 seconds, rest for 5 seconds, then walk for 20 seconds.
b. You walk for 10 seconds, run as fast you can for 10 seconds, and then turn around and walk back toward your starting point for 10 seconds.
c. You walk for 10 seconds, turn around and walk back to where your started in five seconds, and then run as fast as you can away from your starting point for 15 seconds.
d. You walk for 5 seconds, run for 5 seconds, walk for 5 seconds, run for 5 seconds, and so on until 30 seconds are up.
e. You walk for 15 seconds, turn around and walk toward your starting point for 5 seconds, then turn and walk away from the starting point again and walk for 10 seconds.

13. The following graphs show people's activity over a time of 30 seconds. Describe what each person must have been doing. Some of the graphs may not be correct. If a graph does not make sense, explain why.

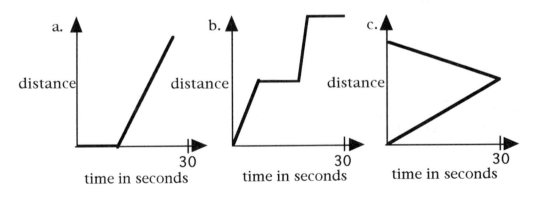

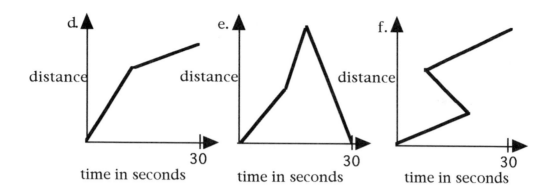

14. Sketch the following relationships.

a. The height of a rubber ball above the ground is related to the time elapsed since you bounced it.
b. The number of pounds of aluminum cans you take to the recycling center is related to the number of dollars you are refunded.
c. How fast you can run is related to how steep a hill you are trying run up or down.
d. The weight of the envelope you are mailing is related to the amount of postage you have to put on a letter.
e. The temperature of your casserole is related to the time that has passed since you put it in the oven.
f. How far you are from your stereo speakers is related to how loud the music sounds to you.

15. In the following situations, sketch a graph to show the way that the changing quantities are related. Tell which one is changing more quickly than the other.

a. Time to do a job increases as the number of workers decreases.
b. The distance required to stop a moving car after you apply the brakes increases as the speed of the car increases.
c. The amount of water in a bathtub decreases as the time it has been emptying increases.
d. The number of dollars you get at the recycling center increases as the number of cans you returned increases.
e. The diameter of a tree increases as the number of years since you planted it increase.
f. The time it takes you to drive to Chicago decreases as your speed increases.

* * * * * * * * * * * * * * * * * * *

STOP   Take some time to reflect on the ideas in this chapter.

Reflection

1. Put into your own words the differences among relative change, average change, and rate of change.

2. Think of a real context in which two quantities are increasing but not at the same rate.

3. Think of two real contexts to illustrate the fact that not all ↓↓ situations are the same.

Chapter 13
Rates

STOP

Children's Strategies

Monica and Ben, two sixth grade students, solved the following problem:

Two bicyclists practice on the same course. Green does the course in 6 minutes, and Neuman does it in 4 minutes. They agree to race each other five times around the course. How soon after the start will Green overtake Neuman?

Analyze the students' work and determine (a) why they came up with different responses, (b) strengths in both approaches, and (c) possible misunderstandings of the problem.

Monica

track : 2 miles long

    N : 20 minutes

    G : 30 minutes

whole race : 10 miles

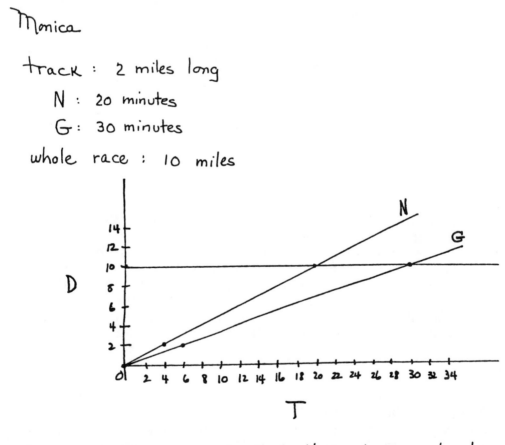

We can see by the graph that N is always ahead.

Ben

I will make the times the same

4 min.   N   once around

4 min.   G $\frac{2}{3}$ around

I will keep adding 4 min. and see when they meet.

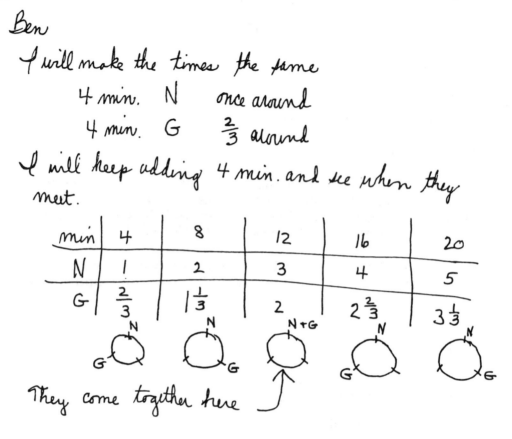

min	4	8	12	16	20
N	1	2	3	4	5
G	$\frac{2}{3}$	$1\frac{1}{3}$	2	$2\frac{2}{3}$	$3\frac{1}{3}$

They come together here

* * * * * * * * * * * * * * * * * * * *

What Is A Rate?

It is difficult to arrive at a single definition of rate on which everyone will agree. If we look at the ways rates are used in everyday contexts and the ways in which the word rate is used mathematically and colloquially, we see a complex web of meanings.

A *rate* can be thought of as an extended ratio, a ratio which enables us to think beyond the situation at hand, to imagine a whole range of situations in which two quantities are related in the same way. In this sense, a ratio can be a specific instance of a rate.

Example

The rule of thumb for ordering pizza at Reggie's Pizza is "Order 2 medium pizzas per 5 people." The rule means to order 4 pizzas for 10 people, 6 pizzas for 15 people, 30 pizzas for 75 people, etc. Serving a party of 10 people 4 pizzas (4 pizzas:10 people) is a specific instance of the restaurant's general rule for how much pizza to order.

Rates can also be thought of as descriptions of the way quantities change with time. They are identified by the use of the word per in their names, and they can be reduced (or divided) to a relationship between one quantity and 1 unit of another quantity. This is called a *unit rate.*

Ex.   30 miles per 5 hours can be expressed as 6 miles per 1 hour. In this case, the unit rate is 6 mph.

Although these examples do not exhaust the nuances involved in understanding the phenomenon "rate," they serve as a starting point. To help students investigate and discuss rate below the obvious level, we need to examine more specific characteristics and develop a vocabulary by which to talk about them.

The Domain of a Rate

When we encounter rates in everyday situations, they may be applied to either a limited domain or an unlimited domain. In a truly proportional situation, rates have a virtually unlimited domain. In other situations, the domain may be implicit or explicit in the situation.

Example. The amount of sales tax you will pay increases in a steady way with the amount of your purchase. This is a proportional situation.

Example. The soccer team has a ratio of 3 wins to 2 losses so far in the season. At this rate, what will be their record at the end of the 15-game season?

The words "at this rate" give us permission to assume that the rate extends proportionally over a limited domain—that of a 15-game season. This means that the rate of 3 wins per 5 games may be applied to 15 games. However, it does not help to determine the number of wins and losses at the end of, say, 8 games.

Example.   As he was driving along the highway, Pete noticed the following road sign.

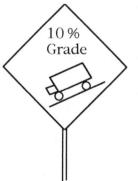

When he saw the sign, Pete did not think that the rest of his trip would be downhill. He realized that the 10% rate or $\dfrac{1 \text{ foot vertical decline}}{10 \text{ feet horizontal distance}}$ would apply only to the hill that he would encounter ahead. In this case, the domain of the rate was implicit in the situation.

Example

ORANGES

3 for $.69
with coupon

Limit: 1 dozen

In this case, the rate of $\dfrac{69 \text{ cents}}{3 \text{ oranges}} = \dfrac{23 \text{ cents}}{1 \text{ orange}}$ will apply on any purchase up to 12 oranges. The domain was explicit.

Example. Mary can run a 4-minute mile. How far can she run in 2 hours?

In fact, this question cannot be answered because we know that even very good athletes do not run at the same high speed for a long period of time. For some interval during the two hours, Mary might run at a speed of $\dfrac{4 \text{ mi.}}{1 \text{ min.}}$, but not for the entire 2-hour interval.

Chunked Rates

Chunked rates are those in which the constituent quantities have been melded and renamed with a single term because there is some basis in perception or experience for identifying them as a single entity. These rates become known by names that disguise their comparative nature. For example, the words "speed" and "density" are used in everyday and scientific contexts to denote single concepts; nevertheless, they are composite quantities composed of two other quantities. Speed (average speed) compares the amount of distance traveled per unit measure of time to denote swiftness of action. Density may be, for example, number as compared to a unit measure of area or volume, used to convey a sense of the degree to which a space is occupied. Many students do not realize that chunked rates are actually comparisons of two quantities.

Constant Rates and Varying Rates

Rates may be constant or varying rates. It is not always obvious to students which are varying and which are constant. Only by encountering enough rate situations can they begin to distinguish those rates that are "standard" and those that change.

> Example. Conversion factors are constant rates.
>
> If 12 inches = 1 foot, how many feet of rope do you have in a piece that measures 156 inches?
>
> The unit rate $\frac{12 \text{ inches}}{1 \text{ foot}}$ applies not only to the 156 inches in this specific situation, but to other situations in which the number of inches may vary. This would hold true for all measurement conversion factors.

> Example of a varying rate.
>
> International monetary exchange rates are constantly changing. The speed at which one is traveling in a car is constantly changing unless the cruise control is on. The rate at which the bathtub fills with water may be slow or fast, depending on how far you have opened the tap.

Dual Rates

When a rate is reduced to answer the question "how many (or how much) for 1?" it is called a *unit rate*. For example if bananas are priced at three pounds for $1.20, we can determine the unit rate or the rate representing the cost for 1 pound by reducing $\frac{\$1.20}{3 \text{ pounds}}$ to get $\frac{\$.40}{1 \text{ pound}}$. But this unit rate has a reciprocal which is $\frac{1 \text{ pound}}{\$.40}$. The dual rate, although it is not the same as its reciprocal, arises from and gives information about the same situation. It is, however, psychologically different. Students find one form of the rate easier to interpret in some situations than in others. For example, if you were wanting to know the cost of some quantity of coffee you wanted to purchase, you might find it easier to use the rate $\frac{\$.40}{1 \text{ pound}}$. But if you had $5.60 in your pocket and you wanted to know how much coffee you could purchase with it, you might find it easier to use the rate $\frac{1 \text{ pound}}{\$.40}$.

Rates as Single Numbers

Sometimes rates are reported as single numbers. Single-number rates are those resulting from the division of the two quantities of which they were originally composed. Students would have no way of knowing anything about these rates unless discussion focused explicitly on them.

Examples

> Her heart rate was 68.
> The birthrate of country A is 12.4.
> The unemployment rate is 3.4%
> The inflation rate is 4.6%.

In these examples, rates are implicit per quantities, but are more like divided ratios or quotients. To reconstruct the comparisons that any of them represent, additional information is needed about how they were computed. A heart rate is the comparison of the number of times a heart beats per minute, usually counted over 10 seconds and then extended by multiplying by 6. In other divided per quantities, where the division results in very small numbers, the result of the division is multiplied by 100 or by 1,000 and the rate is reported as a percentage or as some number per thousand. In some countries, the birth rate is defined as 1,000 times the ratio of the number of babies born alive to the total number in the population (the number of live births per thousand of the population). Similarly, the unemployment rate is expressed as a percentage. It is 100 times the ratio of the number of people who are unemployed to the number of people who are in the civilian labor force, as determined by sampling. Finally, the inflation rate is perhaps the most illusive of these rates. In actuality, many variables figure into its computation, and most people probably have only a "sense" of its meaning, without really knowing how it is computed.

When students encounter these rates, they need to discuss them individually, because they would have no way of knowing how they are calculated.

Equivalence Classes

Suppose that the market has advertised 2 pound of peanuts for $3.00 and there is no restriction on the amount I can purchase at that price. Then I can transform the multiplicative relationship between pounds of peanuts and dollars to get various pieces of useful information:

$$2 \text{ pounds costs } \$3$$

$$1 \text{ pound costs } \$\frac{3}{2} \text{ or } \$1.50$$

$$\$1 \text{ buys } \frac{2}{3} \text{ pound.}$$

With any number of pounds, I can associate a dollar amount by multiplying pounds by $\frac{3}{2}$. For example, 4 pounds will cost \$ 6; $6\frac{2}{3}$ pounds will cost \$10. Of course, many of these ordered pairs are possible, especially because we are not restricted to using whole numbers. As we have done before, we can graph the values of the independent variable on the horizontal axis and their dependent values on the vertical axis. Because of the dual nature of rates, which quantity is the independent variable is a matter of choice, although sometimes that choice has already been made by convention (users' agreement about the way things should be done). In this case, the cost depends on the number of pounds, so put pounds on the horizontal axis, and dollars on the vertical axis.

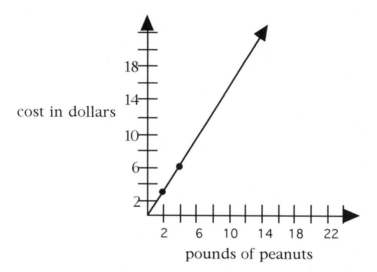

This graph show two points, (2,3) and (4,6), corresponding to the ratios 3:2 and 6:4, and the line determined by those points. When we draw the line, we are imagining the extension of the advertised rate to all of the different amounts of peanuts we might buy, some less than 2 pounds, some more than 2 pounds, some whole numbers of pounds, and some fractional numbers of pounds.

These rates are in the same equivalence class because they represent the same relative comparisons. That is, 3 relates to 2 in the same way that 6 relates to 4 in the same way that 10 relates to $6\frac{2}{3}$. All rates in which the quantities share the same relationship belong to the same class and they reduce to the same ratio. None of them is preferred as "the" name of the equivalence class. We can write $\{\frac{3}{2}\}$ to refer to the equivalence class to which the rate $\frac{3}{2}$ belongs. Because $\dfrac{10}{6\frac{2}{3}}$ belongs to the same class, we could have called the equivalence class $\{ \frac{10}{6\frac{2}{3}} \}$.

Actually, the equivalence class may be designated by placing any one of the rates in the class inside brackets $\{\ \}$. $\{\frac{6}{4}\}$ refers to the entire equivalence class to which the rate $\frac{6}{4}$ belongs. That class includes all of the other rates represented by points on the same line as $\frac{6}{4}$. Be careful! Note that the point (2,3) in usual Cartesian coordinates is not in the class $\{2,3\}$, but rather, in the class $\{3,2\}$.

Note that equivalence of ratios or rates is different from the equivalence of fractions. Recall that equivalent fractions are merely different symbols for the same quantity. All of the names for the same amount refer to a single rational number. This idea is analogous to the fact that a single female person may be referenced by many different names: a friend may call her Jack, her mother may call her Jacqueline, her spouse may call her sweetheart, her child may call her mom, her sister might call her Jackie, etc. But ratios and rates in the same equivalence class do not name the same amount, but rather, the same comparison of quantities.

Example. Bag A contains 4 sweet candies and 6 sour candies and bag B contains 12 sweet candies and 18 sour candies.

A and B clearly do not contain the same number of candies. Bag A contains 10 candies, and bag B, 30 candies. However, in both bags, the comparison of numbers of sweet to sour candies is the same.

On the graph comparing cost to pounds of peanuts, the coordinates of all the points have the same relationship. For example, look at the points whose coordinate rectangles have been drawn and determine their y to x ratios. Can you see that they are $\frac{1.5}{1}$, $\frac{12}{8}$, and $\frac{19.5}{13}$? We call $\frac{1.5}{1}$ the unit rate because it tells us the cost per 1 pound. All of the rates in this class are equivalent and they reduce to $\frac{1.5}{1}$, the unit rate.

Furthermore, the slope of the line is $\frac{3}{2}$ or $\frac{1.5}{1}$. Remember that the slope of a line compares the change in the vertical direction to the change in the horizontal direction. On the graph, if you determine the slope between any two points, say, (8,12) and (13, 19.5), you get $\frac{7.5}{5}$ or $\frac{1.5}{1}$ or 1.5.

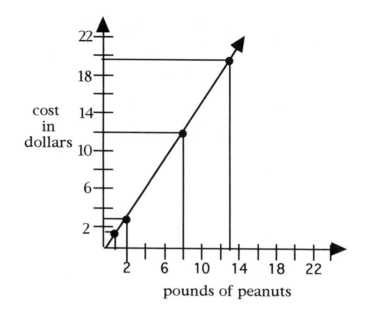

pounds of peanuts

We get the following connections:

• All rates in the same class are composed of different quantities, but they reduce to the same unit rate.
• The slope of the line containing all of the rates in the same class is the unit rate.
• A constant—a number that does not change—is associated with each equivalence class. That constant is found by dividing any ratio from the class. If you know that constant, you may determine the equivalence class and all of its members. That constant is the slope of the line containing all of the rates in the same class as the unit rate.

Comparing Ratios and Rates

The Flavorful Fruit Juice Company bottles various fruit juices. A small barrel of apple juice is mixed using 12 cans of apple concentrate and 30 cans of water. A large barrel of raspberry juice is mixed using 16 cans of raspberry concentrate and 36 cans of water. Which barrel will be fruitier?

This problem asks us to compare ratios. First, assume that both fruit juices taste equally fruity when the same number of cans of concentrate are mixed with the same number of cans of water for each of them. Then the strength of the apple taste and the raspberry taste depend on both the amount of juice concentrate and the amount of water and the proportions of each—that is, you must use relative thinking. To use an extreme example, you could mix 2 cans of apple concentrate with 50 cans of water. Or, you could mix 1 can of apple concentrate with 3 cans of water. Although there was more apple in the first mixture, the second would have a stronger apple taste because the first was more diluted. If the concentrate and water in both barrels are mixed in exactly the same ratio, they should taste the same, even though there is more total liquid in one container than in the other.

One way to think about this question is to try to equalize the two mixtures and then see which has more fruit concentrate in it. We can do this by reunitizing. Another way is to use extend the given ratios to scale the mixtures up and down. Then we could graph the line containing all of the members of each equivalence class and compare the slopes. Begin by reunitizing.

apple:

$$\frac{12 \text{ apple}}{30 \text{ water}} = \frac{6(2\text{-cans})}{15(2\text{-cans})} = \frac{4(3\text{-cans})}{10(3\text{-cans})} = \frac{2(6\text{-cans})}{5(6\text{-cans})}$$

raspberry:

$$\frac{16 \text{ raspberry}}{36 \text{ water}} = \frac{8(2\text{-cans})}{18(2\text{-cans})} = \frac{4(4\text{-cans})}{9(4\text{-cans})}$$

One the ratios we got for the apple drink was $\frac{4(3\text{-cans})}{10(3\text{-cans})}$ and one of the ratios for the raspberry drink was $\frac{4(4\text{-cans})}{9(4\text{-cans})}$. From these, we can see that the raspberry drink must be stronger because 4 parts raspberry concentrate are mixed with only 9 parts of water, while 4 parts of apple concentrate are mixed with 10 parts of water.

Now, solve by graphing. Because it is not clear which quantity depends on which, we may put either quantity on either axis. If we put the amount of fruit concentrate on the vertical axis, then the equivalence classes {12,30} and {16,36} are shown on the following graph. The larger ratio of fruit to water is the steeper line, representing the raspberry mixture.

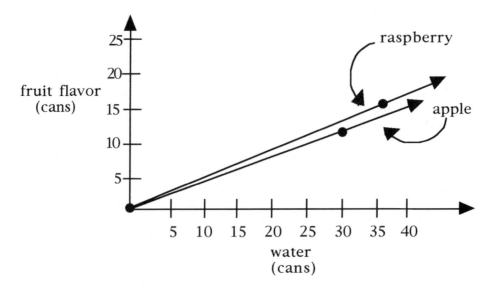

We have already seen that the ratios in the same equivalence class all show up on the same line when we graph them. (0,0) is in every equivalence class, so we can use the point (0,0) on the graph with the x and y coordinates of only one of the ratios of a class in order

to determine the line representing the class. For example, to graph the line representing {16 raspberry:36 water} we can use the points (0,0) and (36,16). To graph the line representing {12 apple:30 water} we can use the points (0,0) and (30,12). The line representing the raspberry mixtures is steeper; its slope is $\frac{4}{9}$. The slope of the line representing the apple mixtures is $\frac{2}{5}$. The slope is the change in fruit juice as compared to the change in water, so a greater slope represents more concentrate as compared to water. The raspberry mixture will taste fruitier.

We can also obtain the equation of the lines representing each equivalence class quite easily. If w is the amount of water and c is the amount of concentrate, we have:

$$\text{apple} \quad 12{:}30 \quad \frac{c}{w} = \frac{12}{30} = .4 \;\rightarrow\; c = .4w$$

$$\text{raspberry} \quad 16{:}36 \quad \frac{c}{w} = \frac{16}{36} = .44 \;\rightarrow\; c = .44\,w$$

Without graphing, we could check the constant associated with each equivalence class. For each class, this constant is given by a divided ratio from the class. The concentrate-to-water ratio for apple is 12:30 = .4. the concentrate-to-water ratio for raspberry is 16:30 = .44. Every ratio in {16:36} is associated with the constant .44. For example, $\frac{16}{36} = .44$ and $\frac{4}{9} = .44$. Every ratio in {12,30} is associated with the constant .4. For example, $\frac{2}{5} = .4$ and $\frac{6}{15} = .4$. This tells us that the ratio of concentrate to water is greater in the raspberry mixture.

If, instead, we had looked at the ratio of water to concentrate for each flavor, we would get:

$$30\,\text{water}{:}12\,\text{apple} = 2.5$$
$$36\,\text{water}{:}16\,\text{raspberry} = 2.25$$

These divided ratios indicate that there is more water in the apple mixture. These numbers also indicate what the slopes of the lines would have been if we had graphed the water on the vertical scale and the fruit concentrate on the horizontal.

In summary, we have several ways to compare the ratios:

• Reunitize both sets of ratios until you get a pair that is easier to compare.

- Graph the equivalence class for each rate and use the slopes to compare.
- Compare the constants associated with each equivalence class.

Distance-Time-Rate Relationships

One of the most common rate situations is the distance—time—rate relationship. Although we all encounter this relationship in some way every day of our lives, research has shown that it is not well understood by most people. In general, the elementary mathematics curriculum has failed to provide any analysis of these quantities and their relationships. Most students have seen the formula

$$distance = rate \cdot time$$

and have mechanically substituted two numbers (without their labels) into the formula to solve for the third.

Children's early understanding of distance is usually based on their experience of how long it takes to get someplace by bicycle or by running, but soon, distances become too large to measure directly or to experience by biking or running. They might further develop a sense of distance by using a watch and a rough estimate of average speed. Later, instruments such as the car's speedometer measure speed, and we do not tend to think much about how it manages to attach a number to the phenomenon. Because we are able to experience speed, we learn to describe certain feelings or experiences by associating them with the number the speedometer gives us.

Students need to encounter the distance—speed—time system of relationships and to explicitly think about and discuss (a) ways to compare speeds of movement, (b) the characteristics of rate discussed so far, (c) the meaning of constant speed, (d) the meaning of average speed, and so on. It has been taken for granted that students understand these ideas, but in in-depth interviews, we find that they understand very little. This is a handicap that can affect their conceptual understanding through high school mathematics and into calculus. This interview with Joe, a freshman in high school, is indicative of many students' shaky understanding of distance—speed—time relationships. Joe's teacher asked him to discuss this problem:

> Mr. Green reset his odometer to 0000 and drove for 2 hours.
> At the end of the two hours, his odometer read 108 miles.
> After another 2 hours, he checked it again and found that
> it read 216 miles. What changed? What did not change?

Joe: The odometer changed, the miles, the distance changed, his car clock, the cities.
T: What didn't change?
Joe: Both times, he checked the odometer after two hours of driving.

T: Anything else?

Joe: I don't know.

T: Do you have any information about Mr. Green's speed?

Joe: (Long pause.) Well, since he went 108 miles, he must have been going fifty something.

T: Can you tell me more about his speed?

Joe: He did 54 and 54.

T: How do you know?

Joe: Because he took 2 hours.

T: Was 54 mph. a constant speed or an average speed?

Joe: Yeah. Constant. Because it was the same for 2 hours.

T: What happened during the next 2 hours of his trip?

Joe: His miles doubled.

T: What does that tell you?

Joe: He must have had his cruise control on, because nobody could be that steady. They couldn't keep their foot on the gas pedal just right so that they could go exactly another 54 and another 54.

T: Can you see anything that didn't change in this situation?

Joe: Yeah. He kept his cruise on.

Most beginning high school students do not realize that speed is a composite quantity, the comparison of a distance to a time. Although students use the words "miles per hour," they think the phrase is just a label for speed and have never thought about how speed is calculated. Ben and Monica, the sixth graders who solved the problem at the beginning of the chapter, are unusually bright, and they had been studying the distance—time—speed relationship for several weeks. Ben's solution was sophisticated. He first determined how far around the track each man would bike in 4 minutes. Then, using a ratio table, he recorded minutes of cycling time against times around the track (rather than actual distance), and using his own notation system, noted the men's position on the track at 4 minute intervals. Monica realized that the track was 2 miles long, and she used that fact to calculate the distance and the men's times in cycling five laps. However, when she graphed total distance against time, she ignored position on the track, as if the men rode their bikes on a country road. Monica interpreted her graph as saying that the men never met and that Neuman was always ahead. It is not clear from her statement whether or not she understands what her graph shows, and we would want to ask her for further explanation. Does she think steeper and "ahead" mean farther or faster?

What does it mean to understand the distance—time—speed quantity structure? The answer to that question is not a list of facts, nor is it the "rule," distance = rate · time. Although the rule captures the relationships among the three quantities at some abstract level, there is a great deal of variation in the way this cluster of relationships plays out in real situations. Knowing the rule does not provide the level of comprehension needed to solve problems. We want students to develop an understanding of the structure of this set of relationships that comes from, but goes beyond, the investigation of specific situations. After sufficient experience, they should be able to make generalizations such as this: if distance doubles, time will have to double if speed remains the same, or speed has to double if time remains the same. In short, there is no substitution for gaining a broad conceptualization of the quantities as well as their relationships through analysis and problem solving in a wide variety of situations.

Characteristics of Speed

Like other rates, speed has a domain. That is, it applies to some explicit domain, which may or may not be the entire trip under discussion. In addition, it is important to take into consideration whether or not a speed is homogeneous over its domain. If you drive a certain distance with the cruise control on, then over that distance, it may be said that your speed was homogeneous. (Technically, even using a cruise control, your speed will not be *exactly* the same for the entire distance, but we agree that it is close enough to call it homogeneous.)

Example. Tom drove half the distance to another city with his cruise control set at 55 mph and the rest of the distance with the cruise set at 50 mph.

Tom's speed of 55 mph was homogeneous for the first half of the trip and his speed of 50 mph was homogeneous over the second half of the trip. This means that it took him longer to cover the second half of the distance.

Example. For half the travel time, Tom had his cruise set at 55 mph and the other half of the time with the cruise set at 50 mph.

Tom's speed of 55 mph was homogeneous for half the time he was driving and his speed of 50 mph was homogeneous for the other half of the time. This means that he covered more distance during the first half of his trip than he did during the second half.

Example. Jack set his cruise control at 65 m.p.h. How far did he travel in 2 days?

Although the cruise control may aid homogeneity during Jack's actual driving times, in a 48-hour period, rest stops will be necessary for a variety of reasons and these will affect its homogeneity over the entire trip.

Example. Jack drove for 3 hours with his cruise control set at 65 mph.

Because Jack's speed was homogeneous with regard to the 3-hour trip, we can say that he traveled a total distance of 195 miles during that time.

We can also determine the distance he had covered at any intermediate time. For example, after 1.5 hours, he must have gone 97.5 miles and in 2.25 hours, he must have covered 146.25 miles.

Example. Marcia drove 195 miles with her cruise set at 65 mph.

Marcia drove for 3 hours.

Example. Mr. Brown's drove from city A to city B to city C and his average speed on the trip was 60 mph.

An average rate of change is usually not homogeneous. In this sense, "average" means "distributed proportionately" rather than referring to an arithmetic mean. That is, it is not equivalent to the average of the speeds over the respective segments of the trip. Average speed is the total distance traveled as compared to the total time it took to travel that distance. The average speed is the speed you would have traveled if you had done the entire trip in the same amount of time, using a constant speed.

Example. You drive at a speed of 35 mph for 15 minutes, then walk back to your origin at a speed of 4 mph.

Your average speed is

$$\frac{\text{total distance}}{\text{total time}} = \frac{8.75 \text{ mi.} + 8.75 \text{ mi.}}{.25 \text{ hr.} + 2.1875 \text{ hr.}} = \frac{17.5 \text{ mi.}}{2.4375 \text{ hr.}} = 7.18 \text{ mph.}$$

Example. Mr. Brown drove from city A to city B to city C using his cruise control.

In this case, Brown's average speed will be the same as the speed over any segment of the trip because his speed was constant for the trip. Traveling at a constant speed means that the rate of change in distance over each like time interval is the same.

Discussion of these nuances in real contexts is essential for helping children to develop a richer understanding of distance—speed—time relationships.

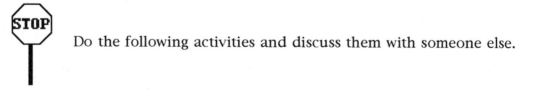

Do the following activities and discuss them with someone else.

Activities

1. Compare each of these rates by reunitizing.
a. Trent mixes chocolate milk every day after school. Yesterday he put 4 teaspoons of chocolate syrup into 6 ounces of milk. Today he put 3 teaspoons of chocolate into 4 ounces of milk. Which drink had the stronger chocolate flavor, yesterday's or today's?
b. Would you rather be taxed $15 on a purchase of $68 or $12 on a purchase of $52?

2. Compare these rates by finding their unit rates.
a. Bill drove 380 miles in 6 hours and Greg drove 565 miles in 9 hours. Who was moving at a slower rate?
b. Stacy's offered a discount of 15% off on a purchase of $100 or more and Boss Store offered $ 20 off a $100 purchase. Which was the better discount?

3. Compare these rates by graphing the rate pairs in their equivalence classes.
a. The Lamplight Theater sold 50 tickets in two weeks, while the Globe sold 150 tickets in 4 weeks. At which theater are the tickets selling faster?
b. The Jones Company had a loss of $500 in 3 weeks, while the McDuff Company had a loss of $700 in 8 weeks. Which company suffered the least?
c. Which solution is stronger, 35 parts ammonia in 55 parts water, or 25 parts ammonia in 45 parts water?

4. Your salary rose $2.50 per hour in your first year with the company, then stayed the same for the next 2 years. What was your average salary increase for the first 3 years?

5. Suppose that while you were driving along, you noted the time at the following mile markers.

Time	Mile Marker
2:00 pm	42
2:29 pm	66
3:01 pm	105

a. What is the average rate of change of distance between mile 42 and mile 66 in miles per hour?
b. What is the average rate of change of distance between mile 66 and mile 105 in miles per hour?
c. What is the average speed of your car between mile 42 and mile 105?

6. Coffee is $4.50 per pound. How much coffee can you get for $1?

7. a. Explain how you would compare drivers' speeds if you were the official in a 3-hour auto race.
b. Explain how you would compare drivers' speeds in a 50 km auto race.

8. On a 6-mile stretch of road, two people started running together as part of their daily exercise routine. You looked down from a helicopter and checked the position of each person every 10 minutes and made the following sketch of what you saw.

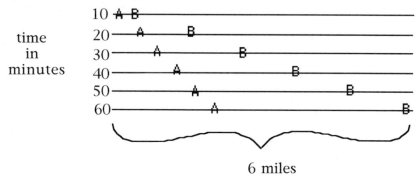

6 miles

a. Who was moving faster?
b. How can you figure out exactly how fast each person was moving?
c. Was that an average speed or a steady pace? How can you tell?

9. A car traveled at an average speed of 28 mph for 7 miles. How long did it take?

10. A car traveled 7 miles and it took 20 minutes. What was its average speed?

11. A police helicopter clocked an automobile for 10 seconds over a stretch of highway $\frac{1}{5}$ mile long. At what rate was the auto traveling?

12. When you went to the doctor's office for a checkup, the nurse counted 32 heartbeats in 15 seconds. What was your average heart rate?

13. Jake went on a 60 kilometer bike ride. After 3 hours, he was 40 kilometers from the start, but he was tired and he slowed down. He did the remaining 20 kilometers in 2 hours.
a. What was his average speed on the first part of the trip?
b. What was his average speed on the second part of the trip?
c. What was his average speed for the whole journey?

14. Charlie got a traffic ticket for a moving violation: traveling 5 mph over the 55 mph speed limit. The officer's citation said that he followed Charlie for 10 miles and that he averaged 60 mph—5 mph over the speed limit. Charlie drove at 80 mph for the first 5 miles and then at 40 mph

for the next 5 miles. Charlie went to traffic court. How did he argue his case?

15. Frank drove from Boston to Washington and back again. He averaged 50 mph on the way and 60 mph on the way back. It took him 18 hours of driving. How far apart are the two cities?

16. A cruise ship headed out for a trans-Atlantic trip traveling at a constant speed of 25 knots. A passenger who missed the departure hired a speedboat to catch up. The speedboat traveled at 45 knots. The speedboat left the dock precisely 2 hours after the cruise ship did. How far from the dock were the two boats when they met?

17. Frank and Flo have a pet fly named Frieda, who can not stand it when the twins are separated, so she flies back and forth between them at a rapid rate of 50 mph. Frank was downtown and Flo was at home—a distance of 10 miles apart—when they both hopped on their bikes and sped along their secret path toward each other. Each was going 20 mph. Frieda Fly started on Frank's handlebars and flew along the path to Flo's handlebars, and then back to Frank's, then back to Flo's, until the twins met each other on the path. How far did Frieda travel?

18. Frieda Fly has a twin who Frank and Flo named Free-To. Free-To Fly looks like Frieda Fly, but he travels at a different rate—15 km per hour. Once when Frank and Flo were 9 km apart on their bikes, Free-To was upset and traveled along their path between them until they met. Frank was traveling eastbound at a speed of 10 mph and Flo was traveling westbound at 8 mph.
a. How long did it take Frank and Flo to meet?
b. How far did Free-To Fly travel by the time Frank and Flo met?

19. Did you ever walk the steps of a moving escalator? In my favorite department store, I found that if I walk down 26 steps, I can get to the bottom in 30 seconds, and if I walk down 34 steps, I can get to the bottom in 18 seconds. How many steps are in the moving stairway? (Time is measured from the moment the first step begins to descend until I step on to the solid platform at the bottom.)

20. My friend and I exercise together and we are always looking for new scenery on our hikes, so we take a bus out into the country and then walk back. The bus travels at about 9 mph, and we walk at the rate of 3 mph. If we have only 8 hours for our trip on Saturday, how far can we go before we get off the bus?

21. When the lights went out, my mother looked for some candles. She found two pillars of the same diameter, but one was $1\frac{1}{2}$ inches shorter than the other. She lit the taller one at 8 pm, and the shorter at 9 pm. At 10:30 pm, both candles were the same height. At midnight, the candle

that was originally shorter burned out. At 12:30, the other candle burned out. Assuming that the candles burned at constant rates, how tall was each candle originally?

22. Jim cuts the lawn in 4 hours. His brother can cut the same lawn in 3 hours. If they work together, how long will it take to mow the lawn?

23. Solve these problems using reasoning alone. Do not use any algebraic solutions or algorithms.
a. Mack and Tom are riding the train and trying to figure out the distance between the different stations. The only information they have is that it is 40 km between stations A and B. They use a watch to find the time between station A and station B (16 minutes) and between station C and station D (36 minutes). Assuming that the train ran at a constant speed, what is the distance between stations A and D?

b. At a recent fox hunt, Prince Charles timed his favorite hound and found that he was running 10 m for every 6 m run by the fox. At one point, a fox was 30 m ahead of the hound. How far did the hound have to run to catch up with the fox?

c. Two workers working for 9 hours together made 243 parts. One of the workers makes 13 parts an hour. If the worker maintain a steady pace all day, how many parts does the second worker make in an hour?

* * * * * * * * * * * * * * * * * * * *

 Think back over the ideas in this chapter

Reflection

1. Name all the ways you can think of for comparing speed.

2. State a simple rule for comparing the graphs of equivalence classes in terms of steepness.

3. Graph the apple-raspberry drink problem with water on the horizontal axis and amount of fruit concentrate on the vertical axis. Explain why the line representing the apple ratios is steeper. (Remember that the line representing the raspberry ratios was steeper in our discussion of this problem.)

Chapter 14
Reasoning Proportionally

STOP **Children's Strategies**
Some eighth-grade children were given four problems to solve and then their teacher was given the task of deciding whether or not each child might be reasoning proportionally. The children used various strategies to solve the problems, but Mason, whose work is shown, consistently used the same strategy. First, solve the problems yourself and talk about them with others in your group. Try to list the characteristics that might help you decide whether a child is using proportional reasoning. Then examine Mason's work and make some conjectures about his reasoning.

Can you solve these problems?
(a) If a bag of topsoil weights 40 pounds, how much will three identical bags weigh?
(b) If one football player weighs 225 pounds, then how much will three players weigh?
(c) If Ed can paint the bedroom by himself in 3 hours. Assuming that Jake works at the same pace Ed does, how long will it take if Jake helps Ed?
(d) If I was charged $1.30 in sales tax when I spent $20, what would be the sales tax on a purchase of $50?
(e) Bob and Marty run laps together because they both run at the same pace. Today, Marty started running before Bob came out of the locker room. Marty had run 7 laps by the time Bob ran 3. How many laps had Marty run by the time Bob had run 12?

Mason

a. $\dfrac{1 \text{ bag}}{40 \text{ p.}} = \dfrac{3 \text{ b}}{? \text{ p.}}$ $3 \times 40 = 120 \text{ p.}$

b. $\dfrac{1 \text{ f.}}{225 \text{ p.}} = \dfrac{3f}{? \text{ p.}}$ $3 \times 225 = 675 \text{ p.}$

c. $\dfrac{1 \text{ man}}{3 \text{ hrs}} = \dfrac{2 \text{ men}}{? \text{ hrs}}$ $2 \times 3 = 6 \text{ hrs}$

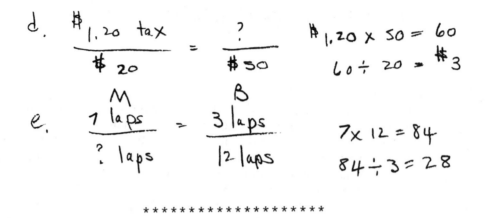

d. $\dfrac{\$1.20 \ tax}{\$20} = \dfrac{?}{\$50}$ $\$1.20 \times 50 = 60$

$60 \div 20 = \$3$

e. $\dfrac{7 \ laps}{? \ laps} \overset{M}{=} \dfrac{3 \ laps}{12 \ laps} \overset{B}{}$ $7 \times 12 = 84$

$84 \div 3 = 28$

* * * * * * * * * * * * * * * * * * *

A *proportion* is typically defined as an equality of two ratios. Most textbooks state that definition and teach students to solve problems using proportions, without first helping them to gain a sense of when quantities are proportionally related and what proportional reasoning is. If you have been following the discussion and activities in this book, then you have been reasoning proportionally.

Problems involving proportional reasoning are of two basic types. The first is a comparison problem: Which vehicle has a faster average speed, a truck that covers 126 miles in $1\frac{1}{2}$ hours or a car that travels 135 miles in $1\frac{3}{4}$ hours? The second kind of problem is one in which three quantities are given and the fourth quantity is missing; hence, these are called *missing value* problems. For example, if Tamara reads 14 pages in 30 minutes, how many pages can she read in 15 minutes? The traditional proportion algorithm is frequently used to solve missing value problems: set up two ratios, cross multiply, and then divide to solve for the missing term.

The ability to set up a proportion and solve it does not constitute proportional reasoning. Hopefully, as you looked at Mason's work, you came to that conclusion. Mason had evidently been taught the algorithm without adequate preparation in the reasoning processes that can lead to it. Unfortunately, once we give students rules, we dramatically decreases the chances of their doing any reasoning to get an answer. Any kind of reasoning entails conscious, purposeful activity rather than the blind application of a procedure to come up with a correct answer.

Part of being able to reason proportionally involves the analysis of the quantities in a given situation to determine that they are related proportionally and that it is appropriate to scale them up or down. All problems in which three quantities are given and one quantity is missing do not call for proportional reasoning. For all five problems he was given, Mason automatically used proportions because he saw three terms and knew a strategy for finding a fourth. However, knowing a strategy that works, in the sense that it produces an answer, is not the same as proportional reasoning.

There are no shortcuts available here! Thought, common sense, and experience must be used to determine whether a situation is proportional or not. You must always bring into play your knowledge about how things work in the real world.

Ex. Jeff runs a mile in 4 minutes. How far can he run in 3 hours?

A person may be able to run a 4-minute mile, but can anyone keep up that pace for 3 hours? We know that runners slow down a bit over time. This means that the two quantities, distance and time, do not continue to increase at the same rate. This is **not** a situation you would solve using a proportion.

In this chapter, using the problems that Mason was given, we develop guidelines for analyzing situations to determine whether or not they are proportional and we identify the hallmarks of proportional reasoning.

Characteristics of Proportional Situations

In a proportional situation, both quantities are increasing or decreasing together. We know that there are many different ways in which two quantities can increase together. Here are just a few.

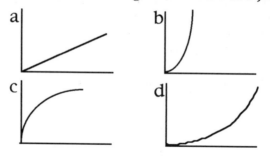

What makes them all different is the rate of change. In graph a, two quantities are both increasing at the same steady rate. On graphs b and d, the quantity on the y axis is increasing more quickly than the quantity on the x axis. The rate of change in the y quantity with respect to x quantity is greater on graph b than it is on graph d. On graph c, the quantity on the x axis is increasing more quickly, so the change in the y quantity compared to the change in the x quantity is decreasing. Because there are many conditions under which both quantities may be increasing, this is a necessary, but not sufficient, condition to identify proportional relationships.

In a proportional situation, two quantities increase multiplicatively. Both are multiplied by the same factor. In the case of the topsoil, the number of bags and the weight of the bags are related because the bags are all identical. The weight of three bags should be three times the weight of 1 bag. In the case of the football players' weights, the weight of three people will certainly be more than the weight of one person, but it will not usually be three times the first player's weight. We know that people's weights are not related to each other that way! We would need to add the weight of the second player and add the weight of the third player in order to determine the weight of three players. This is not a proportional situation at all!

The number of laps Bob runs and the number of laps Marty runs are also related by addition. By the time Bob started to run, Marty had already run 4 laps, but once both men were on the track, they both ran the same number of laps since they ran at the same pace. So Bob's number of laps was always 4 less than Marty's and Marty's number of laps was always 4 more than Bob's—no matter how many laps the men ran together.

Sales tax, on the other hand, is related to the amount of your purchase and it increases in a multiplicative way. If you spend $20, the amount of tax you pay is 4 times as much as you would pay if you spent $5. Similarly, the amount of tax you pay on a $50 purchase will be $2\frac{1}{2}$ times what you would pay on a $20 purchase. The factor which either increases or decreases both quantities is called a *scale factor*.

The requirement that both quantities increase by multiplication by the same factor rules out graphs b, c, and d because one quantity was changing more quickly than the other in each of those graphs. The only graph that describes a proportion is a straight line. But will every straight line graph correspond to a proportional relationship? No. Having a straight line graph is another necessary, but not sufficient, condition. The graphs of proportional relationships are straight lines through the origin (0,0), but every straight line graph does not correspond to a proportional relationship.

Consider the problem about Marty and Bob running laps. If we graph their distances against time, we get a straight line.

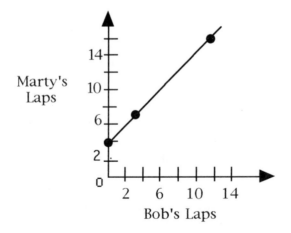

Although the graph is a straight line, Marty's and Bob's laps are **not** related proportionally. In a proportion, both quantities are increasing and maintaining the same ratio, and they must both be 0 at the same time. In this case, it is impossible to include the point (0,0) because when Bob has run 0 laps, Marty has already run 4 laps. At one point, the ratio of Marty's laps to Bob's is 7:3; at another point that ratio is 10:6; at still another, it is 16:12. None of these ratios are equivalent.

In proportional relationships, we can always find a rule that relates one quantity to the other. We can solve the sales tax problem because one quantity depends on the other (sales tax depends on the amount of purchase) and we can express that relationship in a rule that holds no matter what the dollar amount of you purchase. It is called a *function*. The rule tells you how to find one of the quantities when you know the other one. For a proportional relationship, the rule always looks the same:

$$\text{quantity B} = \text{constant} \cdot \text{quantity A}$$

The constant that appears in the rule relating the two quantities is the slope of the line on which lie all of the ratios in the same equivalence class lie. For example, the reduced ratio of sales tax to amount of purchase, which is the same as the slope of the line, will be .065 for every set of coordinates.

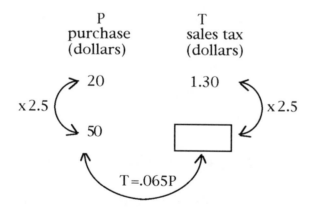

On the other hand, in a non-proportional situation such as the football player problem, you can not find a rule relating the two quantities.

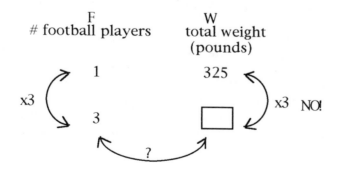

Inversely Proportional Relationships

When it comes to the painting job, we again must use our common sense and experience. Solutions like Mason's result when operations are performed without thinking. If you stopped Mason and asked him to reconsider this situation, he would probably realize right away that his answer was not reasonable. We know that it take less time to get a job finished when there are more people working. Therefore, as the number of people increases, the work time decreases and this is not a proportional situation. It took twice as many workers to cut the time in half, and it would take three times as many workers to finish the job in $\frac{1}{3}$ the time. This is known as an *inversely proportional relationship*. In inversely proportional relationships, one quantity varies with the other, but in the opposite direction. There are two scale factors and they are inverses. There is also a rule relating the two kinds of quantities. That rule always says that the product of the two is a constant. In this case, (#men)(# hours) = 3. A quantity diagram shows these relationships:

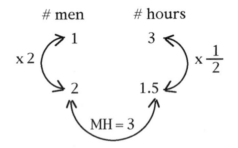

Analyzing Quantitative Relationships

It is important for younger children to think about and verbalize all sorts of relationships and to distinguish relationships that can be modeled by ratios from those which cannot. But by the time students reach middle school, we need to encourage them to think more deeply about quantitative relationships and to develop a notation to aid their analysis.

The following process helps students to take a systematic approach to the analysis of quantities, provides a gradual approach to symbols, and allows students to develop their own representations when appropriate; it encourages the use of intuitive knowledge and common sense, and builds strategies for thinking mathematically, not merely for solving certain types of problems. The following flow chart outlines some simple steps that students can use to analyze a situation.

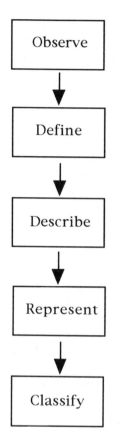

We apply each of the steps in this diagram to the following situation:

> If 1 boy can mow the lawn in 1.8 hours, 3 boys could probably mow the lawn in .6 hours.

Observe. Observing the situation means attending to the quantities given. Depending on the statement under consideration, not all of the quantities might be critical to understanding the situation. Students should be reminded that a quantity always has two parts: a number and a unit of measurement. For example, rather than merely listing "boys" and "time" as the significant quantities in this situation, "number of boys" and "time in hours" should be encouraged.

Define. Defining the situation means making explicit the assumptions needed to keep answers sensible and to ensure that we are all thinking about the same things as we work on the statement. Middle school students are imaginative and they sometimes suggest "far out" conditions: "Suppose one of the boys mowing the lawn is in a wheel chair and has only one arm." Students need to make and agree on certain reasonable assumptions to keep a situation sensible and tractable. In the lawn-mowing problem, we need to assume that both boys are willing and able to do about the same amount of work in one hour. Students should come to appreciate that in mathematics, one always sets out the conditions under which a discussion or proof evolves and that any conjectures or results are valid only under those conditions.

<u>Describe.</u> Describing means making a verbal statement about how the important quantities are related. For example, "If you have more people doing a job, it should take less time to get it finished than if only one person is doing it." To anticipate the representation in arrow notation in the next phase of this modeling process, students should be encouraged to reframe their assertion in terms of an "up" and "down" statement. "As the number of people goes up, the time to do the job goes down."

<u>Represent</u>. Representing entails the use of arrow notation and other modes of the student's choice to describe the relationship between the significant quantities in the situation. In our example, if B represents the number of boys and T represents the time it takes to mow the lawn in hours, the quantities change in the following way: B↑ T↓. Because we know that all situations that of the ↑↑ or ↓↓ or ↑↓ types are not the same, further analysis is needed. Middle school students should be encouraged to create quantity diagrams, such as the following:

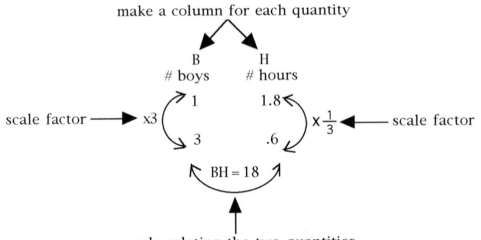

rule relating the two quantities

<u>Classify.</u> Classifying means associating the situation under consideration with other situations that have similar structures and operations. Students may keep notebooks or file boxes in which they group problems whose quantities behave in the same way. In time, after they have analyzed many problems, students see patterns emerging and the characteristics of each type of quantitative relationship become more distinct. By comparing situations within a category (for example, two ↑↓ situations), they discover that their

classification system needs to be refined. Compare the lawn mowing problem to this one:

After the first $1\frac{1}{2}$ hours, the cell count was down to 40. Thereafter, every 3 hours, half of the remaining cells died. time ↑ cell count ↓

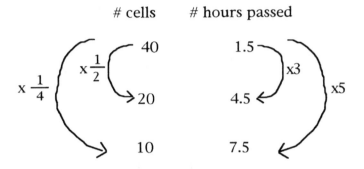

cells   # hours passed

It becomes clear that the multiplicative relationships are different in the two situations. The following work from a sixth grade student documents her differentiation of problems within the ↑↓ category. She was analyzing the following statement:

If one boy can mow the lawn in 3 hours, then 2 boys can do it in $1\frac{1}{2}$ hours.

Nicki°   I think we have a new relationship. Here is my diagram, then I will show how I got it.

# of boys   how long each one works in hours
(B)   (T)

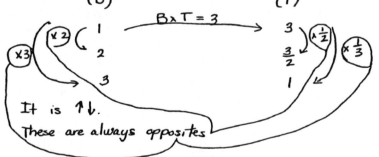

$B \times T = 3$

It is ↑↓.
These are always opposites

And there is a rule $B \times T = 3$

Other people think it works like this: every time you add another person, the work gets cut in half. But here is the right way to do it.

# of boys	how much of the lawn each one does	how long each one works together in hour.	
1	ALL	3	
2	$\frac{1}{2}$	$\frac{1}{2}$ of 3	$\frac{3}{2}$ or $1\frac{1}{2}$
3	$\frac{1}{3}$	$\frac{1}{3}$ of 3	1
4	$\frac{1}{4}$	$\frac{1}{4}$ of 3	$\frac{3}{4}$
5	$\frac{1}{5}$	$\frac{1}{5}$ of 3	$\frac{3}{5}$
6	$\frac{1}{6}$	$\frac{1}{6}$ of 3	$\frac{3}{6}$ or $\frac{1}{2}$

   In time, students begin to mentally group structurally similar relationships. Using their quantity diagrams, they can show why situations are or are not similar. Later, to make it easier to refer to each category of problem they have identified, more conventional algebraic language may be introduced: that type of up—up relationship is called proportional, or that type of up—down relationship is called inversely proportional.

Using Proportion Tables

We know that students can easily apply the proportion algorithm to obtain answers without ever doing any reasoning. Rather than teaching them to set up and solve proportions before they have learned to reason, they need to do more problem solving using ratio or proportion tables. Students should be encouraged to use the reasoning up and down process that we have used throughout the book in order to solve proportion problems. Trace the steps in the following examples to see how this can be done. These tables are merely vertical forms of the ratio tables we have used before. They include an additional column for keeping track of the steps performed. This column serves the same purpose as the arrow notation that we used before in ratio tables.

‖Example. If 15 cupcakes cost $3.36, find the cost of 38 cupcakes.

cupcakes	cost	notes
15	3.36	given
30	6.72	x 2
5	1.12	÷ 6
3	.672	30 ÷ 10
38	8.512	30 + 5 + 3

The cost of 38 cupcakes is $8.51.

It is best not to round before the last step. When you round, you introduce a small error. If you then use the rounded figure in another calculation, you magnify the error introduced by the rounding process.

Example

A famous designer gave away free perfume samples in the mall, and in 15 minutes, 600 people picked up his free gifts at the cosmetic counter. If this give-away is going to be repeated, but this time for 1.5 hours, how many gift packages will be needed?

people	time	notes
600	15 min.	given
2,400	1 hr.	x 4
1,200	.5 hr.	÷ 2
3,600	1.5 hr.	x 3

Example

Cheese costs $4.25/pound. Nancy selects several chunks for a party and when they are weighed, she has 12.13 pounds of cheese. How much will it cost her?

	pounds	cost	notes
a	1	4.25	given
b	10	42.50	a x 10
c	2	8.50	a x 2
d	.1	.425	a ÷ 10
e	12.1	51.425	b + c + d
f	.05	.2125	d ÷ 2
g	.01	.0425	f ÷ 5
h	.03	.1275	g x 3
i	12.13	51.5525	e + h

The cheese will cost $51.55.

Example: Divide 2,624 by 61.

	quotient	divisor	notes
a	1	61	given
b	10	610	a x10
c	40	2440	b x 4
d	2	122	a x 2
e	43	2623	a + c + d
f	.01	.61	a ÷ 100
g	43.01	2623.61	e + f
h	.001	.061	f ÷ 10

i	.005	.305	h x 5
j	43.015	2623.915	g + j

The quotient, rounded to two decimal places is 43.02.

The tables used in these examples are the work of eighth-grade middle school students. Their tables are efficient because they were able to think in large chunks and they had learned to combine operations to their best advantage. Younger students use more steps than are necessary and their tables are longer.

Characteristics of Proportional Thinkers

When students reason proportionally, their thinking is marked by most of the following characteristics. You will recognize these characteristics in the kinds of reasoning that have been encouraged throughout this book.

1. Proportional thinkers do not think solely in term of 1-units or unit rates, such as $\frac{13 \text{ miles}}{1 \text{ gallon of gas}}$ or $\frac{\$1.19}{1 \text{ pound}}$. They think in terms of complex units, such as 3-units or 10-units, and they use composite units, when possible. That is, instead of opening packs of gum and counting individual sticks, they can think in terms of packs. When possible, they reason with unreduced rates such as $\frac{26 \text{ miles}}{2 \text{ gallons of gas}}$ or $\frac{\$1.98}{3 \text{ pounds}}$.

2. They exhibit greater efficiency in problem solving. The ability to think in terms of composite units gives them this advantage. One example is in cases where unit pricing produces nonterminating decimals. If oranges are priced 3 for $.68, it is more efficient to think of the price of 12 as $.68 x (4 groups of three) = $2.72. Finding a unit price and then multiplying introduces error.

3. Proportional thinkers can look at a unit displayed in an array, such as the one shown here, and immediately see how many objects are in $\frac{1}{3}, \frac{1}{2},$ $\frac{1}{4}, \frac{1}{6}, \frac{1}{12}, \frac{2}{3}, \frac{3}{4}, \frac{5}{6},$ and so on.

4. They can flexibly interpret quantities. For example, 3 apples for 24 cents can be interpreted as 8 cents per apple or as 1/8 apple per 1 cent. They can reunitize several times without losing track of the unit.

5. Their ability to think in terms of larger quantities helps them to anticipate the size of a share and a greater ability to use equivalence to

produce shares consisting of fewer pieces. Thus, they are faster to generalize the goals of partitioning:

(a) if p people share n objects, one share consists of $\frac{n}{p}$ of an object;

(b) if p people share n objects, each person gets $\frac{1}{p}$ of the total objects;

and (c) that the number of people, the number of objects in the unit whole, and the size of the shares are related in the following way:

$$n\left(\frac{1}{p}\right) = \frac{n}{p} \text{ and } p\left(\frac{n}{p}\right) = n.$$

These results are not generalized and may be obtained only by a great deal of computation by those who think in terms of many little chunks. For example, if the job is to find one share when 3 people share 4 pizzas, the student who partitions in larger chunks (top) is able to name one share, while to the student who produced the bottom picture, it is not as easy.

6. Proportional thinkers are not afraid of decimals and fractions. Often, students replace the fractions and decimals with whole numbers (nice numbers) to help them think about a problem. They exhibit a kind of fraction and decimal avoidance, while proportional thinkers move around flexibly in the world of fractions and decimals.

7. They have often developed strategies—sometimes unique strategies—for dealing with fraction density problems. That is, like some of the children whose strategies we discussed, they have clever ways of finding fractions between two given fractions.

8. They are able to mentally use exact divisors to their best advantage and can quickly compute, say, $\frac{3}{8}$ if they know $\frac{1}{8}$, 80% if they know 10% or 20%, or add $\frac{1}{8} + \frac{1}{16}$ if they know $\frac{1}{2}$.

9. They have a sense of covariation. This means that they can analyze quantities that are changing together, talk about direction of change and rate of change, and determine relationships that remain unchanged.

10. Proportional thinkers can identify everyday contexts in which proportions are or are not useful. Proportions are not just mathematical

objects or situations to which they know how to apply an algorithm. They can distinguish proportional from non-proportional situations, and will not blindly apply an algorithm if the situation does not involve proportional relationships.

11. They have developed a vocabulary for explaining their thinking in proportional situations.

12. Proportional thinkers are adept at using scaling strategies. For example they are able to reason up and down in situations involving comparisons, percents, and similarity.

13. They can solve both missing value and comparison problems by reasoning, and without resorting to the cross-multiply-and-divide algorithm. If they have developed shortcuts or algorithms, they can use one or more reasoning processes to explain what they are doing.

STOP Complete these activities before moving to the next chapter.

Activities

Use reasoning to solve every problem! Do not use the proportion equation, $\frac{a}{b} = \frac{c}{d}$.

1. Does each situation involve proportional relationships, inversely proportional relationships, or neither? How can you tell?
a. Three pints of milk cost $1.59 and 4 cost $ 2.12.
b. Two brothers drive to the basketball game in 15 minutes, and when John drives alone, he says it takes him 10 minutes.
c. Six people clean a house in an hour and 3 people do it in 2 hours.
d. One boy has 3 sisters, and 2 boys have 6 sisters.
e. It takes me twice as long to do a math problem when I am watching TV as it does when I do my homework in my room.
f. Tom can eat a hard-boiled egg in 20 seconds. In a recent contest, he ate 20 hard-boiled eggs in 5 minutes.
g. Your car averages about 100 miles on 4.5 gallons of gas. On a full tank of gas (15 gallons) you can travel about 333 miles.
h. You spent $5.00 and pay $.30 in sales tax and then paid $2.10 on a purchase totaling $35.

2. Solve each of these problems using a proportion table:
a. If the school makes $1.15 on every raffle ticket sold, how much will it make when 128 tickets are sold?

b. If a can of tennis balls costs $4.49, how many cans can be purchased for a tournament in which $70 has been allotted for balls?
c. Matt runs a 10 km race in 45 minutes. At this rate, how long would it take him to run a 6.25 km race?

3. Solve each of the following problems, if possible, using any method except by solving a symbolic proportion. If a solution is not possible, state why.
a. Mark can type 575 words in 15 minutes. At the same rate, how many words can he type in 1.25 hours?
b. If 3 boxes of cereal are on sale for $6.88, and a day-care provider needs 17 boxes, how much will she pay?
c. If Ellen has 537 points and 60 points may be redeemed for 1 baseball cap, how many caps can she get?
d. If 1 inch on a map represents 195 miles, how far apart are two cities that are 2.125 inches apart on the map?
e. For every $3 Mac saves, his dad will contribute $5 to his savings account. How much will Mac have to put into the account to money before he can buy a $120 bicycle?
f. Five girls drank 3.5 quarts of lemonade on a warm day. If they were planning a party for 14 girls, how much should they prepare for the party?

4. Analyze each situation. Use a quantity diagram to show the multiplicative relationships.
a. A circle has a diameter of 3 feet. If you double the diameter, what happens to the area of the circle?
b. The taxi I took from the airport started with a base charge of $1.50 and increased $.20 for each tenth of a mile.
c. The width of a rectangle is half its length. If you double the length of the rectangle, will the perimeter increase proportionally?

5. If 8 men can chop 9 cords of wood in 6.5 hours, how long would it take 4 men to chop 3 cords, assuming that they work at the same rate as the group of 8 men?

6. In the Robo-Work Factory, robots assemble small sports cars. If 3 robots can assemble 19 cars in 40 hours, how many cars would you expect 14 robots to turn out in 8 hours?

7. Sam, amateur detective, was walking along at the rate of about $3\frac{1}{2}$ mph when a car passed him on the road and tossed a gun out the window. He heard sirens back in town and immediately suspected that it was a get-away car. He counted his steps—29 in all—until the car turned the corner and he lost sight of it. It took him another 203 steps to get to the corner, but by then, the car was gone. He told the police that he was not sure it was the get-away car because it was not moving very quickly. How did Sam know how fast the car was moving?

8. For each situation,
i. determine whether there is a proportional relationship or an inversely proportional relationship;
ii. write an equation relating the two variables.
a. Your weight of 120 pounds is 54.54 kilograms, and your boyfriend, a blocker on the football team, who weighs 320 pounds weighs 150 kg.
b. When lightening strikes at 10 km away, you hear the crash about 30 seconds later; when it strikes 20 km away, you hear the crash after 60 seconds.
c. When you are 150 feet under water, the pressure in your ears is 64.5 psi (pounds per square inch) and at 10 feet under water, the pressure is 4.3 psi.

9. Solve by any reasoning method you wish. Do not use the algebraic representation of a proportion, $\frac{a}{b} = \frac{c}{d}$.
a. In 3 weeks, 4 horses eat 45 pounds of hay. How much will 1 horse eat in a month?
b. Five robots produce 5 auto parts in 5 minutes. How many packages containing 2 parts each, can be produced if 10 robots work for 10 hours?
c. If a hen and a half can lay an egg and a half in a day and a half, at the same rate, how many eggs can be laid by 2 dozen hens in 2 dozen days?

* * * * * * * * * * * * * * * * * * *

  Think, discuss, write.

Reflection

1. Give an example of a linear relationship that is not a proportion.

2. How is an analogy like a proportion? How is it unlike a proportion?

3. Explain what it means for two quantities to have an inversely proportional relationship.

Chapter 15
Applications: Similarity and Percents

STOP

Children's Strategies

Joshua, an eighth grader, talked about the following problem concerning similarity. Solve the problem yourself, analyze Joshua's response, and make some conjectures about his probable misunderstandings.

These rectangles are similar. "Similar" means that they are the same shape even if they are of different sizes. Can you find the missing length on the larger rectangle?

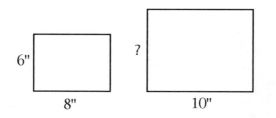

Joshua:

"I think the answer would be 12 inches because the 6-inch side grew to 10 inches, so it gained 4 inches. If the 8-inch side gains 4 inches, it would be 12 inches long. Wait a minute! There is another way to check. If you do 8 take away 6, you get 2, and if you do 12 take away 10, you get 2 again. So 12 must be right."

＊ ＊ ＊ ＊ ＊ ＊ ＊ ＊ ＊ ＊ ＊ ＊ ＊ ＊ ＊ ＊ ＊ ＊ ＊

Proportions have many uses. It would be impossible to list them all. Discussion in this chapter is limited to two topics that are important in the elementary and middle school curricula—similarity and percent.

Similarity

Human beings seem to have a built-in capability to recognize objects whether they are large or small in size. We can also recognize objects whether they are the real thing, or whether they are photographs or models with characteristics of real things sketched on paper. For example, even very small children can recognize that the following sketches are models of a bunny. They will call each one "bunny," implicitly understanding that the picture does not have all of the characteristics of a real bunny—life, movement, furriness, size, and so on.

In our everyday use of the word "similar" we mean showing some resemblance. All of the sketches, whether they convey great detail or whether they show a more abstract style, are all close enough to rabbits that we might identify them as such. However, there is an inherent vagueness in this use of the word similar. At some point the model of a rabbit can become abstract enough that in one person's judgment it may not resemble a real rabbit, but in someone else's opinion, it might. Therefore, abstractness or level of detail influences whether or not a person would call two objects similar. Children can also tell you which of the six rabbits pictured above looks most like a real rabbit, and which least resembles a real rabbit. They recognize that each sketch portrays a different degree of abstraction.

There are nuances in the colloquial use of the word similar, but mathematically speaking, similarity is a more precise notion. Unfortunately, we tend to underestimate the conceptual difficulty of the mathematical idea of similarity because we think we know the meaning from its colloquial use and because the standard textbook definition is deceptively simple: objects are similar when they are the same shape. When we talk to children, we can find out that, in fact, they develop their own notions about "having the same shape" if we are not careful to explore that idea more carefully. Consider, for example, the following observation of an eight-year-old regarding the set of rabbits shown earlier. "These pictures are similar because they are all have the same shape—the bunny shape."

The richness of the similarity relationship needs to be made conscious and discussed and explored, rather than disregarded as simple, basic, and obvious. There is much insight to be gained by engaging children in visual and verbal experiences for a sustained period of time before translating ratios and the notion of similarity into numerical representations.

Multiplicative Relationships in Similarity

By the time we treat similarity in the middle school curriculum, we would like to develop a better definition of what it means for two figures to be similar. The following activities provide some clues that will help to uncover some of the key characteristics of similar figures.

When both parts of an analogy entail the same relationship, we say that the parts are similar. This definition of similarity applies in mathematics as well. Consider this example.

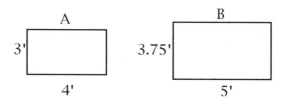

What is the relationship between the widths of the rectangles?

3.75 is 3(1.25)

The larger width is 1.25 times the smaller one or the smaller width is the larger width divided by 1.25.

What is the relationship between the lengths of the rectangles?

5 is 4(1.25)

The longer length is 1.25 times the shorter one.

Both relationships, the relationship between the widths of the two rectangles and the relationship between the lengths of the two rectangles, are the same. In this case, you would call the rectangles similar. We can look at these relationships in a quantity diagram as we have done before.

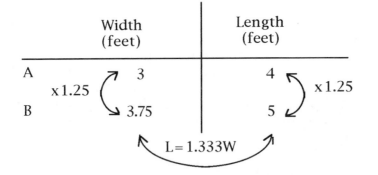

When a figure is shrunk or enlarged, the scale factor is the factor by which all of its dimensions are enlarged or shrunk (1.25). The ratio L:W (1.333) defines the relationship between length and width of all of the members of the same equivalence class—that is, all of the figures, smaller and larger, that could be obtained by shrinking and enlarging so that they are similar to the rectangles we are discussing.

It is clear that we cannot attain this enlargement by adding the same amount to both dimensions of the rectangle. When we add, say 5 inches to each of the dimensions of a 3" x 4" rectangle, we get a rectangle whose measurements are 8" x 9."

	Width (in.)	Length (in.)
+5"	↗ 3 ↘ 8	↖ 4 ↙ 9 +5"

In the next picture, a 3" x 4" rectangle and an 8" x 9" rectangle were both copied at 25% of their size so that they would fit in this book. You can see that the 8" x 9" rectangle is not the same shape as the 3" x 4" rectangle. The height of it is $2\frac{2}{3}$ of the original rectangle and the width of it is $1\frac{1}{3}$ of the original rectangle. By putting copies of the smaller rectangle on the larger one, we can see that the one dimension of the larger rectangles is about $2\frac{1}{2}$ times that of the smaller rectangle, while the other is about $2\frac{2}{3}$ times that of the smaller figure. These rectangles are not similar.

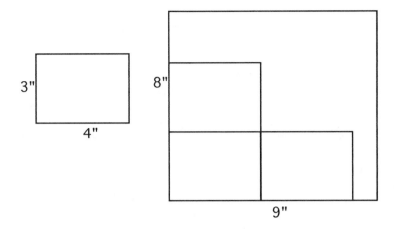

The most difficult idea for children to grasp about the notion of similarity is that the relationship does not involve addition, but rather multiplication. For example, even middle school students like Joshua, have trouble relating shrinking or enlarging to multiplicative, rather than additive increases. But when children have discussed enlarging and shrinking and additive and multiplicative changes throughout elementary school, we hope to see a dramatic decrease in the misconception that shrinking and enlarging are accomplished by addition and subtraction. From Joshua's response, we can imagine how deeply ingrained his additive thinking is. Not only does he think that he can enlarge the rectangle by adding the same amount to its dimensions, but he even finds a second additive argument to convince himself that he is correct!

Part of the trouble is that to check for similarity, many people impose the smaller figure on the larger, as in the next picture, and conclude that they are the same shape. That is, they make a judgment based on the way the rectangles look, rather than applying a definition. To enlarge something and keep the same shape means that sides must maintain the same proportions, but in adding 5" to both dimensions did not maintain the same proportions: $\frac{3}{4} \neq \frac{8}{9}$.

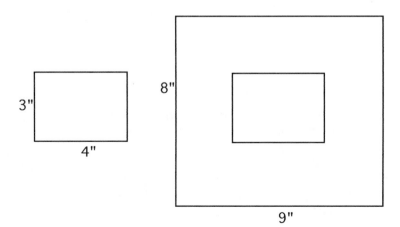

Similarity and Equivalence Classes

When we examined ratios and rates, we saw that they could be grouped into classes such that all the members of a class were either smaller or larger copies of a single relationship. When we graphed one of the components of the ratio on the x axis and the other on the y axis, all of the ratios that shared the same relationship formed a straight line. So, for example, 2:3, 4:6, 9:13.5, 12:36, and a host of other ratios all fall on the same line.

What we know about ratios and their equivalence classes is helpful in analyzing similar figures, because they, too, are just different-sized figures whose sides share the same relationship. Suppose, for example, that we wish to decide which rectangles among the following are similar:

    4'x 6'   6' x 10'   8' x 12'   2' x 3'

We could take those rectangles, put them into a nested arrangement (that is, stack them up according to size), and then put them on a grid so that their shorter sides (W) are against the y axis, and their longer sides (L), are against the x axis.

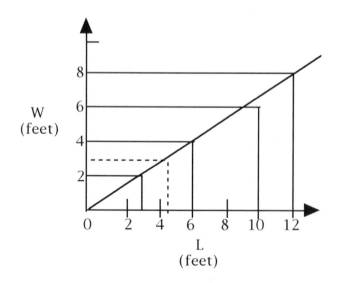

Draw a line through the origin, (0,0) and the upper right-hand corner of one of the rectangles. Extend it so that it goes through all of the rectangles. The line represents the ratio W:L. We can see that the width-to-length ratio for three of the four rectangles we are considering is the same. The ratios 2:3, 4:6, and 8:12 are all in the same equivalence class. The 6:10 ratio is in a different equivalence class. The slope of the line that forms the diagonal of the three rectangles in the same class is $\frac{2}{3}$, and the constant associated with the equivalence class to which the three rectangles belong is .667.   The rule relating width to length is $W = \frac{2}{3} L$ or $W = .667 L$

We can use the line to determine the dimensions of other rectangles that are similar. The dotted lines from any point on the line to the axes show such rectangles. The dotted lines on the graph form a new rectangle, and its dimensions are 3' x 4.5'.

Percent

Percent is a special kind of ratio in which the second quantity is always 100.

Examples

5 percent means 5 out of every 100.
200% means 200 for every 100 —twice whatever quantity you had.
.3% means .3 out of 100 = $\frac{.3}{100}$ =.3 divided by 100 = .003 = $\frac{3}{1000}$.

Reasoning with percents is no different from reasoning with ratios and rates. You are merely looking for a ratio equivalent to some given ratio.

Question	Meaning	Action
15 = ___% of 40	15:40 is equivalent to ? : 100	scale up until you get some number compared to 100
30% of ___ is 24	30:100 is equivalent to 24:?	scale down until you get 24 compared to some number
___ is 48% of 56	? :56 is equivalent to 48:100	scale up until you get some number compared to 56

Ratio tables provide a convenient means of recording your calculations as you scale up or down. Because percent means out of 100, shading a grid consisting of 100 small squares also aids the reasoning process. We illustrate the use of both ratio tables and grids.

Suppose we want to change the fraction $\frac{3}{5}$ into a percent. Begin with a standard part—whole comparison model:

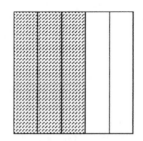

We have two options. We can do it by reasoning or by superimposing the part—whole model on a grid of 100 squares. In our part—whole model, we have shaded 3 blocks out of 5. Using 3 out of 5 as the starting point, reason up to some number out of 100.

shaded	total blocks	notes
3	5	given
30	50	x 10
60	100	x 2

60 out of 100 is 60%. So $\frac{3}{5} = 60\%$. This may be figured out on a 10 x 10 grid by dividing the grid into fifths and shading. Each column of the grid represents 10%. After shading $\frac{3}{5}$, 6 columns or $\frac{60}{100}$ or 60% is shaded.

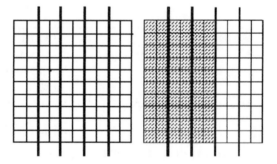

Example. What is 80% of 40?

Begin with 80 out of 100—that is 80%—and reason down to some number out of 40.

shaded	total squares	notes
80	100	given
8	10	÷ 10
32	40	x 4

This means that $\frac{80}{100} = \frac{32}{40}$, so $\frac{80}{100}(40) = 32$. In other words, if we start with 80% or 80 out of 100 and scale down, we get 32 out of 40.

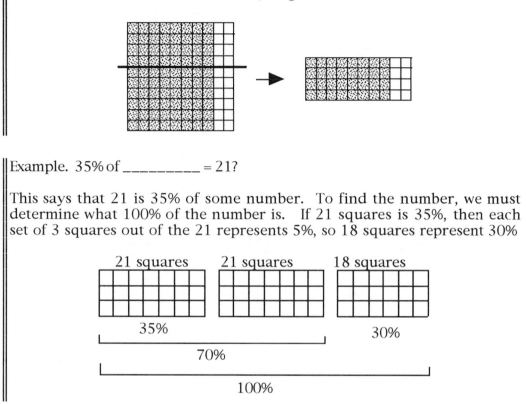

Example. 35% of _____ = 21?

This says that 21 is 35% of some number. To find the number, we must determine what 100% of the number is. If 21 squares is 35%, then each set of 3 squares out of the 21 represents 5%, so 18 squares represent 30%

Example. Another way.

You may also solve by using a ratio table and reasoning from 35 out of 100 (35%) down to 21 out of some number.

shaded	total squares	notes
35	100	given
7	20	÷ 5
21	60	x 3

This means that $\frac{35}{100} = \frac{21}{60}$, so $\frac{35}{100}(60) = 21$.

Example. 31.5 = _____% of 70

This means that if 31.5 squares out of 70 are shaded, how many out of 100 would be shaded? Suppose each of the following boxes represents 10 squares and distribute the 31.5 shaded squares evenly over the 70 squares.

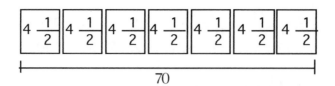

Extend this pattern by another 3 blocks to make 100, then count the number of shaded squares in 100.

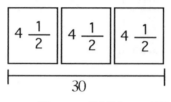

31.5 out of 70 is equivalent to 45 out of 100 or 45%.

shaded	total squares	notes
31.5	70	given
4.5	10	÷ 7
45	100	x 10

Ex. $\frac{5}{8}$ = _____%

shaded	total squares	notes
5	8	given
2.5	4	÷ 2
62.5	100	x 25

Shade 5 out of the first 8 rows. Divide the remaining portion of the chart into eighths and shade 5 parts out of each eight.

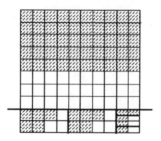

Then, by counting the shaded squares, it can be seen that $\frac{5}{8} = 62\frac{1}{2}$%

Ex. .672 = _____ %

.672 is how many out of 100 squares?

On a percent grid, shade the first 6 rows to represent .6 or $\frac{6}{10}$.

Shade 7 squares to represent .07 or $\frac{7}{100}$.

Divide one square into 100 parts and shade 2 of them to represent .002 or $\frac{2}{1000}$.

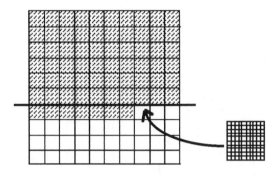

67.2 squares are shaded, so .672 = 67.2%

To do this using a ratio table, you must first read the decimal number correctly. .672 says "672 thousandths" or 672 shaded squares out of 1,000.

shaded	total squares	notes
672	1000	given
67.2	100	÷ 10

STOP   Stop here and work on the following activities.

Activities

1. Devise a test similar to the one we used for rectangles (nesting) to determine if these triangles are similar. How does your test work?

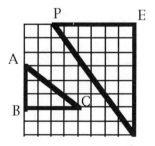

2. An 8-inch square shrinks to become a 2-inch square.
a. What is the relationship between a side of the larger square to a side of the second?
b. What is the scale factor?

3. Measure these abstract designs to answer the following questions.

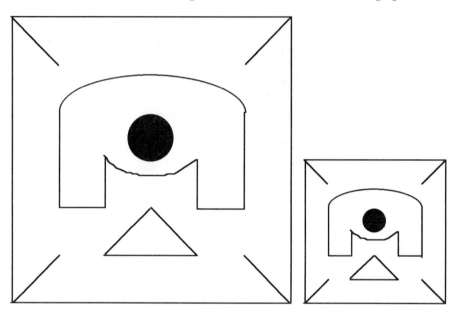

a. Describe the relationship of the second design to the first.
b. What is the scale factor?
c. In the shrinking process, what happened to right angles?
d. What happened to the length of vertical segments?
e. What happened to the length of horizontal segments?
f. What happened to the length of diagonal segments?
g. What happened to the area of the circle?
h. What happened to the area of the square?
i. What generalizations can you make about the effects of shrinking and/or enlarging?

4. In each pair of figures below, suppose the first figure went through a shrinking machine. Would it look like the second figure? Why or why not?

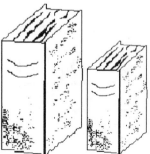

5. a. Use the pizza parlor menu below to determine which cheese pizza is the best buy. All pizzas are round.

Type	Diameter	Price
small	10 inches	$6.80
medium	12 inches	$8.50
large	14 inches	$12.60
giant	20 inches	$28.00

b. Is the price proportional to the size of the pizza?

6. Draw a triangle that is similar to this one, but first describe how you determined what its measurements should be.

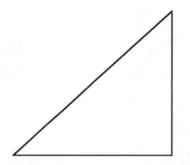

7. When you found the ratio W:L for several rectangles, the ratios were all 1:1. Interpret this information.

8. Which of the following rectangles is most square?
   A. 5.5' x 7.8'
   B. 6.25' x 8.7'

9. How many different sets of similar rectangles are in this list?

2' x 6'	3' x 6'	4' x 8'
5' x 15'	6' x 18'	7' x 14'
8' x 12'	10' x 15'	11' x 22'
	12' x 18'	

10. Are these figures similar? Explain.

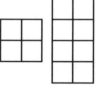

11. In each case, determine what the given measurement must have been originally if the given information is the result of a change in scale.

a. scale factor: $\frac{1}{14}$

2.5'

b. scale factor: 25

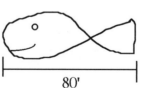

80'

c. scale factor: 4.5

$$A = 25 \text{ sq. ft.}$$

12. Answer each question by drawing a picture.

a. 25% of 80 = _____
b. 15 = _____ % of 50
c. 45 is _____ % of 60
d. _____ = 20% of 70
e. 65% of _____ = 58.5
f. 28 is 40% of _____
g. 15% of 80 = _____
h. 36 is _____% of 90
i. 27 is 45% of _____

13. Write these answers without doing any computation. Do them mentally.

a. What is 50% of 40?
b. What is 200% of 40?
c. What is 150% of 40?
d. What is 10% of 40?
e. What is 60% of 40?
f. What is 260% of 40?
g. What is 5% of 40?
h. What is 15% of 40?
i. What is 55% of 40?
j. What is 35% of 40?

14. The University Book Station prices books according to the following equation. C represents the cost of the book to the bookstore and S represents the price at which they sell the book to students. $\frac{C}{.75} = S$ What is the percent of markup on the books?

15. Use reasoning alone to solve these problems. Do not do any writing. Solve them mentally.

a. There are 50 questions on a test and Jake gets 80% correct. How many did he get correct?
b. If the sales tax is 5%, what is the sales tax on a car for which you paid $15,000?
c. Suppose a special CD pays 8% on your money and you have $1800 invested. How much interest would it pay?

d. They say that the human body is 85% water. If this is true, how many pounds of water are there in a 200-pound man?

16. Use a ratio table to solve the each of the following problems:
a. ? is 62% of 30
b. 136% of 80 = ?
c. 57% of 29 = ?

17. Use a grid to show each fraction as a percent:

a. $\dfrac{3}{20}$ b. $\dfrac{5}{8}$ c. $\dfrac{1}{16}$

18. Can you enlarge a photo whose size is $3\frac{1}{2}$" x 5" so that it is $8\frac{1}{2}$" x 11"? Explain.

* * * * * * * * * * * * * * * * * * * *

STOP   Stop, think, discuss, and write.

Reflection

1. Explain the connections among similarity, ratios, and scale factors.

2. What is the connection between scale factors and operators ?

Bibliography

For graduate students and others who would like to study the development of proportional reasoning and other rational number ideas in greater depth, the following list of professional books, chapters, and research reports provides a basic reading list.

Behr, M. J., Harel, G., Post, T., & Lesh, R. (1992). Rational number, ratio, and proportion. In D. Grouws (Ed.), *Handbook of research on mathematics teaching and learning* (pp. 296-333). New York: Macmillan.

Behr, M. J., Harel, G., Post, T., & Lesh, R. (1993). Rational numbers: Toward a semantic analysis--Emphasis on the operator construct. In T. P. Carpenter, E. Fennema, & T. A. Romberg (Eds.), *Rational numbers: An integration of research* (pp. 13-47). Hillsdale, NJ: Lawrence Erlbaum Associates.

Behr, M. J., Harel, G., Post, T., & Lesh, R. (1994). Units of quantity: A conceptual basis common to additive and multiplicative structures. In G. Harel, & J. Confrey (Eds.), *The development of multiplicative reasoning in the learning of mathematics* (pp. 121-176). New York: State University of New York Press.

Behr, M. J., Lesh, R., Post, T. R., & Silver, E. A. (1983). Rational number concepts. In R. Lesh & M. Landau (Eds.), *Acquisition of mathematics concepts and processes* (pp. 91-126). Orlando, FL: Academic Press.

Behr, M. J., Wachsmuth, I., & Post, T. R. (1985). Construct a sum: A measure of children's understanding of fraction size. *Journal for Research in Mathematics Education, 16*(2),120-131.

Bright, G., Behr, M. J., Post, T. R., & Wachsmuth, I. (1988). Identifying fractions on number lines. *Journal for Research in Mathematics Education, 19,*215-232.

Carpenter, T. P., Fennema, E., & Romberg, T. A. (Eds.). (1993). *Rational numbers: An integration of research.* Hillsdale, NJ: Lawrence Erlbaum Associates.

Greer, B. (1992). Multiplication and division as models of situations. In D. Grouws (Ed.), *Handbook of research on teaching and learning* (pp. 276-295). New York: Macmillan.

Harel, G., & Confrey, J. (Eds.). (1994). *The development of multiplicative reasoning in the learning of mathematics.* New York: State University of New York Press.

Hart, K. M. (1984). *Ratio: Children's strategies and errors. A report of the strategies and errors in secondary mathematics project.* London: NFER-Nelson.

Hiebert, J., & Behr, M. (1988). Capturing the major themes. In J. Hiebert & M. Behr (Eds.), *Number concepts and operations in the middle grades* (pp. 1-18). Reston, VA: National Council of Teachers of Mathematics.

Hunting, R. P. (1983). Alan: A case study of knowledge of units and performance with fractions. *Journal for Research in Mathematics Education, 14*(3),182-197.

Karplus, R., Pulos, S. & Stage, E. (1983). Early adolescents' proportional reasoning on 'rate' problems. *Educational Studies in Mathematics, 14*, 219-233.

Karplus, R., Pulos, S., & Stage, E. K. (1983). Proportional reasoning of early adolescents. In R. Lesh & M. Landau (Eds.), *Acquisition of mathematics concepts and processes* (pp. 45-90). Orlando, FL: Academic Press.

Kieren, T. (1976). On the mathematical, cognitive, and instructional foundations of rational numbers. In R. A. Lesh (Ed.), *Number and measurement* (pp. 101-144). Columbus: Ohio State University, ERIC, SMEAC.

Kieren, T. (1980). The rational number construct--Its elements and mechanisms. In T. Kieren (Ed.), *Recent research on number learning* (pp. 125-149). Columbus: Ohio State University, ERIC, SMEAC.

Kieren, T. (1993). Rational and fractional numbers: From quotient fields to recursive understanding. In T. P. Carpenter, E. Fennema, & T. A. Romberg (Eds.), *Rational numbers: An integration of research* (pp. 49-84). Hillsdale, NJ: Lawrence Erlbaum Associates.

Kieren, T. (1995). Creating spaces for learning fractions. In J. T. Sowder & B. P. Schappelle (Eds.), *Providing a foundation for teaching mathematics in the middle grades* (pp. 31-65). New York: State University of New York Press.

Kieren, T., Nelson, D., & Smith, G. (1985). Graphical algorithms in partitioning tasks. *The Journal of Mathematical Behavior, 4*, 25-36.

Lamon, S. J. (1993). Ratio and proportion: Connecting content and children's thinking. *Journal for Research in Mathematics Education, 24*(1), 41-61.

Lamon, S. J. (1993). Ratio and proportion: Children's cognitive and metacognitive processes. In T. P. Carpenter, E. Fennema, & T. A. Romberg (Eds.), *Rational numbers: An integration of research* (pp. 131-156). Hillsdale, NJ: Lawrence Erlbaum Associates.

Lamon, S. J. (1994). Ratio and proportion: Cognitive foundations in unitizing and norming. In G. Harel & J. Confrey (Eds.), *The development of multiplicative reasoning in the learning of mathematics* (pp. 89-121). New York: State University of New York Press.

Lamon, S. J. (1994). The development of unitizing: Its role in children's partitioning strategies. *Journal for Research in Mathematics Education, 27*(2), 170-193.

Lamon, S. J. (1995). Ratio and proportion: Elementary didactical phenomenology. In J. T. Sowder & B. P. Schappelle (Eds.), *Providing a foundation for teaching mathematics in the middle grades* (pp. 167-198). New York: State University of New York Press.

Lesh, R., Landau, M., & Hamilton, E. (1983). Conceptual models and applied mathematical problem-solving research. In R. Lesh & M. Landau (Eds.), *Acquisition of mathematics concepts and processes* (pp. 263-343). Orlando, FL: Academic Press.

Noelting, G. (1980). The development of proportional reasoning and the ratio concept. Part I--Differentiation of stages. *Educational Studies in Mathematics, 11*,217-253.

Noelting, G. (1980). The development of proportional reasoning and the ratio concept. Part II--Problem structure at successive stages; Problem solving strategies and the mechanism of adaptive restructuring. *Educational Studies in Mathematics, 11*,331-363.

Post, T. R., Behr, M. J., & Lesh, R. (1982). Interpretations of rational number concepts. In L. Silvey (Ed.), *Mathematics for the middle grades (5-9). 1982 Yearbook.* Reston, VA: National Council of Teachers of Mathematics.

Post, T. R., Wachsmuth, I., Lesh, R., & Behr, M. J. (1985). Order and equivalence of rational numbers: A cognitive analysis. *Journal for Research in Mathematics Education, 16*, 18-36.

Pothier, Y., & Sawada, D. (1983). Partitioning: The emergence of rational number ideas in young children. *Journal for Research in Mathematics Education, 14*(5),307-317.

Sowder, J. T., & Schappelle, B. P. (1995). *Providing a foundation for teaching mathematics in the middle grades.* New York: State University of New York Press.

Streefland, L. (1984). Search for the roots of ratio: Some thoughts on the long term learning process (Towards a theory). Part I: Reflections on a teaching experiment. *Educational Studies in Mathematics, 15*,327-348.

Streefland, L. (1985). Search for the roots of ratio: Some thoughts on the long term learning process (Towards a theory). Part II: The outline of the long term learning process. *Educational Studies in Mathematics, 16*,75-94.

Streefland, L. (1993). Fractions: A realistic approach. In T. P. Carpenter, E. Fennema, & T. A. Romberg (Eds.), *Rational numbers: An integration of research* (pp. 289-325). Hillsdale, NJ: Lawrence Erlbaum Associates.

Thompson, A. G., & Thompson, P. W. (1996). Talking about rates conceptually: Part II. Mathematical knowledge for teaching. *Journal for Research in Mathematics Education, 27*(1), 2-24.

Thompson, P. W., & Thompson, A. G. (1994). Talking about rates conceptually: Part I. A teacher's struggle. *Journal for Research in Mathematics Education, 25*(3),279-303.

Tourniaire, F., & Pulos, S. (1985). Proportional reasoning: A review of the literature. *Educational Studies in Mathematics, 16*,181-204.

Van den Brink, J., & Streefland, L. (1979). Young children (6-8)--Ratio and proportion. *Educational Studies in Mathematics, 10*,403-420.

Vergnaud, G. (1983). Multiplicative structures. In R. Lesh & M. Landau (Eds.), *Acquisition of mathematics concepts and processes* (pp. 127-174). Orlando, FL: Academic Press.

Vergnaud, G. (1988). Multiplicative structures. In M. Behr & J. Hiebert (Eds.). *Number concepts and operations in the middle grades* (Vol. 2; pp. 141-161). Reston, VA: National Council of Teachers of Mathematics.

Index